My Life Behaving Badly

My Life Behaving Badly

LESLIE ASH

with Megan Lloyd Davies

The right of Leslie Ash and Megan Lloyd Davies to be
identified as the authors of this work has been asserted by them
in accordance with the Copyright, Designs and Patents Act 1988.

First published in hardback in Great Britain in 2007 by
Orion Books
an imprint of the Orion Publishing Group Ltd
Orion House, 5 Upper St Martin's Lane,
London WC2H 9EA
An Hachette Livre UK Company

1 3 5 7 9 10 8 6 4 2

A CIP catalogue record for this book is available
from the British Library.

ISBN: 978 0 7528 8837 8 (hardback)
ISBN: 978 0 7528 9088 3 (export paperback)

Printed in Great Britain by Clays Ltd, St Ives plc

The Orion Publishing Group's policy is to use papers that are natural,
renewable and recyclable and made from wood grown in sustainable forests.
The logging and manufacturing processes are expected to conform to the
environmental regulations of the country of origin.

Every effort has been made to fulfil requirements with regard to
reproducing copyright material. The authors and publisher will be
glad to rectify any omissions at the earliest opportunity.

www.orionbooks.co.uk

CONTENTS

To my boys Lee, Joe and Max,
and in memory of Ellie and Moe

ACKNOWLEDGEMENTS

There are so many people who've helped me along the way, and in no particular order my thanks go to: my medical team, Agnes, Cherry, Rachel, Wendy, Peter Wells, Daryl Cantor, Louise Smart, Lynn, Jimmy van Dellen and Raj Shakir; my friends Julie, Nathalie, Marti, Louise, Edwina, Anne and Marie, Georgia, Anneliese and Rose-Marie; and my family, Gill and Bill, Denise and Tom, John and Debbie. I also couldn't have written this book without the help and support of Michele, Ivan, Rita, Beryl, Ian and all the team at Orion Publishing. Lastly, the patience award goes to Megan Lloyd Davies, for making the writing of this book such a fun and rewarding experience.

FOREWORD

A blonde bimbo, Trout Pout, a footballer's wife, a Tweenie looka-like, the ultimate girl-next-door, a comedy blonde, a liar who won't admit her husband's 'abuse'...there are so many ways in which you might think you know me, but the truth is, you don't. Forgive me if I'm too direct – it's the way I am and I usually get away with it. But, after all the stories and all the headlines, it's time to tell the truth and finally separate the facts from the many fictions that have been written about me, my life and, most importantly, my marriage. So here it is – the story of my life behaving badly.

PROLOGUE

I opened my eyes. It was about 2 a.m. and the bedroom was half lit. Beside me, Lee was reading with his bedside lamp on and its light bathed his side of the room in a soft golden glow. He was having trouble sleeping. There was a lot going on for him – business was busy at our private members' club, Teatro, and I'd just spent a week in hospital after cracking a rib which had torn my lung.

My head felt heavy and painful. I'd felt ill since coming out of hospital two days ago and had wondered yesterday if there was something wrong when I'd tried to pee but couldn't. Now, I felt sick and needed to go to the loo again, so I shifted on to my side and moved to get out of bed.

But as I flung off the bedclothes, I realised my legs felt numb. Nothing. Signals rushed from my brain to my nerves for action, but there was no response. It felt as if a lead weight was trapping my legs. I touched them. They felt dead, as if the circulation had been cut off. I could see they were there, but they wouldn't respond – like when you wake up and your arm has gone dead because you've been sleeping on it.

Maybe I've trapped a nerve, or it's a side effect of the painkillers, I thought to myself. I'd been married to a foot-baller for years, was used to all the lumps and bumps, the body's odd ways of breaking down and healing, so I looked to Lee for the answer.

'I can't move my legs,' I said to him.

'What?' he replied, as he turned to look at me. 'Have they gone to sleep?'

'No,' I said, my voice tensing as annoyance snapped inside me. 'I can't move my fucking legs.'

Sighing, he got out of bed and moved towards me. I tried again to move.

'Where are you going?' he asked.

'To the toilet.'

'Well, take my arm,' he said, as he moved in front of me.

I knew something was terribly wrong when I went to push on to my feet and started sliding off the bed. My feet had no grip in them, and wouldn't respond at all when I tried to move them.

'Put me back, put me back,' I said, as panic pushed its way into my throat.

Instinctively I turned to my bedside drawer and scrabbled for Mr Nott's card. He was the surgeon who had just been looking after me at the Chelsea and Westminster Hospital and I had his card because I was due to make an appointment to see him as an outpatient.

'I've got to call the doctor,' I said, reaching for the phone.

'But there won't be anyone there,' Lee replied, and the line clicked straight on to voicemail as I tried the number on the card.

'I'll phone the ward I was on,' I said. 'There'll be someone I know on night duty and they can get a message to Mr Nott.'

As I waited for the line to connect, I felt like I had on the odd occasions when danger had threatened my children – adrenaline and fear combined to give a feeling of almost icy calm.

Don't think. Don't panic, I told myself. Get hold of the doctor, get his advice and do what he tells you – one thing at a time, just like Mum always said.

A voice answered and my words came out in a rush.

'I have to speak to the doctor urgently. It's Leslie Chapman here.'

'I can't give you his number,' the voice replied. 'We can't give out doctors' home numbers.'

'Well, can you take a message and get him to call me?' I asked. 'It's an emergency. I've just spent a week in hospital and have woken up and can't move.'

I put down the phone, and Lee and I waited for it to ring. You could have heard a pin drop. Lee sat down beside me and didn't say a word.

The phone rang. I snatched it up and heard Mr Nott's voice on the other end.

'I can't feel my legs,' I said.

There was no hesitation in his voice, no questioning or momentary indecision. 'We've got to get you to an MRI scanner straight away,' he replied. 'The nearest one is at Charing Cross. Get an ambulance.'

Shaking, I put down the phone and dialled 999.

'I need to go to Charing Cross,' I told the operator.

'You can't choose where to go,' the voice replied. 'We've got to take you to Chelsea and Westminster Hospital because it's the closest hospital to you.'

'But I can't go there,' I pleaded. 'My doctor's told me to go to Charing Cross.'

'Well, then, he's got to request it. If he does that, then we can take you, but otherwise we can't.'

I slammed down the receiver and phoned back Mr Nott, who assured me he'd sort everything out.

Lee stood up and started walking to the chest of drawers. 'I should get you some things if you've got to go to hospital – you can't go like that,' he said. 'Can you feel anything now? You'd better put some stuff on. You can't go naked.' He started looking for clothes.

'Not there,' I told him. 'Get me my tracksuit bottoms. They're in the bottom drawer.'

As he searched for something to put on me, Lee carried on talking in a rush of words.

'Can you feel anything yet? I wonder what's going on. I'm sure it'll be nothing.'

I didn't take any notice of what he was saying. His words were like white noise in the background as I fought the fear that was building inside me, threatening to wrench its way out of my throat in a howl of panic. I wanted my mum, my sons.

'For heaven's sake, it's only been a week and another ambulance is arriving here,' I said to him. 'The neighbours are going to think I'm bonkers.'

Unspoken words hung in the air. The press had had a field day when I'd cracked my rib last week. 'Actress injured during rough sex,' the headlines had screamed. What would they make of this?

The ringing phone cut through the silence.

'There's an ambulance coming to take you to Charing Cross, where Professor van Dellen will be waiting to see you,' Mr Nott said. 'He'll do an MRI scan, and if there's anything wrong, then he's the best neurosurgeon you could have. You'll be in safe hands. You're lucky he's working today.'

I wanted to scream, to cry at Mr Nott, 'What's happening to me?' but I didn't.

'OK,' I replied, and put down the phone.

By now I really wanted to go for a pee and it was starting to hurt as Lee dressed me. All fingers and thumbs, he hurriedly pulled clothes on to me while I lay like a rag doll. When the doorbell rang, he went to let the paramedics in to our flat.

'We can't bring in a stretcher,' I heard one of them say. 'The lift isn't big enough to take one. We'll have to use a chair.'

Two men walked into the room and came towards me.

'Can you get into this, or will you need assistance?' one of the paramedics asked, and gestured at a chair with wheels on the back.

'I think I'll need some help,' I told him.

The paramedics came to my bedside and tried to help me up, but I was like Bambi as my heels slid across the carpet and my legs remained completely straight. I couldn't bend my knees.

'Oh, my God,' I said in disbelief, realising with horror that now I couldn't feel anything from my chest down. The paralysis was spreading upwards.

The paramedics helped me back on to the bed, slid their arms round me and put me into the chair. Wordlessly, they tipped the chair backwards and wheeled me down the corridor and into the lift.

'I'll follow in the car,' Lee said, when we reached the ground floor. 'Everything will be all right.'

I didn't look at him as he turned towards the car park. I was just anxious to get to hospital. I was transferred to a stretcher and carried into the ambulance. It seemed to take for ever.

With blue lights flashing and siren blaring, one of the paramedics took my temperature and blood pressure as the other drove.

Why put the siren on? I thought to myself. It's the middle of the night and it's going to wake everyone up.

I wasn't in any physical pain as I lay there, but I felt awful. My neck was stiff, the lights seemed to burn into my head, and sickness kept rising up inside me. Fear spiked, but I told myself to stay calm and the paramedic tried to soothe me. After all, if there was anything desperately wrong, they'd be panicking, like they do in *Holby City*, and shouting, 'Put a line in.'

I must have trapped a really big nerve, I told myself. I'll get to hospital and they'll sort it out. It'll be a bit of swelling from the rib or something. They'll fix it.

Drawing up outside A&E, I was lifted out of the ambulance and taken through double doors into a closed-off area. Lee arrived just behind us.

'We're going to get you into the scanner,' a nurse said, as she put a line into a vein on my wrist.

Professor van Dellen arrived in his operating clothes. 'Mrs

Chapman, we need to see what this is and it will be confirmed by the scan,' he told me.

Panic subsided in me as the professor, who was in his
fifties and balding with glasses, smiled reassuringly. I was in
hospital, the best place for me, and everything would be fine.

'Are you all right?' Lee kept asking as he squeezed my
hand.

'Yes, fine,' I replied.

The nurses took my blood pressure again.

'You'll be all right,' Lee said to me.

I knew he wasn't convinced, but everyone seemed so calm
as I lay on the stretcher. The nurses were bustling around, the
noise level was low, and no one seemed to be shouting
instructions or anything. Anyway, I felt too terrible to take
much notice. I was so hot and my head pounded as it never
had before.

Soon I was put into a gown and wheeled into a room that
contained a huge machine – an MRI scanner. I was put on to
a bench and it slid slowly inside. It felt as if I was being buried
in a metal tomb. All I could hear was whirring until the
bench came to a stop. Those were probably the scariest 20
minutes of my life as I lay there listening to the silence, interrupted only by thuds, beeps and clicks. It seemed to go on for
ever, and trapped in that confined space, I felt more and more
anxious. What was happening to me? Why couldn't I move?
When would I start to feel again? The white metal walls of
the scanner seemed to close in on me. I couldn't breathe and
I pressed the panic button in alarm.

'It's OK,' a voice said. 'We're finished now.'

The bench slid out of the machine and I was put back on
to a trolley and taken into a side room.

'We're going to prep you for surgery,' a nurse told me.
'Professor van Dellen will arrive in a minute to see you, but
we need you to sign this form giving your consent to be operated on.'

Suddenly the calm that had greeted my arrival was shattered and everything went into overdrive as I scribbled my name. With Lee beside me, I was wheeled out of the side room into a dark corridor. To my right, I could see bright lights shining out of windows in a door. I was pushed through it into the anaesthetic room.

What's happening? Why are they doing this? I thought, my brain woozy from the headache and sickness. I had no idea what was going on, why they needed to operate, and I could still feel nothing from the chest down.

Suddenly the professor walked back into the room with a serious look on his face.

'Mrs Chapman, Mr Chapman, we must operate straight away,' he said. 'The MRI scan has told us that Mrs Chapman has an abscess pressing on her spinal column and an infection that is spreading. Time is therefore of the essence and we have to act quickly.'

Lee and I looked at each other disbelievingly. It was like something out of a bad American soap opera. What was he saying? How on earth could I have an abscess on my spine? I'd only broken a rib.

'If we don't operate now, then there could be devastating effects,' the professor continued.

I stared up at him as I lay on the trolley trying to take in what was happening.

'I must tell you, Mrs Chapman, that there are three possible outcomes to this surgery: one is that you will pull through; one is that you will be paralysed; and one is that you will die. I'm sorry to tell you this, but it really is vital that we get you into the operating theatre now.'

Lee's hand gripped mine and my eyes slid up to meet his. I couldn't believe what was happening. I was going into surgery? I could die?

As I stared up at my husband, it felt like a last look between us. Disbelief rushed through my brain. I was going to be put under anaesthetic and I might not come out. I hadn't said goodbye to my children or had a moment with Lee and there was nothing I could do.

Then all I remember is the hustle and bustle of the room and a voice saying, 'You'll feel a sharp scratch.'

As the needle went into my arm, I gazed again at Lee. His look said it all. Everything went black.

CHAPTER I

In the Beginning

The lights burned white hot above my head, and a man held up a black box to my face.

'Hello,' I chirped into it, thinking it was a microphone.

Everyone started to chuckle. I stared around nervously.

'Leslie, darling, that's a light meter,' Mum said gently. She was stood in the no-man's-land of the television studio where shadow meets bright light.

'Oh,' I said, as a blush curled up my face, and I fell silent once again.

I was four years old and in front of the cameras for the first time to make a television advert for Fairy Liquid. All around was a frenzy of activity – men carrying props, a man peering into a camera lens, and a tall woman reeking of perfume standing beside me. She was going to play my mum, but she didn't seem like one to me. My mum, Ellie, was warm and smiling. This lady seemed to look down her nose at me. But then again I suppose she had little choice, given that I was only 3 feet tall.

My memories of that day in 1964 are like the advert itself – all in black and white. It started with me rolling a ball towards some skittles I'd made out of Fairy Liquid bottles as my 'mum' pleaded with me to give the full one back to her. It was all very 1960s, with crazy wallpaper on the walls of the kitchen and my 'mum' sporting an immaculately set hairdo

9

and speaking like something out of a Noël Coward play. A man fed me my lines and I repeated them.

'I can't do the washing-up without my Fairy Liquid,' my 'mum' said to me.

'Why not? You don't put it on your hands,' I piped up.

Seconds later we were together in front of the camera, smiling at the Fairy Liquid bottle, as you do.

I'd got the advert because my mum and dad knew a commercial producer called Morton Lewis. He was a regular at the many parties they threw. I'll never forget his wife, Sally, because she had Chihuahuas and I couldn't get over how little they were. I was small and so were they, like mini dogs made especially for me – unlike our dog, Pepper, who was a Dalmatian and seemed to tower over me.

Anyway, Morton Lewis announced one day over a Harvey's Bristol Cream that they were looking for a new kid for the Fairy advert and so my parents put me forward. I can't remember the audition, but I do remember shopping to buy clothes for the filming day. You know how some childhood outfits stick in your mind for ever? Well, that was one of them. Brown and navy-blue dungarees, white plimsolls, and me thinking that doing an advert was great because you got to go shopping. Even at four I loved the shops, and it seemed like a real treat to get something brand new because I often wore hand-me-downs from my elder sister, Debbie.

So there I was on set in my dungarees with my brown hair cut into a fringe and sideboards, like a long mullet – very fashionable in the 1960s, me being the leader of fashion I was then – and most of the day seemed to involve doing shots of me smiling up at my 'mum' or speaking my lines off camera. The only sentence I did have to say on film must have needed about ten takes to get right because I kept messing it up. I didn't worry, though – I was wearing a new outfit, had got a day off school and was munching sweets. It all seemed great to me. I didn't realise then that it was to be the first step on the long and winding road of a television career that's spanned four decades.

I was born at home in Mitcham, Surrey, on 19 February 1960 at 3 a.m. My mum had refused to have me in the cottage hospital where my sister, Debbie, had been born three and a half years earlier because the nurses had fastened the nappy pin to her skin. So instead she had me at home with her mother in attendance.

My dad, meanwhile, was in bed asleep – untouched by the euphoria of the birth. For him, it was a job for women, and I don't think my mum wanted him there, anyway – it was her moment.

'It's a girl,' my grandmother told my dad, as she put her head round the bedroom door.

'Well done,' he said, turning over and going straight back to sleep.

My dad, Maurice John, known to everyone as Moe, was of the old school. Five feet eight inches tall, he had a stocky build and I always thought he looked like a bulldog when I was growing up. My mum, though, insisted he looked like Tony Curtis. Oh, my God, was she blind? But then they say that's what true love is.

Moe was a South London boy from Balham and his parents ran a builders' merchants. He was a war baby, sent to the countryside with a little label round his neck and a child-sized gas mask. He had a very strict Victorian upbringing. But, for all that, he turned out to be a bit of a rebel. Moe loved tailored fashion – two-tone suits with a 3-inch vent in the back, that kind of stuff. No one quite knows why, but he also grew a porn-star-style tache in the 1960s and, to complete the image, wore splash-it-all-over Brut. Character-wise, he had a great sense of humour and the ability to make people laugh. When it came to his children, he had a short fuse and his word was definitely always the last, but he was cuddly and gentle in equal measure. Never without a Montecristo No. 2 cigar, Moe had lots of true friends, was a passionate golfer and an even more dedicated gambler – he loved the cards and kalooki was his weakness. I'm sure it must have paid the odd school fee because my dad walked a bit wide of the tracks at times. He knocked around with a lot of South London villains, and while he was more of a Del Boy than a Ronnie Kray, he was always keen to make a bit extra on the side. He permanently had an enormous wad of cash in his pocket from flogging alpaca jumpers or posh watches that people had given him in return for a loan. One of my most vivid memories is of the day crime-buster Shaw Taylor appeared on the telly appealing for help in tracking down boxes of dodgy gin. Suddenly my dad jumped up and started shifting boxes from our kitchen into the airing cupboard.

Moe met my mum, Eleanor, or Ellie as everyone knew her, when he was working in a soft-drinks factory in Canada after he'd run away, aged 15, and ended up in the New World. Ellie, who was blonde and spoke in a softly drawling Canadian accent, had a small face, quite a prominent nose and a big smile. She brimmed with kindness and warmth, and was that bit different from the South London birds Moe was used to. Moe and Ellie shared three vital characteristics: a great sense of humour, a love of fun and a passion for dressing up. Just like Dad, my mum was always extremely well turned out – even for the fashion-conscious 1960s – with perfect hair and make-up. Soon they fell in love, married, honeymooned in romantic Niagara Falls and returned to Surrey.

Then, when I was a few months old, we moved from Surrey to a five-bedroom house in Streatham. While my dad went out to work at the family builders' merchants, my mum stayed at home. Life really did seem perfect – it was almost like *The Stepford Wives* in a way, with my dad in charge and my mum the ideal housewife.

It was at night that they really came alive. My parents

loved socialising and some of my most vivid memories are of watching Mum getting ready to go out with Dad for the evening to meet friends in the West End. Most weekends they'd go to nightclubs like the Talk of the Town and the Astor, while my sister and I were looked after by au pairs. However often they did it, those evenings out were always a big deal for Mum, and I remember watching transfixed as she got ready for the night ahead. Evening dress really meant evening dress back then and she'd put on a long, straight skirt, heavy beaded top and strappy shoes before applying her make-up – false eyelashes, the lot – and drenching herself in perfume. Over the years her perfume of choice went from Femme to Estée Lauder to Oscar de la Renta and even now, when I smell those scents, it takes me back to my mum fussing over me with a hanky or holding me close and making me believe everything would be all right. Then she'd put on some gold or diamond jewellery that my dad had bought her, spray her hair – backcombed to the roots, of course – with so much stuff that the fumes caught in my throat as they filled the room and finally slick on 'Pink Meringue' Max Factor lipstick. At last the look was complete and she'd bend down to kiss me, leaving a glossy pink outline on my cheek, before she, the hairspray and my father were gone.

They also loved entertaining at home and there were many nights when I'd lie in bed listening to the sound of people laughing and glasses clinking. Desperate not to miss it all, I'd creep on to the landing and sit there until I fell asleep. Then, in the morning, before anyone else was awake, I'd sneak downstairs to find the place littered with champagne glasses with clear stems and red bowls, which I thought were the height of sophistication. Invariably some would contain the dregs of the partygoers' Babycham, which I'd knock back in a few quick gulps. In later years, after I started experimenting with smoking at about the age of 12, I'd go round the ashtrays looking for long butts, then smoke them with my friend Neil

Leatherdale from next door. Or, if I was really clever, I'd steal a few cigarettes from the box where my parents kept them. My first experience of true shame came one day when I dropped a fag and my dad said, 'I think you've forgotten something.' I felt mortified and put it back.

When it came to the outside world, Debbie and I knew we were ambassadors for Dad's success as a father and there would be trouble if we embarrassed him. So, on the frequent occasions when Dad proclaimed, 'Let's go up West for a slap-up meal,' we made sure we only spoke when spoken to, sat on our hands to avoid accidents and never reached across the table for something. On reflection, I see now that he taught us something we took for granted that is missing in society today – good manners.

Then there were the cold Sunday mornings when Dad would drag Debbie and me out of bed at the crack of dawn to take us out so that Mum could have a rest. Pulling on our clothes over our pyjamas, we'd follow him out to the car and on to the golf course to watch him play his round. I don't really remember talking to Dad much as a child, but whenever I think of him he's smiling.

While Debbie was always a daddy's girl, I was closer to Mum. Maybe it's because Debbie was a few years older than me, but Mum and I seemed to spend a lot of time alone together when I was a child. Her passion was gardening and there were always flowers in the borders – chrysanthemums, roses and sweet peas filling the beds – and a man called Mr Miles came in to help her with it all. At some point in the day, I'd inevitably get under her feet in the house and she'd shoo me out into the garden where Mr Miles would be trying to work and I'd start annoying him instead. In an effort to distract me, he gave me my own patch of garden to look after, where I grew pansies and rock plants. But it wasn't enough to hold my attention and he soon devised a fail-proof strategy for keeping me quiet. In a yard at the side of the house was a manhole cover that you could lift up to see the open drain-pipes below – and of course what was being flushed down the loo.

'If you wait there long enough, you'll see a poo go past,' Mr Miles told me one day. 'And, remember,' he said, his voice dropping to a dramatic whisper and his eyebrows arching, 'if it's got a flag in it, it'll be the Queen's turd.'

With that, he handed me one of the roll-ups he used to smoke (this was way before the days when we discovered just how bad cigarettes are for you) and so there I'd be, sitting for hours with my roll-up waiting patiently for the Queen's poo to float past.

My other favourite pastime was dressing up in my mum's clothes. I'd spend hours rummaging around – as interested then as I would be in later years in the world of make-believe and glamour. One famous day, I eased on her black kitten-heeled boots and mink stole, went to her handbag and got the car keys. Then I got behind the wheel of the stationary car and started pretending I was going out for a glamorous night on the town. I must have been there for hours because even-tually I got tired and fell asleep. Of course, Mum couldn't find me and was soon phoning all the neighbours to ask if they'd seen me. After ringing round everyone she knew, she decided to look further afield and found me asleep in her heels in the driving seat of the car.

This passion for fashion extended throughout my child-hood and Mum always made sure that Debbie and I were impeccably turned out. My sister and I often wore matching outfits from places like Carnaby Street or the King's Road (yeah, baby, yeah!) and sometimes it would irritate me that we wore the same. Mostly, though, I loved those shopping expeditions, and my pride and joy was a pair of red suede boots bought from a shop in the King's Road. I thought they were the best thing ever, and even better was the fact that Peter Wyngarde, the actor who played Jason King in the TV series *Department S*, was in the shop when we bought them. I got his autograph, so it was the ultimate day for me – new boots and some hero-worship.

When the time came for school, I put on the boater, shirt, tie, blazer and grey pleated skirt that made up the uniform of the Virgo Fidelis Convent in Norwood. Run by French nuns, it was a strict but kind school and I enjoyed it there. I wasn't exactly an academic but was always keen to learn and made my stage debut at about the age of six, playing a mouse in the chorus of a school play and wearing an outfit my mum had made me.

I can't remember if it was because of the Fairy Liquid ad or my turn as a mouse, but my mum used to say that she always knew I wanted to be an actress. I didn't think about it like that, but as far back as I can remember I'd put on records in the front room, memorise the lines and sing along. Or Mum would take us to the pantomime and, while I know it's an old cliché, I'd sit and watch, wishing I was Cinderella. It never occurred to me that it involved two shows a day and hard work. All I could see was a world of dresses, wigs, bright lights and wonder.

A big change for us all came when I was about ten and my dad left the family business. It was a bit of a touchy subject, ironed over, but we stopped seeing Grandpa and sold up the house in Streatham. Suddenly my dad appeared in a white van bearing the words 'Unidec Distributors Ltd' on the side in blue – a far cry from the Mercedes we were used to, but somehow more fun. We moved to 165 Clapham High Street in South London, where my parents had used the money from selling the big house to buy a shop. They were going to start a painting and decorating business and we'd live above in a flat. Debbie and I thought it was all a big adventure, but life for my parents changed dramatically. Gone was the glamour as they worked all hours to get the new business going and gone too was the undivided attention from my mum, so I quickly learned how to be independent. Now, instead of playing in our lovely garden in Streatham, I amused myself in the shop, Unidec, pretending to serve customers and transform their post-war semis into cutting-edge 1970s homes. For my mum, it meant going from being a comfortable housewife to standing on her feet selling paint all day, and I don't think being a shopkeeper was exactly my dad's idea of fun either.

Our two-bedroom flat was a far cry from the five-bedroom home we were used to. Now Debbie and I shared a room and we would lie in bed on Saturday nights listening to the sounds of fights when closing time came in the local pubs. Let's just say Clapham then wasn't quite the trendy spot it is today. But we made our room our own – there was an invisible line dividing it, and if Debbie's clothes sneaked over it, I'd kick them back. In true 1970s style, the walls were painted bright tangerine, and we plastered them with posters. While my sister was a one-man woman and favoured pictures of George Best, I couldn't make my mind up between David Cassidy and Donny Osmond. I think David Cassidy won in the end because he had nicer hair. One thing that stayed the same, though, was my school, Virgo Fidelis, but now it meant a long bus journey. Every morning my parents would stand at the bathroom window to wave me off, and on the odd occasion when they forgot, I used to get really upset.

The most important change the move to Clapham prompted was the discovery of drama school. To get Debbie and me out from under her feet when she was working in the shop on Saturdays, my mum decided dancing lessons would be just the thing. She found a place a mile down the road – the Italia Conti Academy of Theatre Arts. Housed in the beautiful Avondale Hall in Landor Road, it boasted a huge ground-floor room with a stage and skylights and a warren of studios in the basement. Debbie and I thought this all-singing, all-dancing place was the best thing ever. We were amazed when we realised that some children went there full-time and spent the morning doing academic work and the afternoon dancing, singing and acting. How fun was that?

Within months Debbie had been bitten by the bug and had persuaded Mum to let her attend Italia Conti full-time. I begged Mum to let me do the same.

'But Debbie doesn't have to wear uniform, so why do I?' I moaned as I trailed around the shop after her.

She wouldn't budge, though, and I had to stay at Virgo Fidelis until the end of junior school and only then could I leave for Italia Conti. I think my dad had the idea that everyone in the acting business wore a cravat and went around calling people 'darling', but he always let Mum make the decisions and she knew I wasn't going to be turning out straight As in O levels and was desperate to go. So, in 1971, at the ripe old age of 11, I started at Italia Conti full-time.

'Miss Brearly won't be here for your English lesson today – she's having her hair done – so you'll all have to read your Shakespeare book or something,' the student announced as she sat down behind the desk and started filing her nails.

Let's just say that the academic side of life wasn't overly important at stage school back then. It's different now, of course, but 30 years ago no one stressed the importance of passing exams in order to support yourself should your stage career flop. In the 1970s, it was all about performance. Ballet, modern, tap, jazz, singing, elocution – I was learning so many new things and loving them.

My favourite class was improvisation, which was taken once a week by Melvyn Hayes from *It Ain't Half Hot, Mum*. I loved those classes. Improvisation is exactly what it says on the bottle – no text, no lines, just do what you feel. Sometimes you'd have to be funny, other times you'd be reduced to tears, and it was a really good way of cutting through all your fears of looking like an idiot. That's the one thing you've got to be able to get over the moment you start performing and that's what Melvyn did for me. He used to say it was like getting into a swimming pool – you know it will be freezing for a split second, but you enjoy it once you're in. He brought out the actress within me and I adored him for it – plus the fact that he was the same size as me.

At a school where past pupils include Noël Coward, Sharon Osbourne and Sadie Frost, I'd like to say that I was a star who shone brightly, but in fact I was no more than a mini glow. I was never tipped for the top at Italia Conti, and whereas some children had parents who pushed them all the way, mine didn't. My mum was laid-back about the whole thing.

'You can only do your best,' she'd say to me. 'That's all you can do.'

So I didn't take it too seriously, and I shut out the hysteria of all the drama queens shrieking, 'Oh, my God,' about the slightest thing. I was always better at listening than talking and was popular because I made people laugh. Among my contemporaries were Bonnie Langford, Lena Zavaroni and Jamie Foreman – son of the former gangland boss Freddie Foreman, who was a friend of my dad's. My two best friends were Tracey Ullman, the great comedy actress, and Rosemary Hetherington, who ended up in Legs and Co. We were the perfect match for each other – Tracey had the most amazing voice, Rosemary was a fantastic dancer, and I was good at acting. The three of us were very close – we'd make up dance routines to the latest hits, sit together in class and head to Wimpy for a Coke float after school.

By the age of 13 I was exploring London alone. If my parents' shop was shut when I had an audition, then Mum would give me a lift, but otherwise I was on my own. Then, as now, the King's Road was my favourite place in the whole city. How could it not be? There was even a shop that revolved, called Stop the World. The whole place was on a turntable and slowly moved round. Eyes out on stalks, I would gaze in the windows of shops like Chelsea Girl and dream about having all those clothes. I was painfully skinny at the time, but it was cool then because the legacies of Twiggy and Mary Quant lived on. My mum tactfully told me I looked like Jean Shrimpton as she sat at the sewing machine taking in clothes to fit my shapeless body. My dad, on the other hand, nicknamed me 'Muscles'. Even though being so independent presented all sorts of chances to misbehave, I never did. I was a bit of a goody two shoes, really – it took me years to learn how to lose the plot. While my sister was the one who pushed the boundaries, I learned from her mistakes and worked out that it made for a far quieter life if I toed the line.

A couple of years into Italia Conti, I got my first big audition. The previous year I'd done a Christmas special for *The Black and White Minstrel Show* – let's just say shows like *Love Thy Neighbour* were still on TV back then. Ernest Maxim was a big light-entertainment producer at the BBC and he decided it would be cute for the principal artists and dancers to perform 'Walking in a Winter Wonderland' while sickly cute kids with wide smiles danced in the background. I was one of those, and step-ball-changing into view, I appeared from the wings with my fellow girl performers. We wore spangled leotards, while the boys wore silver suits, Afro wigs and blacked-up faces. I cringe now when I think about it.

A year later I went up for the lead in *Black Beauty* – apart from the horse, of course. The combination of a lead role and a pony meant that the part was every young girl's dream. It was between me and a girl called Stacy Dorning and I was determined to get it. Riding was pretty crucial for the role and so I had to learn to do it and fast. Quaking with fear, I was packed off to a local stables, but the pony must have sensed how I felt because it ended up bolting down the A3, which put paid to my ambitions to be Black Beauty's sidekick. Stacy got the gig.

Auditions were the lifeblood of Italia Conti, and letters from the principal, Mrs Sheward, or her daughter, Anne, calling people in to see them were posted on a noticeboard at the bottom of the main stairs. If your name was up, you knew you'd got an audition, that you were going to get a crack, and excitement would bubble up inside as you stared at your name. Then of course you'd turn round with a nonchalant expression and make out as if it wasn't that important, while those who weren't on the list struggled to hide their disappointment. Some pupils' names were up there all the time and they would disappear for weeks on end with a chaperone to do a film or TV series. But mine wasn't. I probably did half a dozen or so auditions a year, but it's funny because the people whose names were on that board all the time, and whom we all thought were the right stuff, were largely the ones who didn't end up in the business, while the people who weren't up for so many auditions ended up making a living at it.

Each audition was essentially the same. You'd sing one high-tempo song and a ballad (mine were 'Who Will Buy?' and 'Where Is Love?' from the musical *Oliver!*) before the choreographer walked on and you'd get asked to do some dance steps. At the end, all the hopefuls would gather on stage and stand in a line and someone would start shouting, 'You...you...you,' at various people and you'd know whether or not you were going home or had got through to the next stage. Some girls were gutted when they didn't get through, but I was never one of those. I didn't view it all as a job or a competition. My parents were well aware that 80 per cent of stage-school children didn't make a living from performing and so they never pushed us or filled us with crazy dreams. I told myself that if I didn't get a job, it wasn't because I wasn't good enough, but simply because I wasn't right. That's the attitude you've got to have in the business: you can't take everything personally.

Auditions aside, I loved being at Italia Conti, even though

it was hard work. Modern dance, taken by the aptly named Miss Wivel (or 'Swivel', as we called her), would be followed by ballet, taken by a man who used to chain-smoke the whole way through. Then there were normal academic classes, and we always seemed to be doing speech and drama grades. I did, of course, get some work – most notably eight weeks in a film called *The Boy with Two Heads*, in which I played the boy's best friend. All I can remember is that we found a shrunken head that could talk and brought rain to a dry land. I also did a series called *Switch on for Sweden*, which was shown to help kids learn English. Not quite the dream role that *Black Beauty* would have been, but, hey.

I just wanted to be the kid in the blockbuster musicals with fantastic dancing. *Chitty Chitty Bang Bang*, *Bedknobs and Broomsticks* – every year as I grew up there was a film I loved. During my last year at Italia Conti I hoped I might finally get my chance to be in one when legendary producer David Puttnam came to our school looking for kids to per-form in *Bugsy Malone*. But I was getting ready to leave, was past the cute stage and wasn't right, so I never did appear in one of those films.

Just as kids outside Italia Conti started preparing to take their O levels and think about earning a living, my thoughts also turned to the outside world. I didn't question the fact that I was going to leave school, get a job and look after myself – and somehow acting was going to help me do that. I didn't get too het up about it all, though. I saw Italia Conti as a training school for my trade and now I was going to go out and learn more about it. Acting for a living was something I would work up to: I knew it wasn't going to happen overnight. I'd learned from my parents that hard work would eventually pay off.

I was also lucky enough to know that whatever happened, I would have a steady income. About a year before leaving school, I'd got a Saturday job at Jean Machine on the King's

Road and was working in there one day when the famous page-3 model Jilly Johnson walked in with a man at her side. I didn't recognise him, but his name was Brian Aris and he was a photographer. Today, he's one of Britain's top celebrity photographers and has taken pictures of the Beatles and of the Beckhams' wedding. He even did the Queen's 70th-birthday portrait. Back then, I may not have known his face, but I recognised his name when he handed me his card. The *Sun* was running pictures of Brian Aris's favourite page-3 girls at the time and my heart sank. If there was one thing I never wanted to be, it was a page-3 girl. No disrespect, they kept my dad happy for years, but my hopes were aimed a little bit higher.

'I'd like to do some pictures of you,' Brian told me. 'I know an agency that's looking for girls to do teen stuff like catalogues, commercials and magazines like *Jackie*.'

My look must have said it all because he added, 'And it's nothing to do with taking your top off.'

I felt so flattered and excited. In those days, models weren't the celebrities they are today, but I'd always been into fashion, make-up and hairstyles, so it seemed to me like a golden opportunity.

'OK, I'll give it a go,' I told Brian, and we arranged for me to go to his studio in Old Street to have my test shots done.

Soon I was taken on by a modelling agency called Freddie's, in Knightsbridge, and given a diary in which to write my casting appointments. In the days before mobiles, I had to phone in three times a day to find out if and where I was needed. Soon I was juggling castings and shoots with lessons at Italia Conti. My first Z card – the 'shop window' that was posted to people so that they could have a look at you – showed me with a shiny brunette flick, my heart-shaped face and wearing a sequinned top and scarf. Something about me was right and I did well from the start. As a fresh-faced 16-year-old, I appeared on the cover of *Jackie* for the first time on 10 May

CHAPTER 2

Caught on Camera

More bloody stairs. Puffing and panting, I climbed my way up to the top floor of the Soho townhouse, lugging my portfolio of photographs with me. I was on my way to see another acting agent. Why, oh, why did they all have offices at the top of the tallest buildings they could find? Nevertheless I was determined to make sure that this one took me on. His name was Brookie, and because I was going to be leaving Italia Conti soon, I wanted to get myself an acting agent who specialised in adults. Also, he was the star of the High Karate aftershave adverts and had fought off busty brunettes because he smelled so irresistible – I knew him from the TV so he must be good.

Brookie's offices were in the middle of Soho, opposite a club called the Valbonne, which had go-go dancers swinging on chairs and in cages. Nerves filled me as I walked up the stairs, but I relaxed the moment I saw Brookie – stocky, with blow-dried 1970s hair and a sharp suit, he looked exactly like he did in the commercial. The only thing that was missing was the whiff of High Karate. Thankfully.

'So when are you leaving Italia Conti?' Brookie asked as I sat down.

'Not long – I've just sat my O levels so I've only got a few weeks left.'

'Well, I would take you on, but you've already got an

acting agent at school and you're not supposed to have two, so it might be difficult.'

I wasn't having any of it, though, and he eventually gave in after I'd begged, pleaded and reassured Brookie that I could easily juggle the situation.

It took about a week for the shit to hit the fan. I knew I'd fallen out of favour at Italia Conti when Brookie phoned to say Arlene Phillips was casting a commercial for Levi's. Back then, Arlene, who's now famous as one of the judges on the BBC's *Strictly Come Dancing*, took modern jazz at Italia Conti and had previously asked me to audition for a new dance troupe she'd set up called Hot Gossip. I hadn't made it in because I couldn't get my legs high enough or something, but I knew she liked me. Anyway, now she was choreographing the Levi's advert, but apparently Italia Conti had said I wasn't available for it – that was when Brookie had got involved. Two things were obvious: first, that Italia Conti had found out about him and weren't putting me forward for jobs; second, that I'd have to leave school early if I got the role via him. The Levi's advert was too good an opportunity to miss – they made one big commercial every year, and who knew what it could lead to?

Brookie got me an audition.

I got the part. We spent three days filming at Shepperton Studios, and I loved every minute of it. Directed by Ridley Scott, who'd go on to make films including *Alien* and *Gladiator*, the ad was set in the 1950s to the tune of 'Leader of the Pack'. A whole American street, complete with an ice-cream bar, was built for the shoot and I was the leader of the pack's sickly sweet love interest. With my hair in pigtails, I sipped on a milkshake, mimed the words of the song and stared at him all gooey-eyed when he appeared on his motorbike. The two of us danced, there were shots of our jeans, and then he disappeared. It sounds simple, but so much work went into producing that tiny advert, and everything – from the smell of bacon sarnies in the morning to the hordes of people running around, each with a job to do – interested me. I was bitten by the bug and would go on to make about 30 adverts over the next few years. I enjoyed every one and still remember some of the lines today. For instance, did you know that *'Pickel'* is the German word for 'pimple'? I learned that for a Clearasil commercial. Then there was Nivea with Adrian Lyne, who later directed *Nine $^1/_2$ Weeks*, which ended with me backlit with a slick of cream on my nose, and a famous advert for Harmony hairspray, shot in Los Angeles, where I was walking in a park with my back to the camera, my hair swinging in the breeze, while everyone asked, 'Is she or isn't she?'

Commercials aside, it was my photographic modelling that really took off after I left Italia Conti. I worked for all the magazines – *Mirabelle, Pink, Fab 208, Jackie* and *Mates* – and did everything from fashion and beauty to covers. Every so often a pop star, like Midge Ure or the Bay City Rollers, would be wheeled in for you to have a picture taken with, but they seemed as confused as I was – we were all young and starting off, so there was no 'big star' bit. In fact, my favourite type of modelling was probably foot work because you could turn up looking awful and all you had to do was sit there reading a magazine while pictures were taken of your feet and shoes. Otherwise, it was really hard work and I seemed to spend hours dragging around a suitcase of clothes because there'd always be a brief to bring accessories like white shoes, black shoes or a skirt that a secretary would wear. So you'd pack it all up, carry it around, lug it up the hill to the studio and only use a pair of bloody earrings.

Even so, they were funny times, happy days and I was in demand. My agency gave out a bottle of champagne to any girl who made £1,000 a month and I seemed to have no prob-lem getting it. Still living with my mum and dad, I soon realised I needed to be more mobile and bought myself a white Mini. Over the next few years I had it sprayed acid green and fitted with everything from a sunroof and brilliant stereo to roo bars and chrome wheel arches – I pimped my ride right up!

'Nicky, give us a drag of that fag while you two nitpick about the shot for another hour, can you?'

I lay completely still as the cigarette came towards me and I took a heavy drag. I was lying on the floor of a photographer's studio waiting for a shoot to begin. My hair was spread out in Marcel waves in a halo around me, and I couldn't move because all the hair on the right side of my head was taped to a light stand. The aim was to create a beautiful fan effect for a photo, but in practice it was like a slow form of torture. My friends photographer Chris Duffy and hairstylist Nicky Clarke weren't helping. They'd been staring down at me for what seemed like hours as they moved the lights and discussed frames.

'Anyone would think this was high fucking art rather than a photo,' I hissed, as I dragged in the smoke.

Nicky plucked the fag away. Supertramp boomed out of the stereo. He smoked rough Rothmans, but I preferred Consulate, a bit more sophisticated. Were we ever going to be ready to go?

It was about ten o'clock one autumn night in 1977 and the three of us were working together on some photos for our portfolios. Chris was in charge of pictures, Nicky the hair and me the face – each of us was helping the others out to get what we all wanted. We were lucky we had a studio to work in at all. Chris's dad was the famous fashion photographer Brian Duffy, and not many people have famous photographers as fathers, let alone a top-of-the-range one like Brian. He'd let us use his studio near Regent's Park after work and we were downing cups of tea and chain-smoking because it was going to be a long night. I was trying to be patient, but it was hard

– Chris and Nicky just wouldn't get a move on.

'Nearly there,' Nicky said, as he walked towards me and fiddled with my hair yet again before wandering off.

I'd met him a few months before, when my sister, Debbie, and I had moved into houses on the same road in Tooting. After spending years holidaying in Spain, Mum and Dad had moved there full-time, leaving Unidec, the shop, in the hands of managers, and I'd got my own place. The Tooting houses had belonged to our grandfather and Debbie and I had bought one each at a discount. Both of us had got a lodger to help out with the bills, and Debbie's was a friend of mine from Italia Conti called Edwina Laurie. She was Lulu's younger sister, and in those days Lulu was married to John Frieda. He worked with Nicky, who started going out with Edwina, and Edwina introduced Nicky to me. The thing about Nicky that had made the biggest impression on me was his mass of red hair; but then again I suppose that's what makes an impression on most people. He was a lovely guy – very artistic, always laughing and really proud of his pale-blue Skoda, which he'd bought for £700.

My lodger, meanwhile, was a glamour model called Barbara Molyneux, whom I'd met through friends. You never made a lot of mates in modelling because you didn't have time; it was all done on the end of the phone and very competitive, so you didn't really get a chance to know each other. But Barbara was a great housemate and we were convinced we were living the dream – I'd converted one of the bedrooms into a proper bathroom to replace the outside loo and had done up the rest of the two-bed house in all the seventies styles. Brown was my main obsession and I'd bought two settees in the Liberty sale with Mum. They were covered in a diamond-checked material that was brown, peppermint green and white. They sat in the living room alongside a dark wooden coffee table with a square cut in the middle to put a plant pot in. I'd also got cheap paint from Dad to decorate with.

What with my brass bed and brown shagpile carpet, man, oh, man, I was set up for life.

Barbara was a real dolly bird. Very pretty, with golden hair and a big bust, she had a thick northern accent and a huge smile. Most importantly, she shared my love of music and we soon combined our album collection. David Bowie's *Ziggy Stardust* and Rod Stewart's *Footloose and Fancy Free* were our favourites, and 'Hot Legs' was our anthem. While Barbara jumped around madly to it, I would air-guitar wearing lip gloss and stripy leg-warmers with my Farrah Fawcett flicks swinging to the beat. I never wore black back then: everything had to be brightly coloured, whether it was a pink sweater dress or a multicoloured cardigan, because deep down I was a real show-off. As well as eye-catching clothes, I loved making people laugh and was always mimicking them. My other favourite trick was going for it on the dance floor when my crowd of friends and I went out – usually to the Embassy Club, off Piccadilly, or Legends, off Savile Row. Completely sober because I was always driving, I'd go mad to everything from Abba and the Three Degrees to 'Woman, take me in your arms and rock me, baby'. It took me back to the Saturday mornings that Debbie and I had spent at the Lacano kids' disco club in Streatham, where our favourite song was 'Cinderella Rockefella' by Esther and Abi Ofarim. We used to get so into it that we usually ended up attracting a circle of people to watch, and nothing had changed ten years later – as everyone around me discoed, I'd be doing experimental high kicks and head rolls. I was convinced everyone was staring at me in awe – now I know it was because I looked like a prat.

That was what I was like all those years ago. I wasn't a thinker or an analyser. I knew I was an airhead – that's what people expected and that's what they got. But what they didn't know was that I carried around a dictionary so that if someone used a long word, I could go to the toilet and look it up, or that part of me was really anxious to be liked – I always seemed to be giving people lifts, buying them drinks and things like that. It's all part of growing up, isn't it? I'd spent a lot of time with my parents, who had spoiled me, and suddenly not everyone was doing that now I'd left home and was earning my own living. To the outside world, however, I lived up to being a bubbly 17-year-old and concentrated on clothes, music and work.

Intent on getting an amazing portfolio, I'd spend hours looking enviously at the pictures in magazines. I was happy with the ones I had in my portfolio already, but I still had dreams. Those were the days of David Bailey and Terence Donovan and my sights were set high, so that was why I'd ended up taped to a light stand in a photographic studio waiting for Chris and Nicky to finish.

'Right, we're ready,' Chris said, as he bent down to the lens which was pointed at me.

'At long bloody last,' I moaned.

We must have worked for about five hours that night and I've still got one of the photos today – it's probably my favourite picture of me. It's not a commercial picture trying to sell a product; it's just me looking young with my whole life ahead of me and a nice hairstyle.

We eventually finished at about 3 a.m. and I couldn't wait to get home, so it really irritated me when the police pulled me over about five minutes into the journey. I must have looked so odd – thick make-up, hair done to perfection and wearing an old tracksuit. When I told them I'd been working, I'm sure they thought I was on the game. Eventually, though, they realised I wasn't up to anything and let me on my way.

Benny Hill stood smiling in the living room of his enormous flat overlooking Kensington Gardens. It was a real bachelor pad – all function and Formica, it looked almost lonely. But Benny himself was lovely.

'We're thinking of bringing out a single for the Bennettes, so I'd like you to sing for me,' he said. 'I'm just going to get my mandolin.'

It was summer 1978 and I was auditioning for the king of slapstick. In the two years since I'd left Italia Conti, I'd had only one small part in a film called *Rosie Dixon, Night Nurse* and was keen to get more acting work. I'd gone for another job a couple of weeks before – probably the biggest audition I had had so far – but hadn't heard anything and kept telling myself not to worry, that what would be would be. But it was hard to forget because the part was the lead female role in the latest Who film, *Quadrophenia* – every 18-year-old's dream. I was desperate for it. A big, high-profile film, a leading role – great balls of mozzarella, here I come!

I hadn't got my hopes up too high when I'd gone to a first audition at Shepperton Studios for the director, Franc Roddam. But I had got more excited when he'd recalled me for a screen test because that meant I was down to the last four and The Who would be looking at my tape to decide if I should play the part of Steph, the capricious girlfriend of the main character, Jimmy. (By the way, I had looked up that word long ago after being called it many times.) The audition had been pretty difficult because I had to do a scene where Jimmy and Steph had a big argument and it had been hard to get worked up while the casting director read Jimmy's part like it was a shopping list. I'd done my best, though, and was now just waiting for the phone call. In the meantime, I was auditioning for Benny.

'Right, are you ready, then?' he said, as he walked back into the room carrying what looked like a tortoise with a stick up its bum.

I wanted to laugh as he began playing the mandolin, but straightened my face and started singing. It was surreal.

I never did become a Bennette. I walked away with the job, but a couple of days later got the call I'd been waiting for –

the offer of the part of Steph in *Quadrophenia*. The Who won hands down over the Hill. I was in the middle of doing the washing when I got the news and my piles of whites and smalls went up into the air as I screamed with excitement.

But I came back down to earth with a bump when I read the full script for the first time. The producers already knew I wasn't exactly a pushover, as I'd told them I wouldn't cut my long strawberry-blonde hair into a Mia Farrow crop: I preferred the Jane Asher style. But when I read the script, I realised there was a much bigger problem. The film tells the story of a mod teenager from London called Jimmy who has a boring office job and only comes alive at night when he's out dancing, drinking and taking 'blues', or amphetamines. Fashion and music are everything for Jimmy and his mod friends, and the rockers are their sworn enemies. The film centres on a trip Jimmy and his friends make to Brighton after he's got together with his dream girl, Steph. There, they meet Ace Face – the king of the mods, who they are all in awe of – and get caught up in a riot with the rockers. Here the problem lay, because the film's climax was quite literally going to come during a riot scene when Jimmy and Steph would run into a basement and do the business. The script detailed that Steph would be shown naked. I knew immediately that I wouldn't do it – even if it meant losing the part. It might have been a time when everyone was getting their kit off, but I didn't want to. I have only done one topless scene during my career and that came years later – a decision that I've always regretted.

In the end, the producers agreed to change the scene. They wanted me for the part because I had the right look, and they also knew I was going to stick to my guns. The scene was replaced: Jimmy and Steph do the deed in an alleyway and you don't see any flesh. I was really pleased, but I didn't know then that keeping my modesty intact and filming the scene in just one take would make it so realistic that it would hang was. Most people looked shocked that the question had even been asked, but I didn't know either because all I'd heard of were 'purple hearts' and 'black bombers'. So it was decided that if we were going to make a film based around 'blues', then we had to try one. I dutifully went back to the office a couple of weeks later to do so. I thought I was going to go off my head, but it didn't do much to me – apart from a moment at about 3 a.m. when I thought I could sing like Shirley Bassey. I might be able to hold a tune, but the thought of me belting out 'Goldfinger' at that time is a bit scary.

By the time the nine-week shoot started, we'd all got to know each other a bit and it felt almost like we were at school together, playing at the real world. Today, a young actor would demand a trailer and an assistant, but back then we were herded into minibuses to travel around and told to huddle in the nearest doorway to keep warm on an outside shoot. We filmed a lot at night and it was always freezing, so most of the time we headed for the nearest launderette to keep warm while we waited for our turn. We'd sit smoking fag after fag, creasing our costumes and getting told off by the wardrobe assistants.

The whole thing was so exciting. There we'd be in Covent Garden or somewhere at 1 a.m. with the road closed off and people would stop to watch what was going on. There would be the bright lights on cherry-pickers, the director shouting, and crowds of extras waiting, then you'd step up in front of the camera feeling almost naked – the traffic's been stopped, all those people are standing looking at you, you're waiting for the word 'action', and you know that if you get it wrong, everything will have to go back to first positions. It's a real pressure because the scale is so much bigger than a TV production, but it's a total buzz.

My fellow actors were great – Toyah was always jumping and full of energy, Mark Wingett was bonkers, and Phil Davis was the joker, even though everyone looked at him with real respect because he'd done a lot of theatre work in comparison with the rest of us. We all got on well and grew quite close, but I soon learned a valuable lesson about acting. You spend hours sitting in places you'd never dream of in real life, like a dirty doorway, gassing away about life and the universe because actors are very good at talking about themselves; but, apart from rare cases, the friendships stop as soon as filming does and you walk away back into your own lives.

My main memories of shooting *Quadrophenia* are the crowds that seemed to be in every scene and the first assistant director, Ray Corbett, who was always shouting at me through a loudspeaker. The other thing that's stuck with me is the fact that nearly every scene involved a Vespa and none of the bikes worked. It was a nightmare – they'd forever be trying to film a fast take-off and the bike wouldn't bloody start. Phil Daniels also got really into the character of Jimmy, and I think at times he found it quite oppressive because he was carrying the whole film. Because he was so focused, there wasn't much small talk between us. But I loved doing the big argument scene at the end of the film in which Steph ends up telling Jimmy where to go. A lot of the dialogue in the rest of the film was improvised, but we followed the script for the argument scene and suddenly, instead of dancing and smiling, Steph became a real person.

The other highlight was going down to Brighton to shoot the main riot scene. We all checked into a hotel on the seafront the night before filming started. While the executives lorded up it up at the Grand, our hotel was like the poor man's relation – it was dirty and full of mice. Soon we were all called downstairs to be given our hair and make-up times for the following morning. Sting arrived carrying the biggest ghetto-blaster I had ever seen. Sitting down in a corner, he started playing some songs by a band called the Police. One was called 'Message in a Bottle'.

'I don't really think it's chart material,' I said loudly. Oops.

The riot took three days to film and most of it was terrifying. There were so many people, crowds of actors and extras sprinting around that it seemed as if you'd be swept off your feet at any minute. I started off the scenes wearing cream kitten heels, but I just couldn't run quickly so I changed to flat black shoes. The continuity people picked it up and started complaining, but the director told them I had a lot of running to do and let me carry on wearing the shoes because they didn't have the budget to reshoot everything. In the final version of the film, therefore, I'm wearing cream kitten heels one minute and flat sensible shoes the next.

In spite of everything, my feet and I survived, and nine weeks later and £500 richer, I finished the shoot. It seemed to take for ever for *Quadrophenia* to be released. After all the years of modelling and bit parts, I couldn't wait for my big moment, and Mum and Dad came over from Spain to share it with me. Wearing a cream silk tuxedo that I'd bought on the King's Road, I stepped out on to the red carpet – well, actually, it was more like a rug because it was only about 3 metres long, but I didn't care. I was a film actress at her first première and nothing else mattered. I had arrived.

CHAPTER 3

Career Girl

'I. Am. In. Agony,' I gasped, flinging myself back in the seat.

It was 1983 and I was on a plane to the south of France with the cast of a Thames TV sitcom called *The Happy Apple*. I was playing a secretary called Nancy – a girl-next-door who kept unknowingly coming up with fantastic ideas for the advertising agency she worked for. It was my first big job in a prime-time TV series, but now I was doubled up in pain on the way to the location shoot and the drama queen in me wasn't keeping quiet.

After all my dreams of instant stardom, I'd learned a few valuable lessons since *Quadrophenia*'s release. In fact, I'd been forced to when the phone hadn't rung off the hook and my agent hadn't taken on an extra post boy to cope with the sacks of mail offering me parts. I'd got it all wrong, and instead of being the next big thing, I was just another jobbing actress-cum-model and wasn't going anywhere in a hurry. The point had been driven home to me when I had arrived at Los Angeles Airport a few months after *Quadrophenia*'s release. I'd decided to spend some time in Hollywood to see if I could get work, and had jumped excitedly into a taxi.

'You here on vacation?' the driver asked.

'I'm an actress,' I announced proudly.

'Not another one,' he snorted.

I had lasted three months living in a tiny flat, meeting

agents, producers and casting directors, and had slowly realised that people in Hollywood were like goldfish because they couldn't remember you 30 seconds after you'd met them. The closest I'd got to a star was seeing Ryan O'Neal in a restaurant.

Then there was my new agent, Laurie, who'd sat me down after I'd asked for the thousandth time if the phone had rung for me.

'You can't expect these things to happen overnight,' he said. 'You have to work for it and get your feet back on the ground. Yes, *Quadrophenia* was a good film, but in the grand scheme of things you're just a beginner and you need to come back down to earth.'

His words had really hit home and that, combined with the fact that *Quadrophenia* wasn't a huge success on its release, made me realise that becoming a well-thought-of actress was going to take some real hard work. It was only later that the film became a cult movie, and in the meantime my dreams of being a Hollywood film star set up for life in a house in Beverly Hills had disappeared.

I returned to London and carried on modelling with Freddie's, while slowly learning my craft after joining CCA Management, which looked after my acting work. In the past four years I'd done one-off roles, such as episodes of police drama *The Gentle Touch* and the sitcom *Shelley*, and a couple of TV plays: one called *La Ronde*, which starred well-known actors like Michael Gambon and Daniel Massey, and another called *Cupid's Dart*, in which I'd played the lead female role, Ros Bedwell. Bit by bit I was learning my trade and bit by bit my name started getting around; instead of being 'the blonde kid from *Quadrophenia*', I was beginning to be known as Leslie Ash. Having said that, I still had to prove myself by auditioning for every job I did. I'd even tried out for a part in the car once because I was late for a meeting and the produc-er had to get to another appointment so I gave him a lift and auditioned on the way. That had got me a role in a TV play called *Outside Edge*, which starred established names like Maureen Lipman, Prunella Scales and Paul Eddington, and in 1982 I had played a karate expert called Juleta Shane in the Blake Edwards film *Curse of the Pink Panther*. It turned out to be rubbish, but at least it was filmed on the French Riviera and I'd learned something from doing it. For instance, there had been another reality check when Robert Wagner, who starred in the film with Ted Wass and David Niven, had phoned me at my hotel.

'What are you doing tonight?' he drawled.

I held my breath. Why was Robert Wagner phoning me? He must be about to ask me out on a hot date.

'Mmm...not much,' I replied nervously.

There was a pause.

'Well, would you mind babysitting for my daughter?' he replied. 'I'm going out to dinner and need someone to keep an eye on her.'

So all in all I was shocked when I got the call offering me the part in *The Happy Apple* – no audition, just a straight 'Do you want it?' – an offer of a prime-time six-part series. All I had to do was decide yes or no. I thought carefully for about two seconds. Oh, yes, yes, yes.

But now it seemed as if I was about to breathe my last. An air hostess and the director, Michael Mills, stared anxiously at me. We were due to spend four days filming abroad because in one episode the agency was up for an award at a famous French ad festival and we needed to do outside location shots. I'd been looking forward to it for ages, but was beginning to wonder if I'd ever touch down on French soil, or any other soil for that matter, as I lay in my seat gasping with pain.

'I just need to stay still,' I groaned. 'Do you have any painkillers?'

'No,' said the air hostess. 'I'm afraid you might have appendicitis and I don't want to give you anything before a doctor has had a look at you.'

I couldn't understand what was wrong with me as the plane bumped on to the tarmac at Nice Airport.

'Don't worry,' said Michael. 'There's an ambulance waiting for you.'

'I do hope you get better,' Judith Chalmers said, as she walked past me lying in the seat panting.

What was going on? She must be on her way to make *Wish You Were Here...?* or something. But I didn't care. The pain stabbed into my side while I was stretchered off the plane and into the back of an ambulance.

This is it, I thought. I'm going to die. In fact, I'm going to explode because my appendix is going to burst.

As the ambulance drove me to hospital, all I could do was shallow-breathe. On arrival, I was put into a holding area between a woman who stank of booze and a bloke who was tattooed from head to toe. Luckily Michael spoke fluent French and stayed with me so he could interpret all the doctors' questions. As time ticked by, I realised the pain seemed to be getting a bit better, but I didn't say anything. Who knew when it would come on again, or how long my appendix would hold out? Maybe this was the calm before the exploding storm.

I tried to relax as the hours passed. The doctors examined me again, and a nurse took my temperature the French way – up the butt. Eventually, after Michael had had a long conversation with a doctor, he announced we could leave.

'But what's wrong with me?' I asked. I couldn't believe that everyone seemed so relaxed when I'd been stretchered off a plane in agony only hours before. 'What's the diagnosis?'

Michael looked at me. 'Wind,' he snapped.

Now I really was going to die – but this time of embarrassment.

'That's what was causing the pain. The doctor said you should be all right by tomorrow morning. You just need to...'

'You won't tell anyone, will you?' I whispered to Michael's back, as he turned to leave.

'No,' he said.

I think it was a story he took to the grave, but he managed to get me back when we were on the plane returning home.

'What's that smell?' I asked, as we sat waiting for take-off.

Michael smiled as he opened his bag and showed me an enormous fish he was carrying back to England. Its smell filled the air around us.

I was about to say something – tell him that now the cast would not only think I was a bit strange after my hospital visit but that I also stank of fish.

Michael looked at me.

I smiled back. After my performance of a lifetime on the journey over, I couldn't start complaining now.

The Happy Apple did really well and put me on the map for sitcom. Apart from being another string to my bow, it also meant that I was becoming known as a comedy actress; but it was a call from *The Two Ronnies* that really confirmed my arrival. I was invited to do a guest spot and couldn't believe it – this was the height of light entertainment; these were the people I aspired to, who I'd sat down with my family every week to watch on TV. Soon my dad had started dropping the news in every conversation he had down at the golf club in Marbella.

The sketch was a spoof of *Raiders of the Lost Ark*, with Ronnie Corbett doubling up as Harrison Ford and Ronnie Barker playing a Nazi baddie. I was going to be the heroine. I jumped at the chance to do it and, in the summer of 1983, headed off for a location shoot on a country estate. It all seemed simple enough: wear a white silk nightie and run along a high wall with Ronnie Corbett brandishing his whip. But it got a bit more complicated when we got up on to the wall and Ronnie suddenly announced he suffered from vertigo. Naturally I felt very responsible for him and it was pretty hard to concentrate on my performance when all I was worrying about was whether comedy legend Ronnie Corbett was about to fall off the wall. During a break in shooting, my agent phoned me.

'I've just had a call,' he said. 'I don't know whether it's for you, but *The Tube* wants you to do six months on the show.'

The Tube was a live music programme presented by Jools Holland and Paula Yates on Channel 4. The channel was still so new that sometimes the screen faded to black during ad breaks because not enough had been sold to fill the time. But *The Tube* was a radical new concept in TV, and Paula Yates had really blazed a trail as the first rocky female presenter. My ears immediately pricked up – fashion, make-up and music, my favourite things. Most of my fellow actors wandered around wearing woolly jumpers and rolling their own fags, so it would be good to do something a bit more glamorous. And what could be so difficult about standing in front of a camera and presenting? It wasn't like you had to create a character or anything complicated like that.

'So where's Paula Yates?' I asked. 'And what will I have to do?'

'She's on maternity leave and you'll just have to introduce the odd band. They've asked if you're interested.'

'Absolutely. I'll take it.'

The programme went out live every Friday at 5.30 p.m. from Newcastle, so the day before my first show I got on a plane and travelled up to the studios to be briefed by researchers and do a run-through. I was knackered by the end of it and looking forward to an early night at the posh hotel where everyone stayed each week. I felt so nervous – the next day there was going to be another run-through in front of the cameras before we filmed live – but Jools wasn't letting me go anywhere.

'You can't go to bed yet,' he said as I checked in. 'Come to the bar. I'll introduce you to everyone.'

I couldn't turn down an opportunity to meet Ian Dury, who was drinking with his Blockheads, so I sat down with them and started chatting. I soon realised, though, that I'd never be able to relax properly and so headed up to bed.

The following morning I went downstairs to pay for the sandwich I'd had in my room after leaving the bar.

'That will be £200,' the receptionist said, as she handed me the bill.

What?

I soon realised where I'd gone wrong – I'd put my key on the table when I was in the bar and everyone had got pissed on my room. I never made the same mistake again. Later that day a beautiful bunch of white roses arrived at the studios with a card from Paula Yates – she obviously knew what I'd let myself in for.

Let's just say presenting wasn't quite as easy as I thought it was going to be. In fact, if I had to use one word to describe my performance, then it would be 'crap'. There were so many things to remember, so many bands I didn't know and no autocue to help me out. Even worse was the fact that the show went out live, so everyone knew when I'd made a mistake – and I made so many that they could devote a whole programme of *It'll Be Alright on the Night* to me. My gaffes started a few weeks after I'd begun, when we did a piece marking the 20th anniversary of the death of Martin Luther King.

'Five, four, three, two, one,' the floor manager said, as he waved his hand to show we'd gone live and were beaming into millions of homes.

'Hi,' I said, feeling the nerves rise up in me and straightening my face into a serious look. 'Thank you for joining us tonight on what is the twentieth anniversary of the death of Martha Luton King.'

Shiiiiiiiiiiiiiiiit.

It was the start of so many mistakes that I can't even list

them all. There was the interview with the Eurythmics when I got so nervous that I blanked on live TV and Annie Lennox ended up having to interview me. Then there was the time when I was flown over to the Bahamas to do a massive piece with Robert Palmer at his ocean-front house and called him Robert Plant the whole time. Soon it became a standing joke that I was a bit dizzy, but everyone was really good about it and I refused to get too upset. I hadn't made any promises; I just wanted a chance to look good on TV, but even that was a bit hit and miss. I thought my hair at the time was cool – red at the roots and blonde at the tips, with the sides scraped back and the rest backcombed. As ever, my dad summed it up: 'You look like your head's bleeding,' he told me. I'd say I looked more like an owl.

Then there were the outfits. Some were fantastic – like a huge black studded belt I wore with a skintight black jersey mini-dress – but others weren't quite so successful. I thought I looked great in a cream silk shirt tucked into jodhpurs with red braces and cowboy boots, topped off with a neckerchief, which I'd bought on location in Japan; but I didn't look fantastic at all – I looked like the ringmaster of a bloody circus.

Not all the mistakes were mine, though – like the time I went to New York to interview Marianne Faithful. I knew who she was, but it was mostly in connection with Mars bars, so I wasn't that excited about meeting her. The director, Geoff Wonfor, was beside himself, though – it was no secret that he completely fancied her and couldn't wait for the blonde bombshell to arrive.

The interview took place in a hotel suite on a rainy New York afternoon, and after setting up for what seemed like hours, Geoff ran to the door when the bell went. I followed him as he opened it to a bedraggled woman with running mascara and scruffy clothes. She looked as if it was very definitely the morning after the night before.

'Where is she?' Geoff asked, as he peered down the corridor. 'Where's Marianne Faithful?'

'I'm here,' said the woman, and walked into the suite.

Geoff's face dropped. It perked back up again, though, after I'd spent 20 minutes doing Marianne's make-up in the toilet. He was as transfixed as ever.

I didn't make too many mistakes that time, but it became increasingly obvious that the thing I found most difficult was interviewing people, and that's a bit of a problem if you're a presenter. Jools was so confident and knowledgeable about his subject, but I always felt like I was bluffing and the problem only got worse when I interviewed someone I admired. I always wanted them to like me, so I'd get even more nervous than usual – and never more so than the day I interviewed Paul McCartney.

Because he was so busy and important, the interview was going to be done in a taxi, while Paul and I went on a mini tour of his favourite places in London. It was arranged that we would pick him up at Air Studios in Oxford Street, but when we arrived, Geoff told me there was a problem and I'd have to wait before going up to meet the man himself.

It was then that it really hit me.

Oh, my God, I am about to interview Paul McCartney, I thought. You cannot mess this up. This is the one time you've got to get it right. This is the bloke whose picture used to be all over your furniture, your Beatles furniture – you cannot get it wrong.

Suddenly there was a knock at the window. I turned round and the camera started rolling. Paul McCartney was smiling at me on the other side of the glass. I gasped.

'Well, you caught me by surprise there, Paul,' I stammered, as I opened the door and he climbed in.

The tape carried on rolling, and he looked at me expectantly.

'So, what's your favourite place, then?' I asked.

'London Zoo,' Paul said, and we started driving.

'Tell us about what you're doing at Air Studios,' I said, as we drove through the traffic.

'I'm just finishing my latest album – it's called *Pipes of Peace*,' the man himself replied.

He soon got into his flow and I started to relax as Mr McCartney told me about recording 'Ebony and Ivory' the year before with Stevie Wonder. Minutes later we drove up to the entrance of the zoo, where he'd said he wanted to look at the goats.

'I'm not paying to go in,' he said suddenly. 'If you walk round this corner, you can see them for free.'

So I walked round the corner with the richest man I'd ever met, who wouldn't pay to go into the zoo. We carried on chatting.

This is going OK, I thought to myself. I'm doing all right here.

When it was time to get back into the taxi, I carried on the interview while we drove back to the studios. There was just one thing left to do as we pulled up outside – mention the *Pipes of Peace* album again. Relief washed over me as the camera carried on whirring and I turned to Paul for the last time. I had done something right at last.

'Well, it's been lovely meeting you, Paul McCartney, and I want to wish you the best of luck with your album, *Pipes of Piss*.'

There was complete silence for a few seconds before the musical legend burst out laughing.

'I think we'll do that again,' he said, as he peered into the camera.

Needless to say, I wasn't invited back when my six-month stint on *The Tube* came to an end.

The role that would change my life came in the summer of 1984 – the part of Fred in a new TV series called *CATS Eyes*.

It was going to be the first British all-woman action cop show, a bit like *The Professionals* in skirts, and was a spin-off from *The Gentle Touch*. Jill Gascoine was once again going to play Detective Inspector Maggie Forbes, but this time she'd left the police force and joined a private detective agency that was in fact a front for a Home Office team called CATS – Covert Activities Thames Section. I'd worked with Jill a few years before on an episode of *The Gentle Touch* and was keen to act with her again. But the most exciting thing was that the series was going to be 12 episodes long – which meant the security of months of work for me – and would be shown on prime-time television. The heavy shooting schedule would mean far less time to rehearse than I'd had for any TV work I'd done, but I couldn't wait to get started when I read the script. I could see immediately that there were going to be loads of action scenes and I fancied myself as a bit of a *Charlie's Angels* type. The *CATS Eyes* girls were going to tackle everything from blackmail to murder, with Maggie Forbes in charge. Her sidekicks were Pru Standfast, played by Rosalyn Landor, aka the posh bird, and my character, Fred Smith, who was there to look sexy. One critic described us as the Sloane Ranger and the guttersnipe, but it didn't bother me – Fred was a computer buff, so everyone would think of her as brainy – and I also knew her image would be crucial. I decided she'd have to be a bit of a tomboy and cowboy boots would be her trademark. Worn with tight jeans and huge shoulder pads, it was a very distinctive look and Fred's car fitted the image too: a white Ford Escort Cabriolet – groovy.

Filming for the series was being done at Chatham Docks in Kent, so we were going to have to move down to a hotel in Maidstone during the week. Yet again nerves got the better of me the night before my first day and I decided to go straight to bed rather than wind myself up even more by trying to learn lines. I told myself I'd look at them first thing the next morning, but of course it came and went: I got trapped in make-up and by the time I walked on set I realised I didn't know a single word. It's the kind of thing every actress has nightmares about and now it was happening to me – my big break and I was going to mess up my very first scene. There was only one thing I could do – confess. Thankfully the director put it down to inexperience and agreed to film the whole thing via close-ups of the other actor's face, with me off camera reading my lines. I never forgot to learn them again.

Apart from that, I loved every minute of filming. Jill, Rosalyn and I shared a motor home, where we'd sit and wait for our scenes before stepping outside to do a handbrake turn during a car chase or a karate kick in a fight scene. We blew up cars, fired guns, dropped out of helicopters, abseiled – it was brilliant.

CATS Eyes aired in April 1985 and we knew that ITV had an option to make two more series if the first one was successful. We had our hearts in our mouths as we waited for the ratings, and thankfully they were good. Suddenly, as one of the stars of a prime-time TV series, I became a bit of a celebrity and requests to do magazine shoots and invitations to events started coming in. It was all very different to how it is today – 'celebrity' wasn't nearly as huge – but it was fun and I was glad to be recognised for my work. I don't think anyone can deny how good it feels when strangers walk up to you and say how much they like what you do, and I feel sorry for people in the public eye who say they can't go out because they're uncomfortable with it. Actors are all insecure at heart, and while some say they don't want the attention, in my experience they soon start to complain if they don't get it.

Rosalyn left after the first series and was replaced by Tracy-Louise Ward, who played Tessa Robinson. Once again the three leading ladies spent hours on end together – in make-up, in our motor home, on the set, learning lines – and we quickly became very close. We would always watch out for each other, and if one made a decision, then we'd all be behind it.

On one side of our trailer was a seating area, and on the other were two beds, where Tracy stuck a picture of her boyfriend – he was called Harry, but was known as 'Bunter'.

'What does he do?' I asked her one day, as we sat waiting for our scenes, wearing the granny thermal underwear that kept us warm during the winter.

'He's in property,' Tracy said. 'Why don't you come and spend the weekend with us?'

Keen to get out of London, I agreed to go and we left the set late one Friday afternoon. It seemed to take for ever as we got on to the M25, went along the M4 and into Gloucestershire. Eventually we drove into a beautiful village and through some enormous gates. The drive seemed to go on for miles, and we pulled up in front of the biggest house I'd ever seen.

'Is this where Bunter lives?' I asked.

'Yes,' said Tracy.

We were standing in front of Badminton House – the Duke of Beaufort's home – and Bunter was in fact his son, the Marquis of Worcester. I didn't stop laughing to myself for most of the evening as the opening lines of 'If They Could See Me Now' kept replaying in my head.

Back on set was just as much fun. Each episode featured a different guest and Ray Winstone and Alfred Molina were among the people we worked with. Charles Gray, who played the James Bond baddie Blofeld in *Diamonds Are Forever*, was another, and I was so excited about meeting him. I first saw him at the hotel reception on the Sunday night before film-ing started. He was very posh and theatrical as he stood there holding a long cigarette-holder.

'See you tomorrow bright and early,' he called as I went up the stairs.

A couple of hours later I heard an awful noise in the corri-dor and stuck my head out through the doorway. There was

Charles Gray, completely naked but still with his cigarette-holder. A porter was running behind him carrying his bags like Manuel in *Fawlty Towers*. Charles Gray had decided to change rooms and had walked straight into the corridor – without waiting to put his clothes on.

It was all great fun and I mostly took the success of *CATS Eyes* and the changes it made to my life, like a good income and a bit of recognition, in my stride. But there was one occasion when I let it go to my head. Filming was strictly based around mealtimes because of the unions – breakfast at 7 a.m., tea with biscuits at 11 a.m., lunch at 1 p.m., tea and sandwiches at 4 p.m. – but as the series went on, the days got longer and longer. Jill, Tracy and I were spending hours in make-up – fair enough, because we were being paid to look good after all – but we also kept missing out on breakfast and I was getting sick of it. One morning when the second assistant director came to get me minutes after I'd ordered some food, I decided enough was enough.

'Leslie,' he called, 'we need you.'

Jill was usually the one who stuck up for our rights. She was really hot on extra hours and knew that the poor crew still had to pack everything up if we ran overtime, while we got driven back to our hotel. Now it was my turn. I was a star of this show and I wanted my breakfast.

'I'm not leaving this trailer until I've had my boiled eggs,' I said in my most demanding voice.

The assistant director stared at me with disgust for a second and then started laughing. After that, I made up my mind never to order boiled eggs again – I'd have something quicker.

While life was different for me thanks to *CATS Eyes*, my parents were dealing with changes that were less happy. They'd started off at the bottom again all those years ago with their shop, but had worked hard, done well and then moved to

Spain, where they'd lived an ex-pat life, complete with tennis matches, rounds of golf and a lot of Rioja. By 1985, however, things had started to sour – my dad had lost a lot of money playing cards and the flats and flash cars had all gone. Even their shop, Unidec, was about to go under and my mum was terrified they were going to lose their last bit of security. She returned to plant her roots back in the only place she really knew and beg the bank for a loan to save the shop. She was given the loan and started working all hours again, while my dad stayed in Spain. I don't know what he was up to – whether it was tax bills or dodgy deals – or whether he was just afraid to face up to his ego, but he wouldn't return home and I couldn't believe it.

'You're being a fucking bastard,' I told him down the phone – the first time I'd ever sworn at him.

It was like hitting my head against a brick wall: he wouldn't budge. So my mum was left to do it all alone and came back to England to find my sister living in the two-bedroom mansion block flat my parents had lived in when the going was good. Debbie had married Eddie Kidd, but their relationship had broken down by this time and so she was living there with her daughter, Candy. Consequently, Mum ended up sleeping on the floor. I was livid, but Mum didn't complain and started working as hard as she ever had to get Unidec back on its feet. Deep down, though, I think she knew she was fighting a losing battle. She moved back into the flat above the shop where we'd lived all those years before, and after work each night she'd go upstairs to drink a bottle of cava before falling asleep in her chair.

So, in December 1986, I decided to give her and all her employees a treat. My mum was taking everyone out for their Christmas do, and, just like every year, I was invited along to the local Italian in Clapham with them. Halfway through the evening I was sitting talking to Noel, the shop manager. He told me he'd never been to a West End nightclub and I decided to take them all for a night out at Brown's – the hippest club at the time.

It wasn't very busy when we arrived, so we sat down at a table near the dance floor and I went to buy some drinks. Standing at the bar was a tall, blond man and an equally striking woman with dark hair.

He's handsome, I thought to myself, as I went back to join Mum and the others.

A while later, Jake, the club's owner, came up and said there was someone he wanted me to meet.

'This is Lee Chapman,' he said, and I turned round to see the blond vision standing in front of me.

I'm not saying it was love at first sight, but he certainly ticked all my boxes. Six foot four, Lee was tall, slim and very good-looking. Little did I know as I stood smiling at him that we'd met a couple of months before at Brown's. I'd gone with a friend and decided to leave early because I was tired. Just as I was heading for the door, a tall man wearing a dodgy fringed suede jacket had come up to me. He stood in front of me and swayed his head a bit.

'So what are you doing at the moment?' he drawled.

What a crap chat-up line, I thought to myself.

'*CATS Eyes*,' I replied. 'Now fuck off.' And I left the guy standing in the middle of the crowd holding his vodka and tonic.

I didn't recognise him, but Lee knew exactly who I was. He was a professional footballer for Sheffield Wednesday, and maybe the fact that I'd been so rude when I first met him is what had got him interested. Let's just say he was a bit of a player on and off the pitch and was used to girls being more impressed than I'd been by his chat-up lines.

Soon I found out that the woman with him was his sister, Denise. Lee was down in London for the night because he'd played Arsenal away that day. I'd never met a footballer before and didn't know anything about the game, but I liked this man. He was polite, seemed like a gentleman and made me laugh. So when the end of the evening came and I'd got my mum a taxi, I offered him a lift home.

We got into my Mercedes Coupé – just like the Mini had once been, it was my pride and joy, and, in the days before mobile phones, I'd had a car phone and incredible sound system fitted. The Pretenders track 'Don't Get Me Wrong' started booming out as I drove.

He lives in Sheffield and he's a footballer, I thought as we headed off. This won't go anywhere.

As we got nearer to my home in Camden, however, I decided to invite him back for coffee, and as we walked into my flat, I knew I was never going to let him go.

'You know we've met before?' Lee said.

'Have we?' I replied, thinking that he looked familiar – maybe I'd seen him playing on the telly or something.

'Yes,' he said, and told me about our meeting a couple of months before.

The penny dropped and of course I apologised, but secretly I was pleased that I'd played it so cool at least once. I was sure not many women had said no before and it had won me points. He was fantastic, even if he did have rubbish dress sense. He didn't leave for the rest of the weekend.

A couple of weeks later I filmed the final episode of *CATS Eyes* and Lee came down to the set. Four weeks after that, on Boxing Day, I sped off from my mum's flat at about 6 a.m. to see him. I'd arranged to meet Lee in the centre of Sheffield and follow him to his house, but my heart sank when I saw him climb out of a horrible Renault – it might have been a Turbo V6, but it was still like a hairdryer – and dipped even more when I got back to his house, which was full of smoky glass and black lacquered furniture. It can't have mattered that much, however, because I basically didn't leave again.

With *CATS Eyes* finished, I didn't have any work for the

time being and just wanted to be with Lee. My main plan of attack was to make myself indispensable and I soon started looking after him. Our relationship quickly became domestic and Lee seemed to enjoy it as much as I did. We spent a lot of time together because he had every afternoon free after training in the morning and so we got to know each other very well very quickly. He was kind, funny, intelligent and thoughtful. We also understood one another in really important ways – we were both in the public eye, and Lee's job was like acting because match days were his showtime and he had to perform. Because we weren't competing with each other, though, we could offer support without getting in the way. When we moved into a house he bought for us, I knew for certain I wanted to spend the rest of my life with Lee. I went mad with the homemaking and we were soon living in Laura Ashley central.

It wasn't all completely cosy, however. From day one we were very intense, couldn't get enough of each other and were passionate both physically and emotionally. Our jealousy caused many arguments, and, just as I didn't like the football groupies who suddenly came out of the woodwork, Lee didn't like it when the boot was on the other foot and someone flirted with me. I think it kept us both on our toes. Lee had never gone out with someone like me before – so independent and with such a strong character – and I hadn't known a man like him either. I was used to getting my own way all the time and, coming from the structured, mollycoddled world of professional football, so was Lee. He was the first man who ignored my tantrums and it really got to me. What is the point of having a good hissy fit if it's going to be ignored? Explosive arguments were part and parcel of our relationship and we never quite knew what the other was going to do next.

One famous night out summed it all up. We'd gone to our favourite bar in Sheffield for a drink after the match with some of the players and their girlfriends. I was drinking cocktails and chatting to the girls when suddenly I noticed the men laughing as they looked at a woman who was obviously wearing suspenders. Egged on by the boys, Lee went and twanged them, while the others giggled. I felt my face flush red. How dare he touch another woman in front of me?

'Fuck off,' I screamed as I stormed out in my stilettos.

Once outside, I flung open the door of the car. Fuming, I sat and waited for Lee to appear. I was going to give him a piece of my mind, tell him what I thought.

He'll be out any minute, I said to myself, as I stared at the door of the bar. Any minute now he's going to come out and ask me to go back in. Any minute now he'll arrive.

A quarter of an hour later Lee still hadn't appeared to beg for my forgiveness, so I picked up the car phone and dialled the bar.

'Is Lee there?' I screeched.

I waited, listening to the laughter and the chat until he came on.

'What are you doing?' I shouted angrily.

'Having a drink,' he replied. 'Where are you?'

'I'm outside in the bloody car.'

'Why?'

'Because you felt that girl's suspenders, that's why. How dare you do that in front of me?'

'It was only a laugh,' Lee replied. 'Just a joke. It was silly.'

'Well, how would you feel if I touched up a bloke in front of you?'

'Don't be stupid, Les,' he told me. 'Men don't wear suspenders. Come back in and let's have a drink.'

I slammed down the phone.

Ten minutes later, still no Lee.

I called back.

'What are you doing?' I screamed once again when he came back on the line.

'I'm having a drink.'

'But I'm outside!'

'Well, come back in, then.'

'No.'

There was a pause.

'Hang on,' Lee said.

Through the window, I saw him put down the phone and walk towards the door. That was more like it. I got out of the car.

'How would you like it if I behaved like that?' I screamed.

Warming up to my topic, I started throwing an almighty tantrum, but suddenly noticed that Lee wasn't even looking at me.

'The car,' he shouted as he started running down the hill. In my fit of anger, I'd left the automatic gear in neutral and my precious Mercedes was rolling into the distance. Lee sprinted after it and just managed to stop it before it disappeared.

'Les, you've really got to calm down,' he said, pulling the car up alongside me.

'Hmm,' I replied.

We started laughing and went back inside.

As a footballer and an actress, there was press interest in Lee and me from the start of our relationship. It wasn't anything like it is for couples today, but it was definitely smouldering away. For instance, one mid-week evening Lee was playing in Sheffield, and while I usually went to home matches, I missed it because I'd gone down to London. Lee had said he'd meet me after the match for a night out and, after being sent off, had a bath and drove down in record time. We were photographed walking into Stringfellow's and the sports headlines the next day seemed to imply he'd got sent off deliberately so that we could party. He felt really annoyed about it all and asked me not to fuel the interest by talking about our relationship in interviews. Even so, it felt like the more I said I didn't want to talk about Lee, the worse it got. Other people obviously also started to get wound up by it because when Sheffield lost 13 times in a row, the crowd decided that I was jinxed. It was suggested that I shouldn't go to any more matches. I stopped for a couple, but they still lost so I started going again.

I couldn't miss a game – it was like theatre in the round, with the pristine pitch and the roar of the crowd as the team walked out. I still get goose bumps when I think about it today and thought I'd burst with pride whenever Lee scored. He looked so sexy, so confident, like he was in his element – imagine being a person who could make 40,000 people go wild with a flick of his foot. I loved the fact that he was being cheered on by the fans, who would sing, 'Na na, na na, na na, na na, na na, na na, na na, na na, Chapman,' to the *Batman* tune. I always thought the players were like modern-day gladiators – without the leather skirts, of course – as they were cheered into the ring by thousands of supporters baying for the other team's blood.

One afternoon we got back to the players' lounge and were having a drink when someone asked, 'Did you hear the new chant, Leslie?'

'Yes,' I said. 'The one to the tune of "Knees Up, Mother Brown"? I heard it but couldn't make out the words.'

'Well, they're actually singing "Lee's Up Leslie Ash",' came the reply.

Of course I looked appropriately shocked, but secretly I thought it was quite clever – all those people singing my name! I was proud to be his girlfriend.

The room was filled with voices as I sat in the warmth and drank some more red wine. It was a Sunday in November 1987 and we were having lunch with friends at a restaurant. I was acting with Matthew Kelly in *Of Mice and Men* at the

Sheffield Crucible and it was the only day off Lee and I had together. We'd got into a routine of meeting up with lots of our friends for lunch at a restaurant called Fischer's and this time there were about ten of us.

'So, have you ever wanted to get married?' a Canadian actor from my show, called Dale, suddenly asked Lee.

I looked at him. A year into our relationship, we'd decided we were going to start trying for children, but Lee was insistent he didn't want to get married.

'Maybe one day,' he replied.

I nearly choked on my Burgundy. What was he talking about? He'd always said he wouldn't go down the aisle.

'You belong together. You look so good together,' Dale sobbed, as he started on another bottle of wine. 'Go on, ask her.'

I could see that Lee wasn't sure if Dale was acting or not, but it worked. He was more than a little drunk and fell for Dale's emotional plea.

'Maybe,' he said.

'Go on. You must,' Dale slurred.

'All right, then,' Lee said. He walked round to my side of the table and looked down at me. 'Do you want to marry me?'

I didn't give him a second to reconsider.

'Yes,' I said, and everyone started cheering.

The fish was finally on the hook…

It's strange how you can go out for something as normal as Sunday lunch and your whole life can change by the time you've finished your roast beef.

CHAPTER 4

Footballer's Wife

It was pouring with rain as I stepped out of the hotel in my wedding dress. It was 4 July 1988 – Independence Day for some, but not me – and the deed was being done in Jersey. About 50 friends and relatives had joined us, and my dad was beside me as I walked towards the wedding car. Suddenly the sun broke through the grey. It was a good omen.

Dad and I were on our way to the town hall in St Helier, where Lee and I were going to be married. Then it was on to St Mary's for a church blessing, before going back to the Little Grove Hotel for the reception.

I was wearing an oyster French-lace mini-dress with a fish-tail skirt to put on underneath for the blessing because I'd decided it might be a bit disrespectful to walk down the aisle in a mini. I didn't want to look too racy for my big moment but I whipped the fishtail skirt off as soon as we got back to the hotel and the party started. The champagne started flowing very freely, but I couldn't drink a drop because I was two months pregnant. We'd been trying for a while and Lee had insisted we did everything by the book – literally. He can never do anything without reading up about it and pregnancy was the same – he'd got all the books and, even while we were only trying, had persuaded me that I had to stop smoking and drinking.

I was so excited about starting married life. The next day

we were driving down to France because Lee had signed to a new club called Chamois Niortais. His contract at Sheffield Wednesday had come up, he wanted a new challenge, and while I was worried about missing Mum and seeing French doctors, I was looking forward to being a footballer's wife. In the eight months since we'd got engaged, I'd done the odd bit of work, including a panto and a TV play, but knew deep down that my career wasn't a prime concern at the moment. I was entering a new stage as a wife and mother and my work would have to revolve round my life, rather than the other way round. The only thing I found difficult to accept was that I was now a kept woman. After fending for myself financially ever since starting modelling at 15 and leaving home at 17, I was now relying on Lee. He didn't mind, though, and in some ways it was even important to him to be the provider.

'Provide away,' I used to joke, but part of me also found it hard to be dependent.

I never wanted to end up being let down like my mum had been. Dad was back from Spain for good now and living with her again, but we hadn't discussed why or what had happened in the past. It was a no-go area and all I knew was that my dad, for all his Walter Mitty life in Spain, where everyone loved him, didn't have a pot to piss in any more. But he and my mum seemed happy enough, and anyway she'd never have given up on him. Mum had left school when she was about 13 to look after her younger brothers when their parents had split up and their dad got custody. She had moved out a few years later when her father remarried, however, because she hadn't got on with her new step-mother and her younger brothers never forgave her for leaving. She'd learned a hard lesson about not giving up on people and I think that is why she would never have turned Dad away when he came back from Spain – even if he did spend his days playing golf and visiting friends, while she worked. I didn't understand it necessarily, but I loved them both and was just happy that things seemed to have worked out after all those years apart.

Gradually the wedding party got louder, and Lee and his football friends started getting going as the dancing began and the drink flowed. By about midnight I decided that I was too tired to carry on – the baby was really taking the party spirit out of me.

''Night,' Lee said, as he came up to our room to give me a kiss. 'I won't be long.'

'Don't worry,' I told him. 'You carry on. I just feel knackered.'

I couldn't get to sleep for what seemed like hours. As I lay in bed and listened to the pounding noise, I could hear voices singing something like a bloody rugby song, with one side chanting a line and the other answering – it sounded like it was going to go on all night. What was going on, and who the hell was making all the racket?

I phoned down to reception. 'Excuse me, what is that noise?' I asked angrily.

'It's your wedding party,' the receptionist replied.

'But it can't be. It sounds like a rugby match down there.'

'I assure you it is your party, Mrs Chapman.'

'Well, then, can you tell them to keep the sodding noise down, please?'

Married life didn't get off to the start I'd thought it would – our new life in France was a disaster from the beginning. We arrived at the club's flat to find concrete floors, a sofa bed and a crap kitchenette.

'It's like a prison,' I said, as I looked around and thought of our comfy home in Sheffield.

'It won't be for long,' Lee reassured me. 'We can start house-hunting soon and find somewhere nice.'

I soon began to feel very lonely. We didn't have any friends and I saw far less of Lee now that he trained twice a day. Even when he was at home, I spent most of the time doing hand-washing because we didn't have a machine and I had to soak his kit in the bath. The stains never went – they just moved to a different place.

Who said married life was fun? I kept asking myself.

I got even more down when I started bleeding at a match and was later diagnosed with toxoplasmosis. It's passed on by cats but also via soft cheese and rare meat – the two things I was basically living on – and is a big danger to the baby because it can cause blindness if it's not caught early enough. The doctors told me I was in the very early stages and put me on a course of strong tablets. After that, my blood was tested every few weeks and everything was fine, but it still worried me.

Another problem was money. Lee hadn't received his transfer fee because Niort was in financial trouble. They kept making excuses, but money was suddenly tight and I wasn't making anything either. We'd been used to two incomes, so after being pretty comfortably off, we were now short.

My prayers were answered three months later, in October 1988, when the club decided to sell Lee to help their cash-flow problem. We were going home. Soon Brian Clough was on the phone asking Lee to join him at Nottingham Forest. Lee agreed, but Robert Maxwell, the newspaper magnate, who also owned Derby, Forest's arch rivals, wanted Lee for himself. The big man offered everything he could – a BMW, a private jet home – as two of the biggest egos in football fought to win the battle and sign Lee. But Cloughie was clever because he'd got me on side – he knew how much wives could influence the players.

'Now, then, beauty, how are you?' he would say when he phoned up. 'Are you comfortable? Are you warm?'

'Oh, you know,' I'd lie. 'I'm fine. Do you want to speak to Lee?'

'Nah. What do I want to speak to that ugly bastard for? It's you I'm worried about.'

Cloughie was a right charmer, and, anyway, Lee had already agreed to go with him before Mr Maxwell got involved, so he stuck to his word. Soon we left France for Nottingham.

'How did she get that kid dressed? How do you change a nappy?' I said to Lee, as I stared out of the car window at a mother pushing a pram. 'In a few hours I'll have a baby and I don't have a clue.'

'You'll be fine,' he replied. 'You've got my mum and yours to help when you get home. They've done it before. They'll look after you.'

It was 30 January 1989 and Lee was driving me to the Queen's Medical Centre in Nottingham, where I was going to have a Caesarean because the baby's head wouldn't engage. I was terrified. I'd piled on weight during pregnancy as I'd told myself I was Mother Earth, while deep down I wondered where exactly She was hiding. I'd thought I would suddenly be filled with maternal instinct, that a big neon light saying, 'Mother,' would light up inside me, but it hadn't and instead of feeling excited I just felt like I was going to the electric chair.

'Are you OK?' Lee asked.

'Fiiiiiine,' I lied, and stared straight ahead.

We arrived at the hospital and I was taken to meet an anaesthetist who was wearing the biggest gold watch I'd ever seen. Business must have been good. He was going to give me an epidural because I didn't want to go to sleep and wake up a mother – I wanted to be aware of everything. I couldn't help wondering if I'd made the right decision a little while later as the obstetrician, Mr Filshie, stood staring at my stomach. He was wearing enormous rectangular glasses and I could see my reflection in his lenses, thanks to the bright lights of the operating theatre.

'I'm making the incision now,' he said calmly.

Lee winced as Mr Filshie's hands disappeared inside my stomach.

'And now you may feel some tugging, Mrs Chapman,' he went on.

I certainly did. It felt like he was doing the washing-up inside me. Lee's hand gripped mine tighter and tighter, until suddenly a slippery, white, vernix-covered baby appeared. It took my breath away.

'It's a boy,' Lee said.

There was no chance of getting that wrong. All I could see of my son were his great big purple testicles as he was lifted towards me. But everything fell into place as he was put on to my chest and I looked down at him for the first time. The neon light went on. Hello, Mother! Here was our baby, half Lee, half me. We were a family. I looked at Lee. His face shone like the sun – he was so proud.

My moment with Mother Earth must have been a rush of hormones because I was terrified once again when the time finally came to go home. I'd felt safe and protected in hospital knowing that someone was there to help me while I got to know my son. When I walked back into the real world, however, I felt as if I was playing the board game Operation and that lights would start flashing and alarm bells ringing when I did something wrong.

'We'll be fine,' Lee had kept telling me. 'Bet you can't wait to get home.'

Instead, I felt overwhelmed by responsibility for my son, Joe, and full of fear that I would let him down. My favourite times with him were when he was breastfeeding, and as the world narrowed to the tiny point between me and him, I could feel our bond growing stronger and stronger. During those quiet moments I'd also think about the future and it scared me a little.

This is it, I'd say to myself. Unconditional love. Joe knows nothing about the horrible things in life and we have to protect him.

The whole world seemed to have changed as I stared out of the car window on the way back to the beautiful Georgian farmhouse we'd bought in Dalbury Lees, a few miles outside Derby. Everything might have looked the same, but I knew my place in it had changed. It wasn't just about me any more.

Thankfully Lee's mum, Gill, was there to welcome us and show me the ropes. Soon I started getting back to my old self and my fear gradually disappeared, but I was still really emotional – running upstairs to wake up Joe after watching an episode of *Casualty* which featured cot death and that kind of thing. I'm sure most new mums do things like that, though. Otherwise, I was really enjoying my new life as a wife and mother, and Lee loved being a dad. He was really hands on – feeding Joe and changing his nappies whenever he could, although he wasn't quite so involved if the baby started crying in the middle of the night! Don't get me wrong – it wasn't all great and there were hard moments, but becoming a mother changed me. Joe came first, and that was a big shift in my life.

The only real problem I had was trying to lose all the weight I'd put on. I knew I'd soon have to show off the baby in public and go to the match, where all the other wives would be. The pressure to slim didn't come from them – back then, footballers' wives weren't sex symbols like they are today, they were mums. I put the pressure on myself because I was a model and an actress and had never been overweight. Now I had 2 stone to get rid of and I started dieting even while I was still breastfeeding. It made me feel lousy – really tired and drained – but I insisted on carrying on as I started skipping meals. I found the first stone easy to lose but just couldn't get rid of the second and got quite obsessed by it.

'You've got to start working out,' Lee told me. 'You shouldn't miss meals.'

I didn't listen, though, and it was only when a doctor warned me I needed to look after myself that I realised how stupid I was being. Deep down, I think the weight thing was about the split I felt inside between the mother I was now and the career woman I'd once been. Acting is an insecure business, and when you're not working, you're always worrying that someone will step into your shoes if you leave it too long. Of course I wanted to be at home with Joe, looking after our beautiful six-bedroom house and recreating our very own version of *The Darling Buds of May*, but there was also a part of me that wanted to get back to work. I had always been a grafter and it felt strange not doing it.

After putting Joe to bed at night, I'd start thinking about it all. Back then, there was no 'have the baby, plus instant tummy-tuck and back to a size six within two weeks' – expectations were more realistic and people knew you'd be out of action for a while. Even so, I decided I wanted to put out some feelers and so signed to an up-and-coming agent called Sharon Hamper. Within weeks she called to say that the director of a West End farce wanted to see me. The play was called *Paris Match* and was going to be staged at the Garrick Theatre. I couldn't believe a job had come up so quickly and took the part when I was offered it. The football season had just ended, so Lee could look after Joe during the week with the help of Gill and I would stay with my parents in Clapham. I told myself I'd see my boys every weekend.

I totally misjudged just how much I'd miss Joe. I should have realised I was making a mistake when I cried all the way driving down to London, and it was the same every time I left after that – Joe would hold out his arms and I'd have to go, feeling deep down that I was deserting him. It seemed wrong to be hanging around in London waiting for the two hours every night when the curtain went up instead of being at home with Lee and Joe, and the buzz of the job just wasn't enough to make up for it any more. I was pleased, therefore, when the play didn't do that well and closed after three months. I knew I wasn't ready to break the bond just yet, and I was under no pressure to, so why should I? My career itch had been scratched for the time being and I decided I'd put acting on hold until Joe was a bit older.

When your husband plays professional football, you know you'll never be in one place for long because your life is dependent on which club he is playing for. During Lee's football career, we moved five times in three years and I became an expert at packing up and moving on. After 18 months at Nottingham Forest, he signed for Leeds in January 1990, when Joe was almost a year old. In those days there was no Premiership and Nottingham was at the top of the pile in Division One, while Leeds was one drawer down in Division Two. But Howard Wilkinson, who'd managed Lee back in Sheffield, was at Leeds and had big plans. The club was bigger, had more money and wanted Lee to be their new striker. We were off again.

I'd grown really attached to our house and it took a few months to find something else I liked, but I was happy when we found another farmhouse in the idyllic village of Roecliffe, a few miles outside Leeds. It wasn't exactly my dream home – it didn't have much character and had some pretty ropey décor, including false beams and a disgusting butterscotch bathroom suite – but I knew I couldn't get as attached again as I had to our last house. Anyway, it was spring, the place was covered in daffodils, the nursery school looked over the village green, and there was a pub – what more could we want?

My introduction to country life came a few days after moving in, when the doorbell went and I found a large lady wearing a mac standing on the doorstep holding a dead rabbit in either hand.

'Hello, Mrs Chapman,' she boomed in a clipped voice.

'Angela here. I'm the major general's wife from down the road and wanted to say welcome. I've brought a brace of rabbit for you.'

I didn't know what to say as she held them up in triumph. I'd grown up in Clapham – the only rabbits I'd seen were pet ones and now there were two, all dead and furry, dripping blood on to my doorstep.

'Thank you. What do I do with them?' I asked nervously.

'What?' the woman boomed again. 'You've never skinned a rabbit?'

Thankfully she agreed to skin them for me and took them away – all there was left to do was mop up the blood before the team from *CSI* arrived.

Soon everything got back into its familiar routine. I ran the home, and Lee settled into life at his new club. While I was like millions of other wives and mothers in many ways, there was one big difference – my world was governed by a black-and-white ball. Football is one job that can't be left behind in the office. Marry a footballer and you sign up to being almost as much a part of the team as he is. His playing routine rules your family life together, from how much sleep he gets and how often he trains to the high and lows of winning or losing and when to have sex. There must be no hanky panky the night before a game and Lee always played hungry – and not just for food. Grrr. In fact, food was another big thing in our lives because he had to eat the right things at the right time to maximise his performance. Gone were the days back in Tooting when my housemate, Barbara, and I had lived on pizza and frozen cheesecake. Married to an athlete, I became a real healthy-food addict way before it became trendy.

The other big thing is that footballers are mollycoddled. They're told when to get up, when to train, when to play, when to sleep – although I think they're toilet-trained up to a point. Mind you, I did hear one famous story about a certain footballer's party piece, which involved relieving himself from the top of a hotel wardrobe into a pint glass, and we're not talking a golden shower. This regimented life can make players act like kids at times. There is a real pecking order in every team, and the wicked dressing-room humour would reduce most people to tears. Then again, the players have got to be tough because they know people will be as quick to shout abuse at them as cheer them on if they don't perform. The supporters also take some getting used to, even when you're just a wife. For instance, I never went to away games because of the abuse, and while most supporters at home were great, there were also those who didn't hold back if the team hadn't done well.

'Hey, Lee, what happened today? Team were shite,' they'd say.

It was all very different to my job, where people would blow sunshine up your arse whether you were up to scratch or not.

All in all, football is a funny game, and even stranger is the fact that you don't need any qualifications to do it. In fact, most boys leave school at 15 or 16 after being spotted by a scout and don't further their education. Lee was quite rare in that world because he had a place at Manchester University to study chemistry and business studies but ended up not going when he got taken on by his first club. What happens to the boys who spend their childhoods working towards being footballers and don't make it professionally? Do they all learn the Knowledge and become London taxi drivers? Adult life starts very young for those who do make it – they go professional at 17 and get their pension at 35 – and back then it was common for players to marry their childhood sweetheart. I couldn't get over it when I met the wives before a home match because they all seemed so young. I was 29 and had just had my first baby, while they were about 20 and had toddlers. Footballers' wives then weren't like they are today – 'designerised' and dangerous – and although they were well turned out, their most important job was as a wife and mother. In the days before the Premiership, the money just wasn't there for them to be dressed from head to toe in labels.

The other big thing, of course, is injuries – life is full of conversations about tendons, muscles and bones, and players are always worried they might not be match fit. Lee had got away quite lightly, but about a year into his time at Leeds he had a terrible accident when he was playing away against Spurs in February 1991. I was washing the kitchen floor when the phone rang.

'Hi, it's Mervyn Day here,' the Leeds goalie said. 'Now, I don't want you to get worried. Lee is OK, but he's had an accident on the pitch and has been taken to hospital.

'He's injured his face. It looks a lot worse than it is, but he was also knocked unconscious and they've got to check him. You stay where you are. I'll phone when I get some more news.'

Lee had been injured when he'd gone for a ball with his head and Spurs player Steve Sedgley had gone for it with his foot. They'd met in mid-air; the boot had caught Lee under the chin and he was knocked out. So far so not unusual, but because Lee had been unconscious as he flew through the air, he hadn't put his hands out to break his fall and had slid along on his face on a gravel track that ran round the pitch. He'd swallowed his tongue, torn through his upper lip with his front teeth, broken his nose in two places and ripped off the skin covering it to expose the bone. Howard Wilkinson wanted Lee to be seen by specialists in Leeds and so, after being stitched up in the local hospital, he was laid across the back seat of the coach for the trip home. He was taken to a private hospital. I couldn't believe what I saw when I arrived. Lee couldn't speak because his face was so swollen. It was black with gravel still embedded in the skin, and his lip was sewn to his nose. He looked like Quasimodo.

The amazing plastic surgeon Andrew Batchelor, who was

featured in the TV show *Jimmy's*, operated on Lee and scraped all the gravel out before pulling a V-shape of skin down from his forehead to repair the damage to his nose. I returned the next morning to find Lee so swollen I hardly recognised him, while poor Joe took one look and screamed – he wouldn't go near him. In spite of all this, Lee was playing again within three weeks. Amazingly, given the injuries he suffered, the only lasting reminder of the whole thing is the odd eyebrow hair which grows out of the end of his nose from where the skin was pulled down!

So, all in all, there was quite a lot to being a footballer's wife and I dealt fine with most of it. There was just one area in which Lee's professional life spilled over badly into our relationship. Having Joe had forced us to calm down a lot from the days when we first met, but we could still manage a humdinger every now and again. If I felt Lee was using his dressing-room tactics to wind me up, a cross word mostly exploded into a massive row. He could be really cutting at times. One day we were on our way back from a boozy lunch when it all kicked off. We'd got more and more into food since arriving in Leeds, and, instead of bars and clubs, our social life now revolved around restaurants. But with food comes wine and on this occasion I'd had a few. I can't remember what the argument was about, but it started in the car and I saw red when I decided Lee was treating me like one of the boys.

'Stop the car,' I shouted about a mile from home. 'I'm getting out.'

I can flounce off even when I'm in a car, you see. After making Lee stop and getting out, I slammed the door. I got even angrier as I stood on the edge of the road and he started driving off.

'Go to hell!' I screamed, as I kicked our Mercedes – it was our pride and joy.

By the time I'd walked home, I'd calmed down and felt

really ashamed when I saw the massive dent I'd put in the side of our car.

'You can pay for that,' Lee told me when I walked in through the door.

'I will,' I replied.

Women really do make the worst drunks, they become so argumentative, and I'd seen it with my mum at times. As ever, though, I refused to admit I was wrong and so did Lee.

When Joe was two, he started at nursery and I began thinking once again about work. Worry filled me when I thought about how long I'd been out of the fast-moving world of television acting – maybe my excuse about having time off to have a baby might be wearing a bit thin given that he was now a toddler. I also wanted to do my bit financially. I've realised now that there was no pressure on me to do that, but back then I wanted to keep my end of the bargain as a career woman. I wasn't exactly rushing back to work, though, because I knew I might get pregnant any time. Lee and I wanted another child and had been trying for a while, so once again I'd given up having the odd sneaky fag and quietened down on the booze front to help me conceive. Nothing had happened, however, and it felt as if all we were doing was waiting. One day, when I was in the kitchen and Joe was climbing in and out of his favourite cupboard, the phone rang.

'Hi, Leslie,' said my agent, Sharon. 'I've got some news. Beryl Vertue wants to see you for a part. She met you years ago on *Quadrophenia* and is working on something she thinks you'd be perfect for.'

My ears pricked up immediately because Beryl was a legendary producer. She'd started out as an agent for greats like Spike Milligan, Eric Sykes and Tony Hancock before producing loads of successful comedy formats in Britain and America. Now Beryl had teamed up with director John Howard Davies, another legend, who'd worked on everything from *Monty Python's Flying Circus* to *Fawlty Towers*. If anyone could make it work, then it was these two.

'It's written by a guy called Simon Nye, who's never done anything like this before, but he wrote a book which Beryl thinks would be perfect for a TV series,' Sharon told me. 'They're really excited about it. It's called *Men Behaving Badly*.'

I was silent for a moment. 'What a stupid name,' I replied, as I stared at Joe's bottom coming out of the cupboard. 'What kind of thing is it?'

'Sitcom,' Sharon replied. 'But a new kind of sitcom targeting a younger age group. Harry Enfield has signed up for the pilot.'

'Well, I'll go if they want to see me,' I told Sharon uncertainly, and arranged to meet Beryl and John in London.

It was only when I got in the car to go to the meeting that I realised how much confidence I'd lost. Lee was driving me and I kept staring at myself nervously in the passenger mirror. I looked like I was going to a wedding. After a couple of years of being Mrs Chapman, I'd forgotten the audition game and had completely overdone it on the outfit front. I was wearing a smart skirt and jacket, with my hennaed hair slicked back. My nerves only got worse when I arrived and could see in Beryl and John's faces that they'd expected blonde, bubbly Leslie Ash to turn up, not the mother of the bloody bride with red hair and a worried look on her face.

Men Behaving Badly centred on four characters: Dermot, played by Harry Enfield, who lived with his friend Gary, Gary's girlfriend, Dorothy, and the blonde totty from upstairs called Deborah. I don't need to spell out the part I was up for. Beryl and John were very polite as they discussed the idea with me and told me they'd let me know. Although I really couldn't tell how it had gone, I was pretty sure that I'd cocked it up.

A few days later the phone went again.

'Good news,' Beryl said. 'The pilot is going ahead and we'd love you to play Deborah.'

'Thank you so much,' I gasped. 'I'm really looking forward to working with you.'

I couldn't believe it. I'd got the part! I tried to suppress my excitement as I put the phone down and told myself it was only a pilot – there was no guarantee a series would be commissioned. But I also knew I'd be working with great people back in the world I knew and loved. I picked up the phone once more.

'Can I book an appointment for a full head of highlights?' I told the voice on the end of the line. Leslie Ash was back in business.

It felt like my first day at school when I arrived for rehearsals in Twickenham. We were working at a boys' club and it looked like a church hall, complete with wooden floor and chairs stacked up against the walls. The floor was covered in different-coloured masking tape marking out the set – blue for the bedroom, orange for the hallway, red for the living room and so on. There were also wooden poles standing in for doorways so we could get used to the space and how we had to move around it before filming on the real set.

I'd left Joe at home with Lee and Gill for the week it would take to shoot the pilot and I thought of them as I stood in the kitchen, where everyone was drinking tea. While Harry and Martin Clunes were chatting with Beryl about some show they'd all seen, I could only stand there smiling like an idiot.

I really need to get my bullshit button switched on, I said to myself, as I realised yet again how out of practice I was.

I relaxed immediately when Caroline Quentin arrived, however. She was so flamboyant, so confident and so energetic you had to warm to her.

The one thing that struck me as I stood there was how different everyone was from what I'd imagined. You visualise how characters will look when you first read a script and no one matched the pictures in my head. But I'd still found it far easier to imagine Dermot, Gary and Dorothy than my character, Deborah. She was really difficult to pin down because although she wasn't stupid, she couldn't be so sophisticated and unreachable that she wouldn't be seen dead with Gary and Dermot. The viewers would have to believe in why she hung out with them and it was going to be a fine line to tread.

I felt almost sick with nerves as we sat down at a long table. The lines started to come alive as the other actors read them. My nerves got worse and worse as each page turned and my first line approached.

'Hi, I'm Deborah. I've bought the flat upstairs,' I said. Relief suddenly flooded over me. I was away, it was like riding a bike – I hadn't forgotten how to do it after all.

I'm sure everyone could see the potential in *Men Behaving Badly* even on that first day. As we sat at the table without lights, set, make-up or an audience, you knew there was something in it. Sitcoms back then were basically about the middle-aged and middle of the road, and while *The Young Ones* had been a great success in the early 1980s, it was aimed more at students and teens than young working adults. This was different and daring – it was all about drinking lager, shagging women and being a bit crude. And while I couldn't relate to the first two so much, the third was definitely a bit more me. *Men Behaving Badly* was something new.

CHAPTER 5

And Then There Were Four

All I could see were faces below me, like thousands of sunflowers turned upwards, as a roar of cheering filled my ears. I could see young and old, kids on shoulders and people waving banners as Joe's warm, tiny hand tensed in mine.

'I want to go home, Mummy,' he said. 'I don't like it.'

'It's all right,' I replied, crouching down. 'They're not shouting because they're angry – everyone is really happy.'

Below us, Leeds was celebrating because in just over two years its football team had gone from Division Two to winning the Division One Championship, now called the Premier League – it was like climbing a mountain in double-quick time. Joe and I were standing with Lee, his team-mates and their wives on a balcony at the town hall and pride filled me. I'd never seen Lee so happy. There are certain things every football-mad boy dreamed of, and being champions of Division One was one of them. After all the training, Lee had done it at the end of the best year of his career. The previous season he'd been the top goal-scorer in the league and was also writing a column for the *Observer* and doing TV football punditry. For the man who'd once said tongue in cheek that scoring was better than sex, I knew it couldn't get much better.

'How do you feel?' I said to him, as we looked down at the crowds.

'It's amazing,' Lee replied. 'Look at all these people. I'll never forget this.'

Leeds had won the title the previous Saturday. After winning away at Sheffield United early in the day, they knew they could win the league within hours if Liverpool beat Manchester United that afternoon – otherwise it would all come down to a game the following week. I'd got home from shopping to find Lee, Gary McAllister, David Batty and Eric Cantona sitting on our sofa watching the Manchester United versus Liverpool game on TV. They were being filmed by ITV as they watched, to get their reaction to the result, and looked as if they were going to a bloody funeral as they sat nervously in front of the cameras. But they finally managed to crack a smile when the whistle blew. Man U had lost and they had won the league! That was just a few days ago and now we were at the town hall after a victory parade through the city on an open-topped bus. I felt a bit like a gatecrasher as I stood there enjoying the cheers, but then again I've always loved the thunder of applause – even if it is someone else's.

It was May 1992 and the Chapmans were on a roll. In addition to Lee's successes, I was nearly eight months pregnant with our second child and due to starting filming the second series of *Men Behaving Badly*. My gut instinct about the show had been right and the pilot had gone down so well that ITV had commissioned a series that had gone down well with the public.

I'd gone back to stay in my old woodchip-papered room at my parents' in Clapham during the six-week shoot and Mum had spoiled me with home cooking when I got in from work in the evenings. We rehearsed the show from Tuesday to Saturday, before filming on Sundays, so most weekends Lee had travelled down with Joe to see me and they did stuff with Mum while I worked. Some Saturday nights Lee and I would go out for a meal or something while Mum babysat. After our quiet life up North, I loved those evenings out and they reminded me of when we first met. I couldn't go crazy, because I had to work the next day, but Lee had become a member of the Groucho Club and it was a great place to meet people. You would always know someone in there – it was fab. There'd be Stephen Fry in one corner and Michael Elphick by the entrance. Even Robbie Williams introduced himself one day and at first Lee didn't realise it was the same kid he knew from back home in Stoke. Lee's dad was a footballer for Port Vale and was mates with Robbie's dad, who was a comedian at the local social club. The two families had gone on holiday together, but little did Lee know that his beach buddy was a budding pop star!

Work-wise, the filming of *Men Behaving Badly* series one had been interesting. I had been so excited to be working with Harry but also nervous because I knew I'd lost my way somewhere between the washing machine and the changing mat and become a stay-at-home mother. Even though Harry had definitely been the top dog, the star of the show, because he was an established name, he had put me at my ease by being very chatty and friendly. It had soon became obvious, though, that he hadn't really wanted to be on the *Men Behaving Badly* set and it had put me on edge again.

'I'm doing this one series, but no more after it,' had been the attitude that hung in the air.

I think it came down to the fact that Harry was very good at doing his own material but hadn't felt at home doing someone else's. He had been open about the fact that he wasn't the right person for the series, and what he said was true. There had been no real chemistry between him and Martin – it was like they were both doing one-liners, and in sitcom you can't be too much of a solo performer, can't outshine everyone else; it needs to be a team effort. As the weeks had passed, I began to feel more uncomfortable and Harry had seemed more unapproachable the unhappier he got. I don't know if I was sensitive because I was just starting work again two years after having Joe, but it hadn't felt easy and it had been obvious there was a gaping hole in the cast chemistry.

Like everyone else, I had thought ITV wouldn't be so keen to commission a second series if the big name left. I kept thinking, finally something life-changing comes along and it looks like we're not going anywhere before it's even started.

I had put the idea to the back of my mind, however, finished filming and we had all met up at Beryl's amazing Tudor house in Kent to watch the first episode being aired. It had been so embarrassing standing there not sure whether to laugh politely or keep a respectful silence. Despite all the problems, though, there was something about that first episode and the following five in the series that hit the right buttons, because ITV had commissioned a second series – even without Harry. He'd been replaced by a guy called Neil Morrissey, who I knew as the dark-haired motorbike-riding bloke from *Boon*, and we were due to start work in just over two months.

If my obstetrician and I had done our sums right, it meant I'd have to be back at work within a month of the birth and I'd been really aware throughout my pregnancy of the possibility that I'd have to look the part so soon. Lee, like my very own personal trainer, had given me some gentle exercises to do, and running around with a toddler had also kept me on my toes. But I was worried that it wouldn't be enough to stop me piling on the weight like I had with Joe and so, to be honest, I basically dieted throughout my pregnancy. I know it sounds dreadful, and it's not to be advised, but that's what I did and I'm sure there are a lot of other celebrities who've done the same. I knew I'd done well to pop out two babies within four years of marrying Lee, but I also knew I'd look awful if I went in front of a camera carrying extra baby weight and I was realistic enough to know my looks were crucial to my career. It's not rocket science, and, to be frank, I didn't have time to think about it too much. Acting is a strange industry for women because you're pigeon-holed either as a character actress or 'something for the dads' – and that's what I was in *Men Behaving Badly*. No disrespect to Caroline, but I was the blonde bit of skirt upstairs. I had to fill those shoes and so put pressure on myself to do it.

I took pictures of Demi Moore as my inspiration. The year before, she'd been on the cover of *Vanity Fair* heavily pregnant, naked and looking really glamorous, so, ditching the idea of eating for two, I tried to put on just the baby's weight, which would be about two stone. I was 8 stone 7 pounds before I got pregnant so that would make me 10 stone 7 pounds. I kept to a low-fat, low-sugar diet, semi-skimmed milk, salads, no snacking, no puddings and lots of fruit and vegetables. It had taken a lot of self-control to do it, but I wasn't one of these mothers who popped back to stick thin after having a baby. My body had changed and I still put on 2 stone, but I looked completely different to my first pregnancy – no double chin or bingo wings – and I weighed myself every day to check what was happening. Other than that, I had a fantastic pregnancy, and although the baby was a real kicker, I was much more relaxed about it because I knew what to expect.

All in all, there was a lot to be happy about as I stood on the balcony listening to Leeds cheering and looking down at all the smiling faces. Lee and Joe were beside me, and my soon-to-be-born baby was wriggling inside.

'Have I got time to have a bit of lunch before everything starts happening?' Lee said.

I was lying in the maternity unit of St James's Hospital on 1 June 1992 and wondering what on earth was going on. Just two days before I'd razzed it up in a psychedelic mini-dress at a wedding. The bride's dad was DFS boss Graham Kirkham and it had been a spectacular bash. I'd felt pretty proud that at eight months pregnant I'd lasted all day in my stilettos and had only had to put my feet up right at the end of the evening.

But it must have had more of an effect than I'd thought because now I was in labour. I thought it had started a few hours earlier, when I was at home with Gill – I say 'thought' because I didn't know for sure: I hadn't been in labour before, and, anyway, the baby wasn't due for three weeks.

Gill had insisted that we ring an ambulance and I'd begun to feel quite scared as I was loaded into it for the journey, which seemed to last for ever. The ambulance men didn't want to go down the motorway in case they had to divert to another hospital or something. All I know is that it took ages and I just wanted Lee with me, but he was meeting the editor of the autobiography he was writing and we couldn't get hold of him. He'd eventually arrived a few minutes before the birth to find me lying on a bed with a monitor strapped to my tummy and the sound of the baby's heartbeat pounding from the machine beside me. Now he wanted to know if he could go back and finish his lunch!

The Irish nurse shot him a withering look. 'Mr Chapman, your wife is having a baby and she's having it now.'

'Sorry, I'm only joking,' he told the nurse.

Hmm…I've always wondered if he was, and I'm sure if he'd been told it was going to take hours, then he'd have tried to fit in the rest of his meal! But he didn't have to wait long because I was soon given an epidural and wheeled into the operating theatre to have a Caesarean. I had to have one because I'd had one with Joe and in those days that meant you didn't get the option of a natural birth.

'You might feel some tugging,' the surgeon told me, just like last time, and – pop! – my baby was born. It was another boy and we called him Max.

'He's a bit poorly, Mrs Chapman,' a voice told me. 'We need to get him into an incubator.'

Panic filled me. Why were they taking my baby? I'd only just had him and wanted to hold him. What was wrong? He'd gone from being inside me to being with strangers and I didn't want him to be alone. Lee and I were told Max had to be taken away because he had water on his lungs and jaundice. The doctors assured us he would be fine, but I felt helpless as I was taken to my room and put on to a drip because I was anaemic. I was desperate to see him.

'Can I go and see Max, please?' I'd ask each time a nurse came into the room.

The answer was always, 'No, not just yet, but soon,' and after what seemed like hours of politely waiting, I'd had enough. I wanted to see Max, be with him, not sit in my room looking at the walls.

'Let me see my baby,' I wailed.

At last they put me into a wheelchair and I was taken down hospital corridors into the special-care baby unit and up to an incubator. Inside was a really long baby with enormous feet. He was wearing a hat and looked almost squashed as he lay there sleeping. Relief washed over me that I could finally cuddle him.

I was discharged six days later, but Max was kept in because he was still poorly and I felt desperate at having to leave him. He was so tiny, so vulnerable, and I only had a few weeks with him until filming started. Every day they took blood tests by pricking his tiny heel and I would visit every day to get the results, hoping to take him home, but it was a week before they discharged him and work was looming by then. I had committed to doing the second series of *Men Behaving Badly*, which meant a six-week shoot, and couldn't back out whatever was happening at home, and it wasn't just about obligation – part of me wanted to do it, even though another part didn't want to leave Max.

I told myself that Max was well and gaining weight, the boys would be with Lee, and families weren't just about mums but dads too. Gill and my mum were going to help out whenever they could, and we'd employed a nanny to look after the boys during the day and a maternity nurse to do the nights. We'd started getting nannies soon after Joe was born, but they always seemed to be leaving. To be fair, I don't think I was easy to work for – I was pretty possessive about him! However, both women came with really good references so I tried to convince myself myself everything would be fine. Even so, my heart tugged when I thought of someone else putting my sons to bed.

I told myself that Max would be well looked after during the six-week shoot, but I also knew this was a test. It was all very well being a career mother with just one child, but could I do it with two? *Men Behaving Badly* had the makings of a hit and I had been working towards that for so many years. I wanted to be a mother, but I also wanted to work, and while I know some people might think I should have stayed at home, Lee never questioned my decision and neither did I. He knew I was a career woman when he met me and I'd always said I'd go back to work after having children. If I stopped working, then I wouldn't be the person he had married. Don't get me wrong, if Lee had ever asked me to give it up, then I would have done. But he didn't and I had always been in charge of my own life.

I pushed all my worries to the back of my mind when I went down to London to start rehearsals. Once again I went to stay with Mum and Dad, and once again the tiny flat seemed really crowded with the three of us. After finishing work and ringing Lee, Mum and I would usually crack open the cava and Dad would start moaning about the noise. We would end up drinking it in the kitchen, but as long as Dad was in control of the remote and he couldn't hear us yacking, then he was happy.

As soon as filming ended, at about 10 p.m. on a Sunday night, I'd set off in the car – up the M1, the M18 and then the A1 – by which time my eyes would be closing with tiredness. But happiness always filled me when I pulled into our drive – I was safely home. Then I'd creep into the house, kiss the boys, take off my make-up and slide into bed to take the place that had been empty all week. Cuddling up to Lee's warmth, I'd drift off to sleep knowing I'd spend the next day at home.

It all seemed to be going well until I got a phone call during the third week of filming that made me question what on earth I was doing. It was first thing on the Saturday morning when Mum called me to the phone.

'Please don't worry, Mrs Chapman,' a woman's voice said. 'I'm a nurse at Harrogate Hospital and your son Max has been brought in by your husband.'

'What?' I replied. 'What do you mean? What's wrong with him?'

'They've been in overnight,' the woman told me. 'Your son was brought in during the early hours with severe stomach pain. We've diagnosed him with a bacterial infection. It's under control now, but we'll need to keep him in for a couple of days.'

'I don't understand. What's happened to him? How did he get an infection? Are you sure he's OK?'

'Yes, he's fine – the antibiotics are working and he's settled down.'

'Well, OK, then,' I replied uncertainly. 'Can I speak to Lee? Shall I come now?'

'Honestly, Mrs Chapman, Max is responding to treatment and everything is fine,' the nurse reassured me. 'He'll be well looked after here. There are four nurses to every child, and your husband is with him.'

When Lee came on the line, he also kept insisting that Max was OK.

'He seems much better,' he told me. 'He's got some colour back now at least.'

Lee was due to play the first game of the season later that day and, instead of getting a good night's sleep, had spent it in a chair next to Max's bed.

'But what about the match?' I asked.

'I'll be fine,' Lee told me, and he was. He scored two goals that day and the team won 2–1.

He told me to stay put, do the programme and then head home as usual the following night. Guilt filled me as I put down the phone – how had my baby ended up in hospital? Even now I hate admitting that I wasn't there with Max when he fell ill, and discovering he had been given reheated milk and that that had caused the problem only made me feel worse. It would never have happened if I'd been there. I think most working mums will know how I felt – I'd chosen to be a career mother and at some point you have to pay for the downside of your decision. This was that time for me, and I was in constant touch with Lee until I could go back home and see for myself that Max was OK. I'm still reminded of it today, though, because whenever Max plays up, Lee reminds him that he alone pulled him from the brink of death!

It was a freezing night and Caroline, Martin, Neil and I were sitting in a clapped-out van on a dual-carriageway flyover. It was the start of yet another surreal *Men Behaving Badly* conversation.

'What would I want with a snooker table, anyway? I hate snooker,' Dorothy, aka Caroline, asked right after Martin Dennis, the director, shouted, 'Action.'

It was about midnight and we were in the middle of doing a week-long exterior shoot for the series. The scenes for this episode centred on Gary, Tony, Dorothy and Deborah's trip to a shopping centre. Gary and Deborah get stuck in a lift together while Dorothy and Tony wait for them in his van. They're all there for hours, and after drinking a bottle of cheap brandy, Gary decides to pass the time in the lift by setting up the mini snooker table he's just bought Dorothy. Meanwhile Tony sets his van on fire by mistake. Earlier in the day we'd shot all the shopping-centre stuff and were now doing the final lines of the episode, when the four

My very early days as an angelic toddler and in my first stage role as a Mouse, aged five – I'm the one third from the left. By then I was already a TV veteran, having done my first advert for Fairy Liquid.

ABOVE One of my favourite pictures of my mum from my childhood.

LEFT My parents get ready for a night on the town in the mid-1960s.

A meal out at La Dolce Vita in Soho with our friends the Berlinskies in about 1966. Mum Ellie is second from left, with my sister Debbie next to her. I'm third from right and my father Moe is on the right.

TOP A couple of early portrait shots, but the above picture, taken by Chris Duffy with hair styled by Nicky Clarke is probably my favourite of me – I had my whole life ahead of me, and there seemed to be so many opportunities.

OPPOSITE PAGE, TOP With 'Jimmy' during the shooting of *Quadrophenia* in Brighton. BOTTOM Garry Cooper, me and Sting in Piccadilly Circus when *Quadrophenia* was released. Strangely enough, Sting wasn't asking for my advice on his music career.

THIS PAGE Despite the eventual success of *Quadrophenia*, the job offers didn't come rolling in, and I spent a lot of the next few years doing modelling work.

LEFT With Gareth Hunt and Jilly Johnson in the 1983 series *The Balance of Nature*. Suddenly things were all about to change.

BELOW A still from the film *Shadey* in which Anthony Sher played a psychic. Here I am doing a classic 1980s fitness pose.

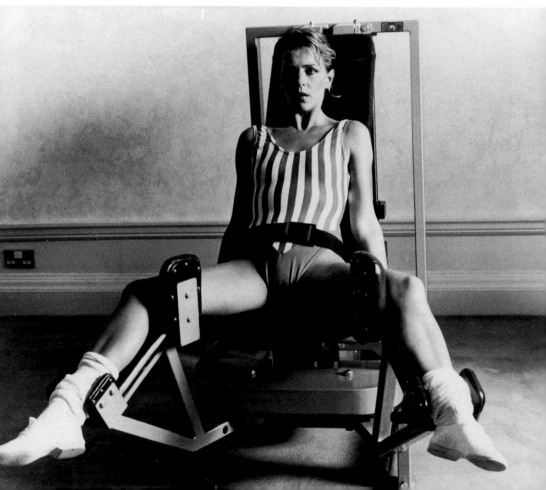

Great days on *The Tube*. Jools Holland takes a keen professional interest in Stevie Wonder in action; meanwhile I try not to embarrass myself too much in front of Paul 'Pipes of Piss' McCartney.

CLOCKWISE FROM TOP **With Ray Winstone during the shooting of** *CATS Eyes*; Jill Gascoigne proudly displays her glamorous thermals; looking forlorn on the phone; yet more hairspray is urgently called for.

characters finally leave the car park, only for the van to break down on a flyover, where they then have to wait for the AA to arrive.

All fine so far...except for the small problem that at the end of a long, long day I was now a little bit tipsy. It had seemed like hours as we'd waited earlier in the evening for the crew to set up, and eventually the four of us had decided a few cheeky beers were in order. I'd kept telling myself I only had one line to do so a small one wouldn't hurt.

It's only one line, I thought to myself. How hard can it be?

Impossible, as it turned out. We'd done the scene again and again and I just couldn't seem to get my beer goggles straight enough to get the words out.

'Snooker is a marvellous game,' Martin replied as the camera whirred. 'Then we could have something in common, or you could use it for putting things on.'

'That's true, actually. We had a billiard table at home we used for that,' said Neil.

'Yeah, we had a table we used to put things on,' Martin told him. 'You know, household objects, cups and plants and shopping and pencils—'

'Oh, yes, thank you,' Caroline cut in sarcastically.

'It's pretty amazing this van when you think about it,' Neil continued. 'One minute it's on fire, the next it's up and running.'

It was time for my line. I took a deep breath. I must get it right.

'Only because we tush-parted it around the par cark for an hour and a half...' I said before starting to laugh. 'Sorry. I've got it wrong again.'

'*Cuuuuuuuuuuuuuuuut,*' said director Martin Dennis for what seemed the hundredth time.

'Sorry,' I told him, as the other three pissed themselves laughing.

In the end, Martin gave up and let me record my line back

at the studio, but I'm not sure how impressed he was by my behaving so badly.

Mind you, that night summed up the chemistry the four of us had developed off screen which was translating well on to it. *Men Behaving Badly* had changed instantly for the better when Neil had arrived. The boys had hit it off in a big way and it was like electricity between the two of them – they complemented each other just as Gary and Tony did, and it was obvious that new life had been breathed into the show. Martin began to change Gary from the yuppy-type suit of series one to the slightly shambolic guy who became a comic icon, while Neil also played Tony perfectly – a bit dippy, but so endearing. Caroline in turn made Dorothy her own, but I had a bit more trouble with Debs because she was a bit flat compared with the other characters. I was working on it, though, and it felt as if everything was falling into place as the writer, Simon Nye, fleshed out the bones and wrote around the bits he knew we were good at. No disrespect, but series one had felt a bit like the *Harry Enfield Show* – he was the big star and *Men Behaving Badly* was about Dermot and three people in his life. Now it was suddenly about four characters, and better for it.

Off screen, the shape of things to come became obvious when the little party thrown to welcome Neil turned into a nearly all-night bender in the bar at the Thames studios. The boys were young, free and single, and determined to have fun, while Caroline and I were both married, so our lives were a bit different to theirs. I'd started giving her a lift to and from work every day because she didn't live that far from my parents and we really got to know each other as we spent hours chatting in the car. We shared a daft sense of humour, and while I can't remember when exactly it happened, it was a trip to the garden centre that finally sealed our friendship. Caroline and Beryl were both into gardening and were always swapping stories about what they'd grown that week. They were really excited because the rehearsal rooms were opposite a massive garden centre. One day Caroline asked me if I could help her pick up something from there.

'It's really big,' she said as we drove into the car park. 'Too heavy for me to get home.'

'We'll get it back,' I replied. 'I'll help you.'

'There it is,' Caroline suddenly shouted, and pointed to a muscular young bloke. 'That's it. But I can't get it home and it's only nineteen!'

I knew then we were going to be mates.

Our working week started with a read-through every Tuesday morning with Martin Dennis, Beryl, Simon and Mary, the floor manager, and anyone else in the episode, like Dave Atkins, who played Les the barman, or Valerie Minifie and Ian Lindsay, who played Gary's colleagues, Anthea and George. It was always hilarious because everyone put so much into it, but I couldn't help noticing that while I'd pored over the script for days – desperate not to mess up, because sitcom is all based on energy and momentum – the others would speed-read it once and say it perfectly. I was amazed they could do that. I had to be really familiar with the script though, because I was the feed for the jokes and you can't get it wrong otherwise there'll never be any laughs. I never got the punchlines, but, as Ronnie Corbett once said to me, being the straight person is more difficult than the funny one, so I'm sticking to that theory! After the read-through, we'd block on Tuesday afternoons, which meant working out where we were going to stand in relation to the camera. Wednesdays and Thursdays were spent rehearsing, before a full run-through on Friday. The next day everyone came in, including the cameramen, make-up and wardrobe for the last bits of fine-tuning. Then, on Sunday, we'd go to the Thames studios and do a really slow line-by-line rehearsal in front of the cameras and a dress rehearsal. At 7.30 p.m., after supper, we'd film the episode live in front of an audience. Mum would always be there watching and I could instantly pick out her laugh from the crowd because it was so distinctive. Once it was over, it would be into the bar for a few drinks and then home.

It all seemed to be going brilliantly. The show was really gelling, living up to its promise, and I was so excited. *CATS Eyes* had been my first bite at prime-time telly and now it seemed I was getting another.

Towards the end of shooting the second series, however, my future on *Men Behaving Badly* looked doubtful once again because rumours had started circulating on set that Thames might lose their franchise when it came up for sale. If that happened, then *Men Behaving Badly* might well be dropped. Suddenly all the cameramen, props guys and make-up girls I'd worked with on and off for years in different shows were worried about losing their jobs, and by the time we finished filming, the atmosphere was really fearful.

The bombshell finally came when I was back at home being a wife and mum once again after series two aired in autumn 1992.

'Thames has lost the franchise,' Beryl said on the phone. '*Men Behaving Badly* has been dropped.'

'I can't believe it,' I replied. 'Just when we were on a roll. It was only going to get better. It's too good to give up on.'

'I know,' Beryl replied. 'But the new people don't want it. It doesn't stop here, though, Leslie. I'm not going to take it lying down. I'll make sure we're back.'

'I know you will,' I told her, but I wasn't convinced. Beryl was just trying to make me feel better. That was it for *Men Behaving Badly* – it would never get commissioned again. I felt so sorry for Beryl. She was passionate about the show – it was her baby – and now something so new and exciting had been dumped.

Another job will come along, I kept telling myself in the weeks and months that followed. In the cockles of my heart, though, I couldn't imagine what would. I really thought *Men Behaving Badly* had been going places, and I had been so looking forward to being part of it. How wrong I'd been.

It was coming up to Christmas 1992 and I was on my way to Darlington to do an evening panto performance when the phone rang.

'Hi, Les,' Lee said, sounding weirdly cheerful. 'I just wanted to let you know there might be a few people hanging around the stage door when you get there.'

'Not more groupies,' I joked.

Lee was silent.

'What's wrong?' I asked.

'We're being door-stepped by the *Yorkshire Evening Post*. They're saying you had an affair with Eric Cantona.'

'What?' I shouted. 'When is this supposed to have happened?'

'Earlier this year.'

'While I was pregnant? That's ridiculous.'

'I know it is. But the rumour's gone round about two of the other wives and I think it's stuck to you because you're well known.'

I couldn't believe what Lee was saying. Eric Cantona had left Leeds a month before for Manchester United. I knew the two teams were arch enemies, but I couldn't believe someone would make up something like this.

'Where has this come from?' I asked Lee. 'They're not going to print anything, are they?'

'No, no, of course not. Don't worry about it. I'll sort it out. I just wanted to warn you in case a journalist turns up at the theatre or something.'

I felt sick as I put down the phone, and really angry too. It wasn't the first time – or sadly the last – that rubbish had been written about me, but it had washed over me before.

Tomorrow's fish and chip paper, I'd tell myself.

This time, though, it hurt – I was married with two children and had other people to take into account. And what would the Leeds fans think? We were so happy in the city and now I'd probably become an outcast for driving away one of their star players.

No one turned up at the theatre in the end, but there was a knock at the door at home the next day.

'I'd just like to ask you about the rumours that your wife is having an affair with Eric Cantona,' the journalist asked Lee as he stood on the doorstep.

'I'll give you five seconds to get off my doorstep. Now fuck off,' Lee said, then slammed the door. I think that was the moment when he really started to hate the sort of journalists who are interested in that kind of story.

Over the next few days we found out the rumour had been printed in a Manchester United fanzine – it was a good way to wind up their rival supporters – and I was really annoyed. It might not have gone in the paper, but everyone knew about it and I was upset that Leeds hadn't come out and said what a load of crap it all was. I'd hardly spoken more than two words to Eric Cantona because a) he didn't speak much English and b) I didn't speak much French. In fact, the only players I knew well were Gordon Strachan and Gary McAllister because we socialised with them and their wives. Other than that, the only time I tended to meet Lee's team-mates was in the lounge after a match, when we'd have a quick drink before going home.

Unfortunately, soon the terraces were ringing with a new chant whenever Eric Cantona came on: 'He's French, he's flash, he's fucking Leslie Ash.' He was certainly the first and second, but there was no chance he'd ever done the third. Just like the rumour about *Quadrophenia*, though, it stuck and for years to come I couldn't walk past a building site without hearing, 'Ooh, ahh, Cantona.' It went on for ages. Over the years I've been linked to so many people – even bloody Jim

Davidson – but there was no truth to any of it. It annoyed me, though, that people joked about it. When I appeared on Baddiel and Skinner's *Fantasy Football* a few years later, they got the whole audience to shout, 'Ooh, ahh, Cantona,' as they introduced me. I felt like telling them to shove it up their arse and walking off. But in the years to come I'd learn the hard way that mud sticks; people really do believe there's no smoke without fire.

CHAPTER 6

The Party Starts

'Hold on tighter,' I hissed at Lee, as he stood opposite me hanging on to the Christmas turkey. 'Keep it steady and I'll stuff it.'

I leaned down and stared at the turkey's backside – somehow there were two of them. I blinked a few times and Lee started laughing.

'Bloody Rioja,' I giggled. 'I shouldn't have drunk so much.'

It was a few minutes before midnight on Christmas Eve and Lee and I were pissed as farts. We'd been out for dinner earlier with his sister, Denise, at the local tapas place, and one bottle of Rioja had turned into two, three and possibly four. Lee had wanted to go straight to bed when we got back, but I'd made him stay up and help – otherwise there would be no Christmas Day. I'd already laid the table and peeled the sprouts – all that was left to do was get the chestnut stuffing up and in the turkey.

'Bull's eye,' I said, as my hand hit the spot. I was home and dry.

It was the end of 1993 and it had been a big year for us because we'd left the North for London, after deciding it was the best place for us to build a future. Lee knew his contract at Leeds was coming to an end and his football career had peaked, while I was wondering what to do now that *Men Behaving Badly* had finished – it had won a British Comedy

Award, so I still felt sore about it being axed. Part of me was terrified about leaving Yorkshire – we'd had a quiet life since getting married and I was worried that our relationship would change in a place like London, with all its pitfalls. But things move on and Lee had joined Portsmouth in August for a few weeks, before moving to West Ham. It had taken ages to find a house, so Lee had had to live with my parents during the working week, while the boys and I stayed up North. This time, our move was going to be permanent and I wanted a place we could stay in for years. In the end, we had decided to rent for six months while I looked and eventually I'd found the place I knew we'd call home – an eight-bedroom Victorian villa on Balham Park Road with a small garden at the back leading on to Wandsworth Common. I had found it by chance after taking a wrong turning but had known it was right from the moment I had crossed the threshold, and Lee had bought it for me. It needed a lot of work and we couldn't move in straight away, so we remained in the rented house for the time being. I was so pleased when the boys and I finally arrived in London – I knew the M1 far more intimately than any woman should.

To get into the swing of things, we'd taken Joe, who was nearly four, and 18-month-old Max to Harrods to have their picture taken with Father Christmas. After queuing for an hour and a half, Father Christmas turned out to be about 21, ginger and so strange that Max didn't want to sit on his knee. Mishaps aside, I was determined to make this Christmas perfect. It was going to be a real family affair. My parents, Gill and her partner, Bill, Denise, Debbie and my nieces, Candy and Holly, were all expected round in the morning.

I must get everything right, I told myself, as I weaved around the kitchen checking a few last things before heading up to bed with Lee.

Just as we opened the bedroom door, I remembered one crucial detail.

'Father bloody Christmas,' I screeched, and lurched back downstairs to nibble the carrot, bite the mince pie and neck the sherry Joe and Max had left out. Everything was done.

I tiptoed upstairs and into our bedroom. Lee was already asleep when I slid in next to him. I closed my eyes and sighed with relief...

'Happy Christmas, Mummy!' Joe shouted as he stood centimetres from my face with Max. 'Santa's been. Can we open our presents now?'

'Merry Christmas, darlings,' I rasped. What time was it? It couldn't be morning already. I looked at my watch – 6 a.m.

Lee stirred. 'I'll take them down,' he said.

'Well, I'll come too,' I replied. 'I want to see them open their presents.'

My stomach lurched as I sat up.

'Come on, Mummy,' Joe said, disappearing through the doorway. 'Daddy's coming with us.'

Breathing deeply, I staggered downstairs to watch the boys open their presents.

'Go back to bed,' Lee told me, as they started playing. 'I'll sit here. You look awful.'

'Are you sure?' I asked. This was a first.

'Of course,' he replied.

I didn't wait around to argue and just dragged my sorry arse straight back to bed. I had about two hours before I had to be up again. Bliss. I closed my eyes.

'Have you done the sprouts?' Denise, Lee's sister, seemed to scream as she stood over me. Surely the two hours weren't up already, were they?

I scraped myself off the bed, dragged on some clothes and left Lee lying asleep. He must have come to bed when someone else had arrived to take over the kids.

'I'm going to pass out,' I said to Denise, as I turned on the oven. My hands were shaking: I had alcohol poisoning.

'You'll be fine,' she laughed. 'We had a skinful, but not too much.'

She may not have felt hungover, but I wanted to die as people started arriving and the kids made whoopy Christmas Day noises. Lee also seemed fine when he eventually got up, had a shower and started opening more wine.

I must be a complete lightweight, I thought to myself.

'You want to get those sprouts on,' my mum kept insisting as she sipped her sherry.

'All right, Mum,' I snapped. 'But I don't want stewed sprouts so I'll leave it a while. Lee likes them al dente.'

'Well, I think you'd better get them on soon.'

I stayed silent, concentrating on the voice in my head, which kept repeating, 'Get this done and you can lie down. Everyone falls asleep after Christmas lunch.'

The time passed in a haze of steam and popping champagne corks. The smell of turkey made me want to heave as it filled the kitchen, but at least it meant the oven was working – I hadn't used it before.

At last everything was ready. Lee started carving and I herded people towards the dining table. Plates were piled high and glasses filled. My dad pushed a forkful of food into his mouth.

'These bloody sprouts aren't cooked,' he complained. 'They're raw.'

'Well, just be thankful you've got anything at all,' I said, my voice rising. 'And I might as well tell you now there's no Christmas pudding because I forgot to buy one.'

Silence fell. My dad started gnawing on his sprout. He knew better than to argue with me in that mood.

Later, after everyone had eaten, I collapsed on the sofa and fell asleep. Thankfully when I woke up it seemed the wine was finally working its way out of my system.

Never again, I told myself, as I walked into the kitchen to start tackling the mess.

Instead of piles of washing-up, though, everything was lovely and tidy. It had all been done and put away. That's the nice things about families – they look after you when you're down. Or hungover.

Beryl was as good as her word about *Men Behaving Badly*. After promising us all she'd get it back on the telly, she never gave up. For nearly two years she talked to the right people, took them out to lunch and used her charm, until the BBC commissioned another series in early 1994.

'I told you I wouldn't let it go,' she said when she phoned to tell me the good news. 'It's all the same crew, same routine – should be easy. How are you fixed? Are you available?'

I couldn't believe she'd done it. Resurrecting the show on the BBC was the best thing that could have happened. It would surely be a hit now.

The third series of *Men Behaving Badly* was due to start in July, so a few months after moving to London, I met up with Martin, Neil and Caroline at our new rehearsal rooms in Kensington. The scripts had arrived about a week before we started rehearsing and I realised there weren't going to be any huge character changes when I saw that the first episode required me to wear an aerobics outfit and a swimming costume. Luckily I'd dieted frantically before filming started – more worried about the size of my bum than my performance as usual.

It was great to be back with the old team. There was as much sense of fun as ever, and soon Martin and Neil had developed a joke they'd use on me for years to come. Lots of my scenes with them were shot in the lobby of the flat, and one or the other, or both, would often fart before shutting their front door and leaving me to stand there waiting for my cue. Martin, the director, though, did all he could to keep everyone in line during rehearsals and make sure no one's comedy juices ran out of control. Refusing to come down to the boys' level, he didn't get wound up when they stole his favourite biscuits from the tea tray every morning. To stop such immaturity, he simply licked the ones he wanted.

Meanwhile Caroline and I would sit down on the all-important sofa in Gary and Tony's living room to read the prop newspapers. Once again she and I, Martin and Neil, had naturally fallen into two pairs. Caroline was so full of energy and fun that we seemed to spend the whole time laughing during our drives into work.

On set, though, it could get a bit boring as we waited around for hours some days while scenes we weren't in were rehearsed. We soon found a sure-fire way to make the time pass. If Caroline or I weren't required, or if there were problems working a scene, she'd have a little lie-down on Gary or Tony's bed and I'd go on the other. It seemed such a great idea, until the day the rehearsal had to stop because I was snoring so loudly. I woke up to find everyone standing around me. All I can say is that hanging around is tiring. Why sit in a hard chair when there's a comfy bed to lie in?

The hard work paid off because the third series of *Men Behaving Badly* did well when it was shown on BBC1 in the summer of 1994. It had been given the right slot, the comedy was fresh, and the ratings were good. It felt like everyone was talking about it, and while some reviewers were desperate to label *Men Behaving Badly* sexist, the public knew it wasn't. The show was so brilliantly played by the two boys, and Dorothy and Deborah usually came out on top. The audience were invited to laugh at the boys and their loutish ways, not cheer for them. *Men Behaving Badly* was on the way to big things.

Hurry up, I thought, as the taxi driver crawled through the traffic. We're going to be bloody late again.

Try as we might, Lee and I just couldn't seem to turn up on time when we went out with our new crowd of friends.

About a dozen of us had started going out together a lot, and most Saturday nights started off with a meal in somewhere like Quaglino's, off Piccadilly – it was the place to be seen and everyone went there. Tonight was the same, and, as always, Lee and I were running late. I was sick of arriving after everyone else. How was it that some people managed to turn up early week after week and bag the best seats, while Lee and I ended up at opposite ends of the table, squeezed in facing a wall? We walked into the crowded restaurant which was full of the buzz of Saturday-night chatter and I saw everyone sitting at a long table. Yep, crap seats yet again.

Saturday nights were the new big thing for the Chapmans. It had always been the one night of the week that Lee could relax after a game, but things had moved to a whole new level since arriving in London. Where before the night had been about a meal and a few drinks, in the bright lights of the capital it now meant a meal, a nightclub, a VIP area, drinks and maybe more drinks.

Lee had met our new crowd of friends while I was still living up North and was really friendly with them by the time I arrived. So friendly, in fact, that I soon nicknamed them 'the In Crowd' because it seemed like we couldn't go anywhere without them. Johnny and Bertie Ekperigin, at the centre of the group, were like our social secretaries – informing me of what was happening, when and how. The phone was always ringing, dates being put in the diary and plans being made.

I'd first met them in the summer of 1994 when they'd invited the whole family to their house for a barbecue. Bertie had met us at the door when we arrived at their huge house – she was beautiful with long, blonde hair and a great figure. It came as no surprise to me when I found out that she was a model.

'Come in, everyone's in the garden. Grab a drink, kids,' she said, then turned and led us to the back of the house.

Joe and Max shuffled off in the direction of the lawn, which was full of toys, kids and already slightly sozzled adults. Johnny and Bertie were obviously used to catering for large numbers – that was his world because he was a partner in the famous Julie's Restaurant in Holland Park – and I got the feeling this barbecue wasn't so much of an annual thing but possibly a weekly one. Everyone seemed very familiar with the routine.

'Hi, Leslie, I've heard so much about you,' Johnny said, as he walked up with a bottle of wine in his hand. 'It's nice to finally meet you.' He handed me a drink before turning to Lee. 'Lee, come and join the boys,' he said, and they walked into the lounge.

'Men!' Bertie exclaimed. 'What are they like? Let me introduce you to the girls.'

I soon realised that all the women were just like Bertie – designered up to the armpits – and I felt a little out of my depth as I chatted to them. Would we have anything in common? Don't get me wrong, I liked looking good, but I also had two young boys and loved jeans. It was strange that all the women were in the garden with the kids, while the men were holding court in the house – like cows fussing over their young as the bulls guffawed together in the parlour.

Even Joe and Max seemed to feel a little out of place as the afternoon wore on – they were used to being rough and tumbly but were suddenly sitting really quietly. By about 5 p.m. I decided I'd had enough. Soon it would be time for their tea, bath and bed, and I didn't like messing with their routine – well, that was my excuse and I stuck to it. But Lee obviously didn't want to be enticed home and you could have cut the atmosphere with a knife as we got into the car.

'What's up?' Lee asked, as I sat silently at the wheel.

'Well, where should I start?' I snapped. 'One, I felt annoyed at being forced into a mother and toddler group all afternoon; two, Joe kept asking to go home every five minutes; and, three, you left me alone while you, Johnny and all the other testosterone-filled males sat drinking some very nice wine when I couldn't drink because I had to drive the pissing car home. Do I need to say more?'

It wasn't the best of starts, but I told myself to make an effort with the In Crowd and so I did. I went out to drinks, dinner and clubs, and joined in the fun. But the sense I'd had of not fitting in on that very first day never left me, even as the months passed. The girls would appear for a night out in mini-dresses and I'd be covered up – I was never a big flesh-flasher – or they'd discuss their latest Brazilian and could have been talking about their gardener for all I knew. I just wasn't like them. We spent hours talking, but I couldn't tell you what one conversation was about.

The separation of the sexes also continued to bother me. It reminded me of a wine-tasting Lee and I had got invited to in Yorkshire once, when the men and women were shown into different rooms. I felt like I was at a fucking knitting circle as I sipped tea while the men tasted fantastic wines next door and I thought I was going to cry. I know it sounds pathetic, but I was so used to doing everything with Lee, I knew he was in the other room and hated being forced apart from him. It was strange, but this still went on in certain places at that time. I don't know if it's like it today, but I can remember one game of golf when I wasn't allowed in the bloody bar after-wards because 'the laydeez' were not invited. It was like that with the In Crowd – the girls sat down in a club, the men stood at the bar; the girls stayed in the kitchen at someone's house, the men went into the lounge. I don't think Lee noticed it – he's a bloke's bloke after all – but I was really aware suddenly we had gone from spending every moment together to hardly seeing each other on a night out, and as time wore on, I began to feel more and more like he was being taken from me.

'But why can't we stay in tonight?' I'd ask.

'Come on, Les,' he'd tell me. 'It'll be fun. We're going for dinner and then to Brown's. It'll be a laugh.'

'But I'm bored of going out all the time.'

'Well, what do you want to do? Sit in watching TV? What's wrong with you?'

I think there were lots of reasons why it happened. The guys were on power trips and Lee loved the competition of all that. They also knew how to party hard and Lee had never really done that. He'd been a footballer since he was a teenager and now, for just one night a week, was allowing himself to relax a little more than he'd been used to. Maybe things were also happening inside his head that he didn't want to focus on as his career came to an end and this was a bit of escapism. But, in truth, I don't really know exactly why it all happened – it just did. Somehow cracks started appearing between us. I couldn't believe that a relationship that had been so rock solid could deteriorate so quickly. Instead of talking about it, I just ignored it – refused to look closely at the problems because they scared me too much. It was the first time that Lee and I had faced a real problem in our relationship, and we both stuck our heads in the sand. I told myself things would settle down.

Feelings have a way of coming out somewhere, though, and the one thing I couldn't control was my possessive streak. Lee and I had always been jealous types, and the unhappier I got with the In Crowd, the more jealous I became. I'd long been aware of other women finding Lee sexy – it's weird how some women will flirt with your husband when you're standing right next to him – but our new social life in London meant there were far more opportunities for that to happen and I didn't like the fact that he allowed it to. He'd tell me not to be stupid, that I was winding myself up, but I got more and more insecure about it – sometimes it felt like me against all these women.

'Hi,' I'd say, as I walked up to whichever girl had made a beeline for him. 'And you are?'

I was like a shadow – just letting her know he was attached and she could piss off. As 1994 rolled into 1995, I became increasingly possessive – trying to cling on to Lee in the worst possible way as he and I started to drift apart. The closeness that we'd had throughout our relationship seemed to be falling to pieces now that we were out of each other's pockets.

Things finally came spectacularly to a head one Sunday morning when I woke up to the sound of Lee coming into the bedroom. It was 6 a.m. It was daylight. It was the first time that he hadn't come home all night. I couldn't believe he'd disappeared like that.

'Where the hell have you been?' I said, as I turned and saw this smelly, ravaged drunk man standing by the bed.

'The Groucho. Vic and Bob,' he said. He was completely pissed.

'Let's try that again,' I replied sarcastically. 'Vic and Bob who?'

Lee opened his mouth to speak and the smell of stale alcohol and fags blew in my face.

'Reeves and Mortimer,' he replied. 'They were staying at the Groucho, so we could stay drinking as residents. Then I think we went down to Jerry's.'

'Oh, Vic, Bob and Jerry, is it now? You expect me to believe that shit?'

There was no remorse on his face as he spoke to me – that was his story and he was sticking to it.

'So were there any women with you?'

He hesitated. 'Oh, fuck off. What do you think I've been doing, you silly cow?'

'Well, I don't know.'

I didn't like where this was going.

'Here, phone and ask if you don't believe me,' he shouted, pointing to the phone.

I clambered out of bed as Lee got in. 'I will. I bloody well will call, seeing as how it's a bloody hotel and someone will be there who'll tell me,' I screamed.

'Do what you want,' Lee told me as he turned over. 'I'm going to sleep.'

I wanted to throttle him as I stood there with the phone in my hand. How dare he stay out all night and act like I was the one with the problem?

'If the boot was on the other foot, what would you say, eh? Eh?' I shouted.

No answer.

'Eh?' I shrieked.

Still no answer.

I raised the phone in my hand over him – threatening to throw the whole bloody thing if he didn't answer.

'Go on, then,' he sneered. 'You haven't got the bollocks.'

Fuck him. I'd throw the phone at the wall and wouldn't care if I broke it. Maybe that would get the message home. Now he'd see. He'd have to listen to me.

'You bastard,' I shouted as I threw it.

Everything went into slow motion. The base left my hand and headed for the wall as planned, but the receiver seemed to have a mind of its own as it flew through mid-air, twirled and turned on its curly flex and found its way into Lee's mouth, which was open as usual. His hand flew up.

'You've knocked my teeth out,' he said quietly.

'Oh, shut up,' I hissed back.

'You have – you've knocked out my teeth,' he replied. This time he spoke considerably louder.

What had I done? I hadn't even aimed at him. My stunt had backfired. I stood there silently. Slowly he drew his hand away and I saw that his two front teeth were badly chipped. He'd played football, a contact sport, for over 20 years and they had been OK, but now I'd managed to ruin them. I felt sick as I looked at him. What had I done? How could I have hurt him like that? I'd slammed a lot of doors, driven off in the car, that sort of thing, but never anything like this. I felt so ashamed of myself.

That was the first time Lee stayed out all night. After that, I learned to shut out the anger, and the issues went even more unspoken than before. I stopped asking questions and Lee stopped talking.

Our arguments got worse and worse. We both refused to admit we were wrong. The pitch got louder and the tone got nastier. We'd throw horrible insults at each other, trying to hit where it really hurt by talking a load of bollocks – criticising faults that weren't even there. The difference between us was that while Lee could be just as nasty and aggressive as me, he never lost it like I did – and when that happened, I knew he'd won the battle and it made me even angrier. Ashamed as I was about the phone incident, there were still times when I'd lash out at him, beating at his chest in frustration.

'What's wrong with *me*?' I'd scream. 'There's nothing wrong with me. What's wrong with *you*? All you do is go out.'

'Well, what am I supposed to do? I'm having fun and you're just moaning.'

'But we're living separate lives. I want to see you, Lee. I want us to be a proper family again. I'm sick of this.'

'Well, then, maybe you should fuck off.'

'What? I'm not going to leave. If anyone goes, it'll be you. I'll have the house and the kids and you can just fuck off.'

'You're mad, Leslie. If you want to go, then go, piss off, but I've had enough of this.'

Lee knew exactly how to wind me up, and always did. One night he even locked me out in the garden during a row dressed in just my pants.

'You can stay there until you calm down,' he said in a

singsong, wind-up voice as he shut the door. 'Are you going to say sorry now? Say I'm right and you're wrong and then I'll let you back in.'

The condescending sod – patronising me as I stood there, knowing I couldn't shout back because otherwise the neighbours would take a look. Eventually he let me back in.

In early 1995 another wedge was driven between us when I agreed to do a ten-week tour of the Noël Coward play *Present Laughter* with Peter Bowles and Helen Atkinson-Wood. It coincided with a difficult time for Lee. He'd always said he didn't want to work his way down the divisions, but in January 1995 he had left Premiership team West Ham for Premiership strugglers Ipswich. It must have been hard to go from the roar of the Leeds crowd to a team that was finding it hard to stay up in the division. Looking back, I shouldn't have taken that job. Lee was going through a massive period of change in his life and needed me. I was so unhappy and determined to be independent, to make the most of my career high, that I agreed to go on tour even though I knew Lee missed me terribly when I was away. With the boys being looked after by a nanny and no more nagging, it only made it easier for him to go out and forget things. Suddenly he was partying even harder and wasn't in when I phoned. I missed him, Joe and Max and was so pleased to get home when the play ended. When I got there, however, it seemed as if Lee was even thicker with the In Crowd than ever. We were never alone any more, someone was always with us, and the only time we ever spent together was in bed after another night out. Lee still didn't seem to want to listen when I tried to talk to him and so I usually ended up nagging, which only made things worse.

'She's got to calm down,' I heard Bertie say through the serving hatch, as I tidied up in the kitchen after lunch one Sunday.

We'd had some of the In Crowd round and they were all sympathising with Lee as they sat at the table. We'd made a really big deal of it. After all the building work had been completed, we wanted to show off our lovely new home, and I'd done the table while Lee had picked some fantastic wines – his passion for it was growing and by now he had nearly a thousand bottles in our cellar.

'She's got to let you do what you want to do,' Bertie continued. 'She can't rule your life.'

How dare she? I'd just cooked her lunch and she was sitting in my house saying this? After all the months of socialising and seeing each other, they now felt so comfortable that they could criticise me in my own home. I walked back into the room.

'If you've got something to say, Bertie, then say it to my face,' I said angrily. 'I should lighten up, should I?'

'Calm down, Les,' Lee said. 'It's nothing. Sit down.'

'No,' I insisted. 'If there's something to say, then she should just say it.'

Johnny and Bertie looked at me uncomfortably.

'I'd like to know what I should do to get on with everyone, with you too, Lee,' I shouted into the silence.

'It's just that you need to be a bit more understanding,' Johnny said. 'You're going off to work, but you don't want Lee to come out with us. We're only taking him out for a meal and a drink. He's not getting up to anything.'

'Yes, you've got to let him be himself,' Bertie went on. 'You can't tie him to you. You're pretty hard on him, you know.'

They were like members of a secret club – Lee included – that I wasn't part of, and as they stared with accusation in their eyes, I felt so hurt that the fight left me. There was no tantrum, no screaming match. Instead I simply sat down calmly as if nothing had happened, and, relieved that I'd shut up, everyone started chatting again.

Over the following weeks, however, I couldn't stop

thinking about that day. Maybe what they'd said was true – I was the problem. I knew I was trying to hold on to Lee too tightly, that I had to let him go and see what happened. Deep down, though, that was what I was afraid of. I was used to being in control and now something was happening that I didn't understand. It had all come out of the blue, and the In Crowd seemed to know there were problems better than I did.

I can remember the point when I finally had to let it all go. It was another normal night – we'd been out with everyone for drinks and dinner before going on to a club and I was sitting chatting to the girls. Out of the corner of my eye, I saw one of the guys' girlfriends head over to Lee. She was one of those – big tits, miniskirt, loads of hair – and I couldn't take my eyes off her. I got more and more wound up as she talked to Lee – giggling and leaning into him as she chatted. I knew all the signs; I'd seen them before. This was my cue to defend my patch.

'Hi, how are you?' I said as I walked over. 'I haven't seen you for ages.'

'I was just telling Lee about a great place we went for dinner the other night,' she replied, almost visibly recoiling as the boobs went down and the giggles stopped.

Job done, I went back to my seat.

Later, however, she came up to where I was sitting and bent down to speak to me.

'Well, all I can say is that you must be a really good fuck,' she said, and turned on her heel.

I looked at her retreating back. What the hell did she mean? I could only think that because I was a bit older and not as glam as the other girls, then all I had going for me was my performance in bed. I didn't know whether to smack her or thank her.

Of course, Lee and I had a massive argument about it when we got home.

'She didn't mean any harm,' he told me. 'I'm sure she was only joking.'

Was he having a laugh?

I was still fuming the next day when I saw Mum and ranted on at her for ages while she sat quietly.

'You know, you've got to watch it,' she told me, when I'd finally calmed down. 'Jealousy is the worst thing for any relationship. You've got to stop it, otherwise you'll lose Lee. You've just got to trust him.'

That took the wind right out of my sails. Mum told me to grow up and be an adult. I also knew she was right. If Lee did me wrong, then that would be it, but otherwise I had to keep my mouth shut and let him live the life that he obviously wanted – with or without me.

I smoothed down the edges of the duvet for a final time as I looked around the bedroom. It was clean and tidy – now I could get on with the boys' room. They were out for a walk with the nanny, and Lee was training. Once everything was done, I'd phone Mum for a chat. Series four of *Men Behaving Badly* had just finished airing and she loved hearing about everything that was happening now it was doing so well. I felt like I was in a band as requests to do interviews and openings came in. Everyone seemed to know who we were, and I'd had to laugh a couple of months earlier when I'd offered to drive Martin, Neil and Caroline to a photo shoot in my convertible. Suddenly I realised that people were staring as we pulled up at some traffic lights – Gary, Tony, Dorothy and Deborah were cruising down Kensington High Street instead of sitting on the sofa.

'They really do live together,' I could almost hear people exclaiming.

If only they'd known what it was really like! I think a lot of people would have been disappointed if they'd known how different real life was from our on-screen antics. Of course, we were mates who had a great laugh together, but it wasn't all about beer and farting – life on *Men Behaving Badly* was hard work. Admittedly the boys were a bit more wild on the party front, but the craziest thing Caroline and I got up to was a few too many wines with a meal after rehearsals. It was all far tamer than people imagined it would be. Instead of getting drunk before filming, we watched *Antiques Roadshow* to get us in the comedy mood, and instead of eating curry and chips, we had the home-grown tomatoes Beryl used to bring in for us. The only thing missing were cucumber sandwiches – boy, we were crazy! But because we were all friends on screen, people expected us to be like that off it as well, and while Neil and Martin were good mates and Caroline and I were close, it wasn't like we were down the pub together every night. I was a mum of two boys, and even though I spent a couple of months a year doing *Men Behaving Badly*, my life still revolved around looking after my children and running my home.

It was exciting, though, because series four had done really well and more and more things were beginning to happen on the back of *Men Behaving Badly*, like guest appearances on talk shows, and Mum loved hearing all about it. I took one last look at the room before turning towards the door. The phone's sharp ring cut through the silence.

I picked up the receiver by the bed. 'Hello?'

'Hello,' a man replied. 'Mrs Chapman?'

'Yes.'

'I'm sorry to call you, but I am a lawyer and have been instructed by your agent, Sharon Hamper, to act on your behalf with regard to a story that is going to appear in the *News of the World* on Sunday. It concerns your husband.'

'What about?' I asked. 'Something about him playing?'

'No, Mrs Chapman, I'm afraid not. The newspaper has a photo of your husband in bed with a woman and they are going to print it.'

The man carried on talking, but I didn't hear anything else. My heart started to thud. I felt light-headed and sick. I sat down, making a dent on the newly made bed. The voice continued. I heard the words 'Ibiza', 'weekend', 'bed', but nothing that I could understand.

'I'll be in touch, Mrs Chapman,' the voice said. The phone clicked and I dropped the receiver.

This was it – the end. I couldn't believe it was happening. Admittedly it had been hard over the past few months because watching Lee had been like watching someone on a one-way path to destruction and all I could do was sit by as he continued to live life to the full. But I never thought he'd be capable of betraying me like this.

I knew exactly when those pictures had been taken. A couple of weeks before, we'd been to Ibiza for the weekend with Johnny and Bertie. It had been a total disaster. First, Lee had argued with them on the Saturday evening. Later that night he and I had also had a massive row. It was about 4 a.m. and after going to our favourite club, Pacha, he'd wanted to try out a new place called Space. I had hated it when we got there and wanted to go back to the hotel. It was hot, late and we were both really pissed. I'd had enough. Lee, though, had no intention of leaving and we'd had a massive row on the dance floor before I left him to it. If he wanted to carry on that much, he could do it without me.

The party obviously still wasn't over when I woke up alone later that morning, but I didn't worry too much – Ibiza is the kind of place where you can club all day as well as all night. As afternoon turned towards evening, however, I started getting really anxious. It wasn't like him to be gone so long. Johnny and Bertie were still pissed off with him and all they kept saying was that he could look after himself. I was of course worried, though, and in the end I asked a guy from the hotel to ring around the hospitals and police for me. Nothing had been reported, and there were no unidentified blond men lying in any of the hospitals. I went to bed and told myself I'd just have to wait. Lee would be fine.

He still hadn't turned up the next morning and I was even more panicked. One minute I saw him lying in a ditch in my mind's eye; the next he was still partying. All I knew for sure was that I had a flight home booked in a few hours and had to get back for the kids. It was Joe's sports day and I couldn't miss it. I waited until the last possible moment before going down to reception and tearfully paying the bill. I left Lee's ticket and passport at reception for him.

'I don't want to go,' I told Johnny and Bertie when we got to the airport.

Suddenly I looked up to see Lee walking towards me. He looked awful – dopey and almost out of it – and my relief lasted a split second before anger filled me. Where on earth had he been? Lee didn't say a word as he walked up to me and I didn't dare let myself speak – I didn't want another public row. He could go fuck himself.

It went on like that for nearly 24 hours after we got home. We'd got past the point of talking about the bad stuff for a while now and both of us stayed silent as we went to sports day. When we got home, Lee collapsed asleep in bed while I sorted out the boys. I couldn't stop wondering what he'd been up to. Had he been with another woman? I couldn't bear the thought.

'I met a crowd of people and we just carried on drinking,' he told me when he finally woke up the next day. 'We went all over the place and all I know is that we ended up back at a flat in the evening. I was so pissed that I passed out cold and woke up the next morning. That was when I jumped in a cab, went to the hotel and they told me you'd gone to the airport. I can't really remember much more than that.'

'Were you with a woman?' I asked him quietly. For the first time in a long time, there was no shouting – this could be make or break for us and I had to stay calm.

'Leslie, I really can't remember much,' Lee said as he turned to look at me. 'But I'd know if I'd been with someone else and I wasn't. I wouldn't do that to you or us.'

I knew I had to trust what he said, but there was no way he was getting away with it that easily. I didn't ask any more questions, but I let Lee know he was going to have to pay the price for worrying me. The whole house was quiet as I threw myself into getting ready for Max's christening the following weekend. We had 50 people coming for lunch in the garden, a jazz band playing, and I was doing all the catering – I wasn't going to let anything spoil the day I'd been planning for ages. Caroline, who was going to be godmother, had loaned me a fish kettle and I started poaching salmon while Lee kept himself to himself. He knew he was in the doghouse.

Even though everything was far from OK, there was also part of me that was relieved – maybe the In Crowd would be out of our lives now that things had finally come to a head. Lee knew he'd done wrong and things could start getting back to normal. We'd be as close as we'd always been before the move to London, and if that was the case, then the whole bloody thing would have been a blessing.

Then the phone rang.

I felt completely empty as I turned and walked out of the bedroom. Mechanically I walked down the stairs and into the kitchen. I couldn't believe this was happening – Lee had betrayed me and it was going to be splashed across newspaper pages. I picked up the phone.

'I've just had a phone call from a lawyer,' I told Lee. 'He says the *News of the World* has pictures of you.'

'I know,' he replied.

'What? But what are these pictures of?'

'I don't know. I haven't seen them. I've only known about it for a few hours, but Sharon thought it was best if the lawyer spoke to you first.'

'I don't understand,' I told him. I was so confused. 'He said the pictures were taken in Ibiza and you said you weren't with anyone.'

'Let's talk when I get home,' Lee replied. 'We can't talk properly now. I won't be long.'

I felt anxious and sick as I put down the phone. What was happening? Why wasn't he telling me what was going on? I tried ringing Mum and Sharon, but they weren't picking up, so all I could do was sit it out until I heard Lee's key turn in the door.

'What's all this about?' I asked as he walked in. 'I don't understand.'

'Nothing happened,' Lee replied steadily, but I could see fear on his face. 'I don't know how they got these pictures, but I do know that nothing happened. It's like I told you – I drank all day, went to a party. The only other thing I can remember is a flash going off when I was in bed and me saying, "No." Then I woke up the next morning.'

'What?' I said quietly. 'You were so pissed you don't remember? Then how do you know you didn't do anything?'

'I just do. I'd know if something had happened and I know it didn't.'

'So what the fuck did happen, then?' I shouted.

'I've told you everything I can remember. There were some guys there and they bought me drinks. We moved on somewhere else. There were some girls with us. We went back to a flat. I was gone. I could hardly speak. I don't know if they'd given me something or not, but I was out of it. I was set up, Les.'

I looked at him in disgust. I didn't want to be in the same room as him, be anywhere near him.

'Well, we'll know if you're telling the truth when we see the paper, won't we?' I said as I walked out.

Suddenly I realised that everyone – Lee, Sharon, the lawyer – had known about this and I was the last to be told. I felt so humiliated. Of course I knew that stories that were only 2 per cent accurate were printed as 100 per cent true – it had happened to me before – but I had to ask myself, What if Lee has been unfaithful?

I'd always told myself I'd leave, but as I found myself contemplating the worst, I realised I didn't know if I'd be able to.

'I don't think you should see it,' Lee said. 'You're not going to like it.'

He walked into the kitchen, where I was waiting with Mum. I'd asked her to come because I needed her with me. I was standing in front of the sink. She was sitting at the table and Lee put the newspaper in front of her. I didn't move.

'I don't think you should,' Lee kept muttering to me, as Mum opened the paper and started reading.

I waited silently for her to finish before walking over and picking up the paper.

'I've got to,' I said quietly.

'Night Lee behaved very, very bedly,' the headline screamed across two pages. Blurry pictures showed him with his arm draped round a girl who was wearing a thick pearl choker. Another showed him kissing a woman in bed. I couldn't believe what I was seeing. I said nothing as I stared down.

The whole article was a blow-by-blow account of their day's drinking. Lee had apparently been at the club until 4 p.m. and drinking until 11.30 p.m. – a full 24 hours after we'd started. You could see from the pictures how out of it he was. Despite the pictures, the 'friend' who'd talked to the newspaper hadn't said that Lee and the girl had had sex. I was sure that if he'd actually slept with her, then they would have printed every tiny sexual detail. Whatever mess he'd got himself into, it wasn't that.

Even so, anger filled me as I read. How could Lee have been so stupid? How could he have allowed himself to be set up like that? He knew that our private lives made it into the newspapers. Didn't he care about the boys and me? How could he be so irresponsible?

'This is important, Leslie,' Mum said quietly, as I stood staring at the pages. 'What are you going to do? Do you want this marriage to end, or do you want it to work?'

I looked once more at the newspaper and took a deep breath. I had a choice to believe in Lee or walk away. I chose the first because I trusted him. We'd both made mistakes over the past year and now we had a chance to start again. We had two sons and years together. This was just a drunken night with some chancer.

'From this day forward no one ever mentions a word about this again,' I said. 'Nothing. I'm not going to allow this piece of shit to split up my family. Now take the fucking paper away.'

CHAPTER 7

In a Spin

The wind machine started blowing a gale and a hundred lights flashed as the opening bars of the song boomed out.

'If you want him to be…always by your side,' I sang, dropping my weight on to my left foot and nearly going flying. My stiletto had got stuck in a hole on the stage. There was nothing I could do but carry on bobbing around – one foot trapped and about to break a leg.

Beside me, Caroline swayed to the music – the *Men Behaving Badly* girls were on the way to being pop stars! After Martin and Neil had done a book, we'd recorded a version of the 1960s pop song 'Tell Him' to coincide with series five of *Men Behaving Badly*. Caroline and I had been asked to do a book as well, a sort of *Girls Behaving Badly*, but we'd decided it wasn't a good look for ladies in their thirties, so we'd recorded the single instead. After three days in a studio, we'd done a photo shoot for the publicity material and then the video. We were so excited about it – where would we be going? Ibiza like Wham! in 'Club Tropicana', or the Caribbean like Duran Duran for 'Rio'? Clacton was the answer. We should have known.

It was still fantastic fun. Our hair was backcombed to buggery, we had false eyelashes – you name it, we had it. A costume designer called Boo had also made us beautiful 1950s-style dresses. Mine was white with multicoloured splashes of colour on it and an orange trim; Caroline's was the same with a pink trim. We'd even had stiletto shoes made to match our trims and had really hammed it up during the shoot at an old holiday-camp ballroom. Everyone was pleased with the result.

There was just one problem with project 'Pop Stardom' – the B-side of the single. Caroline and I had turned songwriters after being told we would get more royalties if we wrote it.

'How hard can it be?' we'd asked as we sat down with a bottle of wine at Caroline's kitchen table to write a hit. The tune had been given to us by the producer, Jon Astley; now all we had to do was think up some lyrics.

'We could just write anything,' Caroline suggested, as I stared at the blank piece of paper.

'Yeah, but let's try and do something good,' I urged.

Time ticked on as we downed the wine and inspiration failed to strike.

'We're running out of time,' I said anxiously, looking at my watch. 'I've got to get home soon.'

'Come on,' Caroline said. 'We've got to think of something. This can't be that difficult. We could do anything like "Get Your Shirt Off"?'

'Nooo,' I laughed. 'We can't do a song about getting your kit off. We must be able to think of something better.'

Another half an hour passed as we stared into space.

'All right, then,' I said, looking at Caroline. '"Get Your Shirt Off" it is.'

We thought it was hysterical, but funnily enough other people didn't get the joke and a few years ago I heard our song played on a radio programme about the worst B-sides in history! We'd been a bit miffed when the single was finally released and Radio 2 had put it on its play list – we wanted to be on *Top of the Pops* and Radio 1. In the end, 'Tell Him' only got to number 25 in the charts. Needless to say, the only winner was the record company.

In the summer of 1996 it seemed as if *Men Behaving Badly* was everywhere. Premières, parties, promotions, interviews, photo shoots, paparazzi…it was all happening for us and I was determined to enjoy it. There had been bad times, of course, that year. Sharon Hamper's agency, the one I'd signed up with years before and which represented Caroline and me, had gone into liquidation and we were both owed money. I'd also had to sit in the car while Caroline practised for her driving test – scary! On the other hand, series five was proving as popular as ever and we were all in demand. Advertising voiceovers were the newest thing we were being asked to do and I'd go on to do everything from sanitary towels to *The Times*. The four of us did one for a clothing company owned by Cartier and were given beautiful watches. Martin, though, was the most in demand, and, in the days before mobile phones, he had a pager that used to keep beeping in rehearsals. As he rushed off to the pay phone to call his agent about yet another job, we'd all shout, 'Kerrrrrrrrrrrching.'

The other good news was that Caroline and I had won equal pay with the boys. We'd known for a while that Martin and Neil earned more than us, and one day the subject came up yet again when we were all sitting on the sofa.

'But it's a series about four people, not two,' Caroline said.

'I totally agree,' Martin replied.

'Well, we've all got to stick together on this,' I added.

The boys agreed 100 per cent and Caroline and I got ourselves a pay rise – we were part of the show's success after all, and what a success it was. The previous year *Men Behaving Badly* had won a National Television Award, two British Comedy Awards for Martin and Caroline as Top Television Comedy Actor and Actress and a Writers' Guild Award for Simon. In April we'd also gone to the BAFTAs, where Martin had won Best Comedy Performance, while the rest of us got pipped by *Father Ted* for Best Comedy Series. We'd celebrated Martin's win in style and run up such a massive bar bill that the story made it into the papers. At another awards ceremony, we weren't allowed to return to the auditorium after winning, so we asked someone backstage to get us a drink. We were told to wait in what looked like a cupboard and Caprice, who'd presented the gong, was with us. She looked so amazing in an almost see-through dress that Caroline and I had taken a step back – mind you, we couldn't have got any closer because the boys were almost on top of her.

'Wanna hear a joke?' Caprice suddenly drawled.

'Oh, yes,' the boys said eagerly.

'Well, two southern hookers – Dolores and Charmaine – are talking about their men as they stand waiting for business on a street corner.'

Martin and Neil stared at Caprice in awe.

'"What ya call ya man, Charmaine?" Dolores asked.

'"I call ma man Big Ben," she replied.

'"Why ya call him Big Ben, Charmaine?" Dolores asked.

'"Because he's big and his name's Ben."

'So then Charmaine turned to Dolores and said, "What ya call ya man, Dolores?"

'"I call ma man Drambuie," she replied.

'"Why ya call him Drambuie, Dolores? Ain't that some fancy liquor?"

'"He sure is," said Dolores.'

Caprice started giggling while the boys went to seventh heaven. They couldn't believe such a beautiful bird had come out with such a filthy joke.

The only other award we scooped was one at the Variety Club and I snuck that one home. I felt I deserved it – Caroline had won a British Comedy Award, Martin had got a BAFTA, and the only thing I'd been presented with was a bloody Gotcha. I'd got it the year before while I was touring in *Present Laughter* and was asked to do some work on an educational kids' TV programme about Bedouins. In order to get the 'desert feel', the shoot was at a sand works near

Chichester and soon I was crawling over 'dunes' and hopping on and off a bloody camel as I talked to camera about the Bedouins. After what seemed like hours of retakes, my final piece to camera was in a tent. As I dutifully talked about harems, Noel Edmonds walked in dressed as a sheikh. It was only then that it finally dawned on me that the whole thing was set up. I felt like smacking Noel – I'd been on and off a camel, making a fire with its shit and a fool of myself. But of course I soon saw the funny side and was pretty touched in the end that I'd won a Gotcha at all. Even so, that had been my only award-winning moment and so when *Men Behaving Badly* scooped the Variety Club gong, I decided the time was right to nab it!

While my career was going well, life at home wasn't quite as peachy. Things with Lee hadn't changed in the ways I'd hoped after I'd chucked the *News of the World* in the bin a year before. I had thought it would mean the end of the In Crowd, that Lee wouldn't want to see them, would be all mine again and we'd go back to the kind of quiet life we'd enjoyed in Yorkshire. It had become clear, however, that he didn't want to slow down and I was the replacement for the In Crowd. It was the price I had to pay for us to move on from them and I started partying more than I'd ever done. Lee and I now did our socialising behind closed doors, and everything became quite controlled as we hid away from the press.

I told myself there wasn't time to talk about things – there were always other people around, and we were both working – but in reality we just didn't face up to what was happening. It was a case of 'Let's just carry on the way we are and pretend it never happened', and cracks that had appeared before Ibiza weren't so much papered over as plastered and redecorated. I don't think we were that different from lots of couples with young children – life was busy and we just got on with it.

There were moments, though, when I still felt as close to him as ever and one was on Valentine's Day, when Lee had rung to say he was taking me to lunch in the country.

'Where are we going?' I'd hissed down the phone. I'd arranged for a dozen red roses to be sent to him and knew he'd miss them if we went out.

Lee wouldn't take no for an answer and I was really pissed off by the time I picked him up from the station after training and drove into the country – he'd ruined my big surprise, I'd cancelled the roses, and now we'd be going for some stuffy lunch at some stuffy restaurant.

He sat hunched over the map as we got near Sevenoaks.

'Left,' he told me. 'Right.'

I drove silently, about to blow my stack at any second.

'Here we are,' he said, gesturing to a sign at the side of the road for a kennels.

I couldn't believe it. I'd been on about getting a dog but Lee had always said no because it would be too much of a tie. Caroline had one called Olly who went everywhere with her – it was so friendly I'm sure it was half human – and I knew the boys would love a dog, but I never thought Lee would go out and get us one just like that.

'It's a Valentine's present from me, Joe and Max,' he said with the biggest grin as we drove into the car park.

I couldn't believe how thoughtful he'd been. It was so out of the blue, so kind and he knew how much it would mean to me. It was a complete surprise.

Just one puppy caught my eye as we looked at the litter of tiny cocker spaniels. They were black and white – the posh term, for some reason, is 'blue roan' – and Lee picked her up as the others jumped around.

'She's the one I want,' I said as I looked at her huge eyes and started to cry. We called her Charlie and she still gives me the same look today.

'Pleeeeeease can we keep her?' Joe screamed after he and

Max found Charlie waiting for them in the boot room when they got home from school.

'Of course we can,' I said, and that's how Charlie joined the family.

Looking back, though, I don't think Lee and I ever really stood a chance of getting back to normal after Ibiza because our lives were going in completely different directions. As *Men Behaving Badly* got bigger, it seemed to take up more and more time. What with that, other bits of one-off work like appearing in shows like *Shooting Stars*, promotional stuff like cutting the ribbon at a supermarket, media work including my first big interview and photo shoot with *OK!* magazine, and looking after Joe and Max, I was pretty much emotionally and physically occupied.

At the same time Lee's career was coming to an end and it was a big change for him. Weeks before 'Tell Him' came out, he'd played the last game of his career for his final club, Swansea.

'I'll score for you today,' he told Joe as he got out of the car.

He was as good as his word and got a goal in the final seconds of the game. But I bloody missed it because I bent down at the crucial moment to tell Max to behave. That was the end of Lee's career, and while it must have been really emotional for him, he hid his true feelings about it. We just couldn't seem to find a way to talk about it and Lee was left alone to work out how to deal with the end of an 18-year career at the age of just 36. There would be no more cheering crowds and the adrenaline of winning a match – he hit his career low at the very moment when mine was at its peak. His dad, Roy, a professional player himself, would have understood exactly what his son was going through and helped him adjust. But he had died at only 49, when Lee was 21, and while I wanted to be supportive, I just couldn't seem to find the right things to say. Lee never admitted anything was wrong, but he slowly drifted away from me as the months passed and I was caught up in the rush of my success.

I told myself that I was doing what he wanted – chilling out and leaving him to it – but really there was a selfish part of me that still wanted to punish Lee for what had happened in Ibiza and almost resented him for stopping me from enjoying my success. I'd worked for years to reach that moment and didn't want anyone or anything to take it away from me, so I threw myself into *Men Behaving Badly*, my other work and my children.

The longer it went on, the more independent I became and Lee found that very difficult. We'd always relied on needing each other and I think for the first time he began to wonder if I didn't need him any more. I'd throw the money I was earning in his face or have a photo shoot plastered across a magazine and it couldn't have happened at a worse time. I was also getting a lot of attention about how I looked and even made it into *FHM*'s 100 Sexiest Women – at number 51, I was below Kate Winslet but above Michelle Pfeiffer! For the first time in my career I was being seen as a bit of a sex symbol, and, to be honest, after two kids and at the ripe old age of 36, I secretly thought, Yessss!

Just as I'd experienced insecurity and jealousy in the past, the tables were now turned and Lee felt the same at times – particularly when we'd been drinking. As the months passed, I realised it was becoming more and more of a problem, but I told myself things would eventually come good – I loved him, he was my husband, the father of my children, my mate, who was at a difficult point in his life. OK, it wasn't ideal, but marriage isn't always – my mum had taught me that you make your bed and you lie in it – and I'd made my decision to stay after Ibiza. We'd had so many happy years together and I knew we'd get back to that. It wasn't a bad time in my life; it was just a bad time with Lee.

*

'This is going to be amazing,' I said, as I stood in the huge, empty car park.

Lee and I were in the first-floor parking area of the valuation offices on Shaftesbury Avenue. Work was due to start in a few weeks to transform it into our new business venture – a bar and restaurant called Teatro. With us were Michelin-starred chef Gordon Ramsay, who was going to be Teatro's consultant chef, and his business partner, Claudio Pulze.

'The bar will go in over there and the restaurant will start about here,' Lee said, as he gestured around the concrete shell. 'I know it's hard to imagine, but the builders have only got four months to get everything done.'

I looked at Lee as he carried on talking to Gordon and Claudio – he was so excited, so full of plans, and it was good to see.

Maybe this is what we need, I thought to myself as the three men wandered off across the echoing floor.

It was a year since Lee had retired from football and he'd thrown himself into life after the game. Five months after leaving the pitch for the final time, he'd opened his first bar with Denise's then boyfriend, David Newton, a property developer. They'd come up with the idea on a drunken night out and the next thing Lee knew David had found a site in Walton Street, Brompton Cross. They had turned the tiny space into a really stylish place and Barfly had opened in October 1996. It had been filled every night, with everyone from Rod Stewart to Michael Hutchence and Yasmin le Bon popping in. Three months later Lee had doubled his money when he had been bought out and knew for sure there was life after football.

But his new line of work also meant that drink had now become an official part of our lives and it had created a whole new set of problems. I'd been worried that we would be like kids in a sweetshop and we were in some ways, because the bar almost became an extension of our home. Released from match days and training, Lee enjoyed himself even more, and almost without realising what was happening, I did too. A cold beer in an iced glass, wine with a meal, then brandy or sambuca before getting into a taxi and going on to the Groucho. Then it was vodka and slimline, bourbon and Diet Coke, caipirinhas or mojitos and back to our place to carry on drinking.

The parties were great, and the police were even called one particularly loud night when our music disturbed Nappy Valley. The officers said they'd been called to a disturbance and asked about the woman's shouts the neighbours had heard. I told them that it was only me telling my husband to turn the bloody music down, but it was like being told off as a naughty teenager and I felt really silly. When the police left, we all picked up our glasses again and carried on partying – a bit more quietly.

There were lots of nights like that, when, smoking cigarettes one after another, I'd match Lee drink for drink. At least I knew where he was. I was working hard and now playing harder than I'd ever done before, but it was dangerous mixing alcohol with the game we were still playing – me thoughtless about my newfound independence and success, him enjoying his new kind of freedom now that the strict discipline of football training had ended.

By the time Lee sold Barfly, it felt as if there would always come a time in the evening when we'd had a few drinks and one of us would have a problem with something the other had done. Neither of us could listen or see sense in what the other was saying, and our rows were always sparked by too much drink. Our arguments were as noisy as ever, and even when we weren't officially having one, we'd verbally spar. It drove Mum mad and she'd always be telling me to shut up. But in some ways I knew those sparring sessions were important because they let us know the other cared – however fucked up it was.

Life, though, was as busy as ever and I didn't have a lot of time to think about it all. While Lee concentrated on his new career, I was focused on mine and had done an episode of the BBC action show *Bugs*, in which I played heiress Kitty McHaig. I'd also had a real laugh with Caroline doing an exercise video for Comic Relief Day in March. It was called *Women Exercising Madly*, but for me it was more a case of *Exercising Limpingly* because I'd burned my bloody foot on a piece of coal barbecuing chicken for Mum and the boys a couple of days before filming started.

A few weeks ago we'd also finished filming series six of *Men Behaving Badly* and that had been as fun as ever. It had been a bit of a shock when the scripts had landed on the doormat because Tony and Deborah were finally getting it on and in a big way. There seemed to be references to shagging all over the place. It was more *Debbie Does Dallas* than *Men Behaving Badly* and my heart had sunk. I'd always liked the chase between them, the comedy value of Tony's desperate attempts to bed Deborah, and I thought the public did too. I was forever getting stopped in the supermarket by people asking, 'So when are you going to get together, then?' It was as if a national question mark hung over whether Tony would get his wicked way and I felt quite upset that he was finally going to. It would mean a massive shift for the show as it would now be about two couples. Could it be the end for *Men Behaving Badly*?

Each new series had felt like a bonus after the show's rocky start, and although Simon kept coming up with the goods, we all knew he couldn't spin it out for ever. There was only so long the show could stay on such a high, and so much of the comedy relied on the jokes that centred on Tony *not* getting it on with Debs. But no one knew for sure how long *Men Behaving Badly* would continue, because that's how TV works – you only find out a series is finished when it's screened and isn't re-commissioned – and so in the meantime we'd all gone back into the studio to start filming.

I'd ended up spending loads of time with Caroline and it had created more tension between Lee and me. He could sense my disloyalty and, just as I'd once felt about the In Crowd, began to resent my acting friends. We argued about it at times, but never discussed things properly and it only increased the void between us.

But if we don't talk, we don't argue, so that's a good thing, I tried to reassure myself as the silence between us became deafening.

I knew something was in the air, could sense something was wrong, on the night of 15 October 1997. I'd just met up with Lee after driving into London from Windsor with my friend Marti Webb, who'd come to watch me on stage in *My Cousin Rachel*. We were on our way to the Groucho and I was trying to find a parking space, but Lee seemed impatient.

I'd had a good day at the theatre – knackering, because we'd done two performances, but good. It hadn't always been like that and I'd dried up on the first night because I had felt so terrified of going back on stage after years in telly.

'What's the line?' I'd whispered to a young whippersnapper in the cast, hoping he'd help me out. No such luck.

'Get out of that one yourself, TV queen,' he'd smirked as I stood staring at the footlights and thinking I was going to die of embarrassment. In the end I'd walked off stage to get the line before going back on and it had seemed like for ever as I took those steps, but the audience hadn't noticed too much. Bit by bit I'd got over my nerves and now loved being in the show. The only downside was that I didn't see so much of Joe and Max. They'd get back from school just as I was going out to work and I missed chatting to them about their day and being there with them. It also meant that Lee and I had hardly seen each other.

We found a space to park and headed into the Groucho,

where I ordered a cocktail. One followed another, and, as ever, the alcohol in my bloodstream made everything seem funnier and the night brighter. Marti and I sat and chatted, enjoying the buzzy atmosphere and seeing the odd face we knew. Lee also seemed fine now. Maybe this was going to be a good night after all.

A couple of hours later, however, I looked across the bar to see a guy I had a score to settle with. He'd once spread a rumour saying I had put it about a bit before I'd met Lee – such a lie – and anger rose up inside me as I looked at him laughing and joking.

'I'm going to confront him,' I said as I stood up and started walking away.

'No,' hissed Lee, but it was too late. I was up and away.

'Hello,' I said, when I reached the guy's table. 'I hear you've had a lot to say about me and I was wondering if you'd like to say it to my face?'

'What?' he snapped, looking at me coldly. 'I think you've heard wrong, Leslie.'

He obviously wasn't going to get into a row and I felt drunk and a bit stupid as I stared at him. Embarrassment washed over me. I turned and headed back to Lee and Marti. Had anyone seen me get the knockback? Shoulders back and head high, I was determined not to lose face.

'You silly cow,' Lee said through clenched teeth as I sat back down. He looked really angry. 'Why did you do that? I fell out with him ages ago. We don't speak any more. There was no need to get involved. Why did you do that?'

'She wasn't to know, Lee – no harm done,' Marti said soothingly.

I could see that Lee wasn't having any of it, but how was I supposed to know he'd stopped talking to the guy when he'd never told me? I sipped my drink and started chatting to Marti again, hoping to smooth over my embarrassing outburst, but Lee was obviously still upset. He hadn't finished the row and I knew it was time to go home, otherwise we'd start having it out in public.

'Let it go,' Marti urged Lee, as she gave him a kiss goodbye and we walked out of the front door.

I realised how drunk I was as the cold evening air hit my face. Lee said nothing as he hailed a taxi.

'Come on,' he snapped as it drew up beside us. 'We'll leave the car.'

I felt like a child waiting to be scolded.

'You made yourself look really stupid,' he shouted as the cab drove off. 'And you made me look really stupid. I've said all I've got to say to him and there was no need for you to get involved.'

'Well, you could have told me,' I screamed back. 'How was I supposed to know?'

That was it. We launched into a blazing row as the cabbie kept his eyes forward.

'Do you want everyone to know our business?' I eventually hissed, aware of the driver being forced to listen to it all. 'Can't you just wait until we get home?'

'What?' Lee shouted back. 'I wasn't the one who just lost it in the Groucho.'

I'd had enough. 'I'm not sitting here listening to this shit,' I shrieked as we stopped at some lights and I grabbed the door handle. It was time to make a dramatic exit.

'Where are you going? Come here,' Lee said. He took my arm and pulled me back. 'You can't just storm off, Leslie.'

I was determined to go, though, and the more I struggled, the more he held me. I finally broke free and wriggled out of the cab backwards, wrenching my little finger from his grip.

'Just fuck off,' I shouted, and slammed the door in his face.

There was no reply. I heard the taxi drive off behind me and I looked around the empty street. What on earth was I going to do now?

CHAPTER 8

Drama Out of a Crisis

I felt totally on my own. I'd stormed off loads of times before, but this time I wasn't going to rush back home and Lee wasn't going to come after me.

Sobbing, I pulled out my phone and called Caroline.

'What are you doing?' I cried when she picked up.

'Having a dinner party,' she replied. 'Are you all right? What's wrong, Leslie?'

'I've had a row with Lee. A massive one. And now I'm standing in the middle of the street. I've nearly broken my bloody finger.'

'What?'

'My finger. It really hurts. But I can't see Lee until he's calmed down. I don't know what's got into him.'

'Come over here and join us.'

'But I don't feel like it,' I wept. 'I don't want to see anyone.'

'Well, then, just go up to my room and watch TV,' Caroline replied. 'Come on. You can't go wandering the streets.'

I was still in floods of tears by the time I arrived and she gave me a bag of frozen peas to put on my finger before taking me upstairs to her bedroom. She and her sister were having dinner with a couple of male friends Caroline had met on holiday in Australia earlier that year. They were staying a few days, but I didn't want to see anyone.

'I don't know what happened,' I sobbed. 'Lee was so angry. I don't know what to do.'

'Look, stay here tonight,' Caroline replied. 'Let him calm down and then you can talk about it tomorrow when you're both sober.'

I got into bed and she left me to it, but came back into the room a while later.

'Lee's been on the phone,' she said. 'He wants to know if you're here. We've told him you are and you're in bed, but he won't stop ringing. He keeps calling and calling.'

'Well, I don't want to speak to him. Tell him I'll talk to him in the morning.'

She turned and left the room as I lay back down again. Suddenly our row had become a public thing – other people knew about it, were speaking to Lee about it and it felt strange. I'd stormed off loads of times before, but had always gone home, and because our arguments were usually behind closed doors, this all seemed a bit dramatic and serious. I didn't know what to do, but I was exhausted. Eventually I fell asleep.

As I got up the next morning, had a bath and started sorting myself out, I couldn't stop wondering what my next move should be. Should I ring Lee or leave it a while? But there was no time to decide because when I looked out of the window, I saw a minicab pulling up, the door flying open and Lee getting out. I couldn't believe how he looked.

Striding up the path, I could see he was even angrier than the night before. Shirt hanging out of his jeans and obviously still two sheets to the wind, he looked like a madman as he rushed towards the door. The blood drained from my face. What the hell was he going to do?

'Lee's here,' I called to Caroline, panic sharpening my voice.

'You stay in here,' she told me as she came into the room. 'I'll go down.'

I could hear Lee screaming outside the house and he pressed the doorbell again and again.

'Leslie? Are you there? I want to see you. Leslie?'

He sounded furious. I knew I should be the one to open the door and talk to him, but I just couldn't. I'd woken up feeling embarrassed about the night before, but could see that Lee hadn't calmed down at all. He'd lost it and there was no way I was going to face him in that state. I didn't know what he'd do and I didn't want to find out either. It was the first time in my life that I'd felt scared of my husband. He sounded so full of rage. I'd never seen him lose control before – I was the one who did that and now he had I didn't know what to do.

'I want to see my wife,' Lee shouted. 'Where's Leslie? Get me my wife. I want my wife. I want to talk to my fucking wife.'

Fear made my stomach tighten as he banged on the door, screaming and shouting as he hit it.

Downstairs, I heard male voices calling to him. It must be Caroline's friends.

'All right, mate,' a voice drawled in an Aussie accent. 'Calm down.'

Suddenly I heard an almighty crack as Lee's foot went through the door. Kick, kick, kick. He screamed and ranted as he tried to stove the door in.

'Let me see Leslie. Where is she? I want my wife. I want my wife!'

I didn't want this to be happening. Lee just didn't lose it like this. I'd never even seen him get into a fight, so what was he doing? For the first time in all the years we'd been together, I didn't know what he was capable of. The Lee I knew had gone. This was a stranger and I was terrified of him. I just didn't recognise my husband as I stood in that quiet bedroom and listened to his screams outside.

'I've called the police,' Caroline said, coming back into the room.

I looked at her. Oh, my God, this was serious. I'd brought all my shit and laid it at her doorstep and this was the result.

I just stood in the bedroom as Lee carried on screaming and kicking, yelling and swearing for me, desperate to reach me, until suddenly a police van screeched up outside and seven coppers jumped out. Did Lee really need all of them to calm him down? One or two would have done, surely?

The officers walked towards the front door, where Lee was, and disappeared from view. Everything went silent. It was weird. One minute Lee's rage was echoing around the street and the next it was gone. I carried on staring down from the bedroom window, wondering what was happening, until suddenly Lee came back into view. He was being led away by the police, shoulders slumped, head bent. It still makes me want to cry today when I think about the worst day of my marriage – how wounded he looked in that moment, like someone whose spirit had been broken. How had the man I'd watched score in front of huge crowds, the man who'd cradled our baby sons, the man I loved, come to this? He'd finally been sucked into my dramatic world after all those months of punishing him for Ibiza, of giving him the space that Bertie and Johnny had insisted he needed, but I knew he hated. With a police officer on either side, Lee was put into the van and driven off.

I felt empty as I stared down the road. A woman police officer walked into the room.

'Mrs Chapman?' she asked.

I stared at her. What was happening? How had things gone this far? I wished I could rewind everything to that moment in the taxi, find some way to calm Lee down and go home with him like every other night. But that was never going to happen.

The police officer sat opposite me as I cried at the kitchen table. She was with a male officer and they were from the domestic violence unit. They needed to take a statement. Lee had been arrested for criminal damage to Caroline's door and common assault because of my finger – it's the least serious form of assault because a person can be charged with it even if they just scratch someone. I felt sick, shaky – I didn't want all this.

'It's only because he's drunk,' I told her. 'He'll be fine when he sobers up. You don't need to do all this.'

Despite my protests, there were things that had to be done now that the police were officially involved. They had obviously done this before: they fired questions at me, and statements were taken from Caroline and her friends in another room. I just couldn't concentrate and was still crying when Mum arrived. I couldn't believe what had happened. Was this the end for Lee and me?

'The other thing you can do, Mrs Chapman, is to take out an injunction against your husband,' the officer told me after we'd finished.

'What?' I replied.

'It's something a solicitor can arrange for you. You apply to a court for an order to stop your husband coming near you. It gives you time to organise yourself and work out what you are going to do next.'

I looked at her. I was confused about what to do for the best, but maybe what she was saying was right, maybe it was what Lee and I needed. Things had got so out of hand, this was as bad as it could get, and maybe some time apart would help us.

'Come on, darling,' Mum said. She took my hand and led me outside to her car.

'I didn't recognise him,' I sobbed, as Mum started driving. 'I just didn't know who he was. I think he's finally lost it. This is what it's all been building up to. It was like a volcano – he just erupted. I've never seen him like that before. He was like a madman.'

'But why didn't you come to me?' Mum asked gently.

'I didn't want to bother you when I was pissed in the middle of the night and we were having another row. I don't want to involve the family. We should be able to sort this out alone.'

'But Lee was on the phone to us at three in the morning asking where you were,' Mum replied. 'We're all involved now. You know you're going to have to sit down and think about this, Leslie. You can't live your life like this. I had no idea things were this bad. You two are really going to have to make some decisions – you've got two lovely children, a lovely life. I could bang your heads together, but you've got to think.'

'I know, I know,' I told her, as we pulled into our road. I saw a reporter and a photographer outside the house.

I carried on crying when we got inside and Mum started making tea. I couldn't get pictures of Lee out of my head – his angry face, him being led away, him stuck in a police cell. I was totally confused about what was going to happen now. How long would the police hold him? Was this the end for us? Dully, I thought about the injunction the police had told me about. I had to contact a lawyer – they'd explain it all to me. Maybe it really had to come to this – we'd finally hit rock bottom and it was what we needed. Something had to change because it couldn't go on like this.

This is either an end or a beginning, I thought to myself.

I had no idea how marriages split up, but I knew things between us were desperately wrong. There had been difficulties ever since we'd moved down to London four years earlier, and maybe a week apart would clear our heads, allow us to decide whether we loved each other or wanted to go our separate ways. It also felt like everyone around me was saying that I should do it.

'It's not the end of the marriage just because you agree to this. It gives you a week to think about it.'

'You need time apart. Something's got to give. You can't go on like this.'

'You can't let him get away with behaving like that – he's got to learn.'

Voice after voice kept telling me to do it – even Mum, who had always adored Lee. I felt so close to telling them all that I couldn't be bothered. I'd had enough. Maybe this was finally the end and we weren't supposed to be together. But I also knew my marriage was worth fighting for and so I rung our lawyer. He said he'd go down to the police station to see Lee, but he gave me the number of another solicitor who could apply for the injunction. I had no real idea of the road it would be taking me down, but I wanted to find out.

A couple of hours later the phone went.

'It's me,' Lee said.

He was sober.

'Hi,' I replied.

'They've just let me go. I've been charged. I don't know what's going on. What have you done? Why are the police involved? And what's this about an injunction, Leslie?'

'What do you mean, what have I done?' I exploded. 'What have you done? You can't go around kicking people's doors in.'

'Well, I've got nowhere to go. I'm driving around and apparently I'm not allowed to come home. What am I supposed to do – sleep in the car?'

'I don't know, Lee,' I snapped. 'This is what happens. You're not meant to phone me up and ask where to stay. Find somewhere yourself. You'll have to go to a hotel or something.'

'But what's this about an injunction? What are you doing?'

'Well, the police and the lawyer have advised it. We need a week to think about things.'

'But what am I supposed to do? This is ridiculous, Leslie. I don't have to be somewhere else to sort this out.'

'I think you do, Lee. You lost it this morning, and if you come straight home, things will just go back to how they were. As far as I'm concerned, our marriage is over, and if we want it to work, then we'll have to think about it properly before we talk.'

I slammed down the phone in anger. People were right – we did need time apart because otherwise this would all be my fault and he wouldn't realise that it takes two and he'd been wrong.

By the end of the day the papers were lined up outside. I couldn't believe our mess was public again. The neighbours even had to ask journalists to get off their drive. I'd never seen so many before. Every now and then the doorbell would go and there'd be a couple on the doorstep. What did they think? That I'd invite them inside and tell them about my husband flipping his lid? I shouldn't have been surprised – my whole career had been played out in the tabloids – but I wasn't going anywhere. I spent the day at home with Mum until the kids arrived back from school.

'A man's just taken our pictures, Mummy,' Joe told me as he rushed in.

'Don't take any notice of them, darling. Now, there's spag bol for tea, so why don't you go and play with Charlie while I get it ready?'

A few hours later I climbed into bed. It was horrible being on my own and I knew it might be for a lot longer than one night. Was this what life would be like as a one-parent family? All the people I knew who'd split up came flooding into my head as I lay in the dark. Marriages seemed so easy to end and then you were on your own. I didn't like the thought. I just wanted Lee, but things had gone into motion and were sweeping us up. Maybe he'd be the one to turn round and say he wanted out.

As I closed the bedroom curtains around midnight, I peeped out to see the final journalist walk away. I knew they'd be back the next morning and I couldn't get to sleep that night. It felt so strange being alone and in the end I went to get Max. My son lay warm and sleeping beside me as I wondered where it would all end.

I felt almost as if someone had died when I woke up the next morning and realised it wasn't just an awful dream. I couldn't understand what had happened. Lee's behaviour had come completely out of the blue and I kept replaying that night to see if I could find out why. Horrible thoughts about selling our home and dividing everything up kept running through my head. What would happen to us all? Even the boys were quiet while they got ready for school. They knew something was up as I discussed with the nanny how to get them out of the house with the press still camped outside. This whole thing was a gift to the journalists – *Dinner Dates*, a TV series Lee and I had made together about restaurants, was due to start in a few days, and series six of *Men Behaving Badly* in a couple of weeks. A footballer, a telly stunner whose marriage had previously been rocked by her man behaving badly...the tabloids were covered in the latest twist to our story and the news that Lee had been charged with common assault and criminal damage.

'When's Daddy coming back?' Max asked as he ate his cereal.

'He's away for a few days. He'll be home soon,' I told him.

In the end the boys and the nanny had to walk out of the front door – there was no other way. They were so young, it wasn't fair. But I had to smile when they made faces and eight-year-old Joe suddenly stuck two fingers in the air. Where had he learned that?

Once again I stayed in the house all day with the shutters closed as thoughts continued to run through my head: is this is it? Will we ever get back to normal? Have we made love for the last time? Will Lee live in this house again? Will I have to move?

The lawyers were getting the injunction that day and I felt so mixed up. One part of me felt that although Lee's behaviour had terrified me, it was also a one-off and in my heart I'd already forgiven him for it. I knew that if we split up, I'd be taking his life away for one moment of derangement. Another part of me, however, questioned whether we really were right for each other.

We just clash, I thought. We can't make this work. Think about the kids – we can't argue in front of them the whole time. Things haven't been right for a while.

All I wanted was for Lee to say he'd behaved appallingly, that drink wasn't doing us any good and then we'd have a chance. We just had to draw together again and become as united as we had been in the first few years of our relationship. But my hopes weren't raised when the doorbell rang and a bunch of flowers arrived. The nanny walked into the kitchen and handed them to me. They were from Lee – talk about sticking a plaster over a gaping stab wound.

Later that day Caroline came to see me and I apologised for getting her mixed up in all our drama. The police then came and took a picture of me holding the finger I'd hurt up to my face, and I also had a red mark on my cheek. I didn't know where it had come from, but in the papers it became a great big black eye. Just as the visit from the police during the noisy party a year before had become a 'bust-up'.

Lee's eyes slid away from mine as he sat down in a chair. It was Sunday, three days since I'd seen him being put into a police van, and we were meeting with lawyers in an office in Holborn. I felt shaky with nerves. I looked at him, but he wasn't giving anything away. The day before, Debbie had taken the boys to see him at the hotel where he was staying.

They'd loved going swimming with Daddy, but I'd felt so sad as I sat in the empty house. It felt like we'd been apart for ages and the kids were visiting Lee on a custody weekend or something.

'Does Mr Chapman understand why my client has brought the injunction and abide to stick by it?' my lawyer asked. 'She does not want the marriage to end, but wants to know what he's going to do. She does not want to start divorce proceedings.'

Lee shook his head as he listened. I knew he still couldn't believe what was happening and anxiety washed over me again. Was he still angry with me? Would he want a divorce even if I didn't?

'My client agrees,' his lawyer replied.

It was as if a black cloud lifted off me in the moment I heard those words. Lee didn't want out; he also wanted our marriage to work; we had a chance. Suddenly, as the lawyers carried on talking about the injunction and other legal matters, it finally hit home what we'd got ourselves into. Solicitors, police, court orders...if I didn't take control, pull the reins in, then everything would spin out of our hands again. The fact that it had all started was enough – surely it had had its effect on both of us and didn't need to go any further. Two lawyers were talking to each other about our marriage and they would be the only winners. There were even columnists giving me advice on the pages of national bloody newspapers. This was nobody's business but ours – we were the only people who knew the truth.

I talked it over with Mum and came to a decision. The next day I withdrew my statement and told my lawyers to stop the injunction. It was up to Lee and me to sort this out – no one else.

I felt almost excited hours later as I walked into the restaurant. Lee was taking me out for dinner and I'd bought a new outfit –

a black jersey dress and velvet puffball coat. I can't explain the feeling. It was as if our relationship had been stripped bare and now we were starting again. Finally we had a chance to put all the turmoil of the previous few years behind us. I hoped this would be the first day of the rest of our lives.

'I'm sorry,' Lee said, as he sat across the table from me.

'But what happened?' I asked him. 'I just don't understand.'

Lee told me that he'd gone home after I stormed out of the taxi and carried on drinking. When I hadn't come back, he'd started ringing round to find out where I was and the Aussie guys at Caroline's house had answered the phone.

'Just leave her alone, mate,' they had told him. 'She's here with us. She doesn't want to see you. She's with us now.'

Drunk and jealous, Lee had kept phoning back and had got more and more wound up.

'Look, mate, she isn't going to talk to you,' the men had said. 'Just leave it. We're looking after her. You're not going to talk to her tonight.'

'Once I heard that, I kept phoning again and again,' Lee told me. 'I thought you were there with them, laughing with them, partying with them, and I couldn't get to you. I thought I was going to come round and find you with them. I really believed you were being unfaithful.'

'But I was in bed asleep,' I replied. 'Nothing was going on.'

'I know, but all you had to do was talk to me. Why didn't you? I really thought you'd betrayed me. Anyway, they were taking the piss. They knew they were winding me up. I had to come and get you. But I'm sorry. I shouldn't have gone off like that.'

Heidi, our nanny, had tried to stop Lee from going to Caroline's house, but he hadn't listened. He just hadn't been able to see sense.

'This jealousy has got to stop between us, and so does the drinking,' I told him. 'We're not like this until we have a drink.'

'Well, what would you do if you phoned up to find out where I was and strange women came on the phone?' Lee asked.

'Look, I can see how they provoked you, but it still doesn't justify your behaviour, Lee. I was scared of you. I've never seen you like that. And the worst thing about all of this is that it means you don't trust me, and that is a problem.'

'But I do trust you, Leslie. I've been stupid. We've been through too much to throw it away. We're soul mates. We're good together.'

I looked at him. 'Something's got to give, Lee. Drink is what sparks all our arguments off and something's got to change, otherwise we'll never survive. We've got to quieten down because we just wind each other up. It's like Liz Taylor and Richard Burton sometimes.' I took a deep breath. 'I've thought about it a lot and I'm prepared to stop drinking if you are,' I said.

'I'll never get that drunk again,' Lee replied slowly. 'And I know we've got to cut down, but I can't stop completely. Teatro's opening in a few weeks – it's just unrealistic. But we'll stick to wine with meals from now on and I promise things will get better. I know it's all come to a head, but we've survived it and I will cut down.'

'Well, we've both got to really mean it,' I insisted. 'We've got to slow down. It's too much.'

Deep down, I'd always known that we could never stop drinking completely. We were in the bar business and part of making it work was being there with the customers with a drink in our hands and giving them the smiles, chat and show they wanted. But I also knew we could make a real effort together. I'd seen a side of Lee I never wanted to see again, and, for my part, I knew that as usual I'd helped to light the touchpaper after having a few drinks. As we sat at the table, I was confident that we both knew we could never go there again.

We laughed together so much that night after we'd done all our talking. It was like the days when we'd first met and I was so happy I'd got my husband back. After dinner we went back to Lee's hotel and he came home with me the next morning. We'd gone as low as we could go and now the only way was up.

Sadly, my friendship with Caroline never recovered. I blame myself completely for laying my problems at someone else's door – quite literally. I'd involved her too closely in my personal relationship, told only one side of the story, and sometimes you don't want to hear the advice you're given by someone who can never fully understand what is going on within a relationship. It was a hard lesson to learn, and after that my relationship with Caroline was strictly professional.

CHAPTER 9

Out of the Frying Pan

There's a scene in series six of *Men Behaving Badly* in which Tony and Debs are standing in the kitchen of the boys' flat just after they've finally got together.

'Looks like you've worn me down,' she tells him.

'Debs, how come you turned me down for so long?' Tony asks.

'Well, I always liked the way you looked, I just had a problem with the things you did and the things you said, and I suppose if Dorothy is prepared to marry Gary, then I might as well give you a try.'

There's a pause as they stand looking deep into each other's eyes.

'What are you thinking about?' Debs finally asks Tony.

He fixes her with a serious expression. 'I'm just wondering what colour your bush is,' he says.

The line may have got a massive laugh, but I wasn't smiling a few days later when a headline appeared in one of the papers: 'What colour is Leslie's bush?' My mother might be reading! Readers must have been disappointed by a picture of me planting a bush of the leafy kind at our house. That's what being in the public eye is like – when you're in the spotlight, even something as boring as gardening can make the papers.

I understood it was all part of the game, but it is a difficult one to play. The newspapers had been interested in me from the early days of my career, and I, like every other person in the entertainment business, knew the power of publicity. Six weeks after the argument at Caroline's, Lee and I did an article for *OK!* magazine giving our side of the story. The police had announced the charges against Lee had been dropped and we felt it was only right to have our say. I said we intended to cut down on our socialising but didn't go into the ins and outs of the problems we'd had. That was our business and all I wanted was the chance to put the record straight. Unfortunately, there was no way it was ever going to be that simple, and in the years to come the injunction I'd given the go-ahead to was used by the newspapers to imply my marriage was violent. The official legal language had forbidden him from 'molesting', 'harassing' or 'pestering' me and that meant the papers could draw all sorts of conclusions that weren't right – and point to the injunction if anyone complained about it.

It's hard when you become well known, because your fame affects everyone in your family – and Joe and Max in particular didn't like the attention. They thought all mummies and daddies were like us. Joe piped up to a little classmate on his first day at nursery: 'What football team does your dad play for?' They couldn't work out why we were so interesting that people stared as we walked by or stopped me for an autograph when we were going round the supermarket. I learned early on that I couldn't afford to rush in for a packet of sausages with my hair scraped back and no make-up on, just in case there was a photographer lurking, and the general public didn't seem to like it either if they saw me being an ordinary woman, instead of glamorous Debs.

'Doesn't she look different?' they'd try to whisper as they wheeled their trolley by me, but I could always hear. And so I got into the habit of wearing a bit of slap to do the shopping.

'Are you going shopping as Leslie Ash or Mummy?' Max

asked me one day. 'You don't look like Leslie Ash without make-up.'

In the end Joe found being stopped by TV fans so embarrassing that he refused to go shopping with me, and in later years Max made me sit in the car during football matches because he didn't like people looking. Nowadays they hate it if I put on sunglasses and a baseball cap.

'You're trying to look like a celebrity,' they squirm.

The only time the attention really pissed me off was when my sons got dragged into it all. Like the day the press were camped out on our doorstep after the events at Caroline's or the time I was snapped coming out of the dry-cleaner's. I was walking down the steps of the shop with Max, who must have been about three, and Joe, who was about six. Neither of them would hold my hand and so I put the cleaning between my teeth and made a grab for them. Snap! The picture appeared in the newspaper under the headline 'Boys behaving badly'. I didn't like it that my sons were caught up in my crazy world, but all I could do was try to limit its effect on them.

Other than that, I was a pretty normal mum. We had a nanny throughout the boys' childhood because I couldn't keep employing people when I was working and letting them go when I finished, only to find someone else when the next job started. Mostly, however, I was just like every other mother, doing everything from the washing to the school run. Other people sometimes didn't seem to think so, though, and I remember one day when I took the boys to school in Clapham. The headmistress used to stand outside the front door to shake each child's hand as they went into school. I waited in line beside all the mums with their headscarves and anoraks on, then walked up to her in my ripped jeans.

'And whose nanny are you?' she said, looking coldly down her nose at my trousers. She didn't take her eyes off my knees the whole time I spoke to her.

Ripped jeans or not, Joe and Max were stuck with me and no day was more important than Sundays. That was the day for a real family affair and Mum, Dad, Denise, Debbie, their kids and whoever else would all come over to ours. Short of an earthquake, I always made lunch and some days ended up cooking for loads because you might as well make a meal for 14 as four. I loved those days when the house was full of children's voices, my dad and Lee would be watching the golf or reading the newspapers, and I'd be in the kitchen chatting to my mum as she swigged her cava.

The other important time was our holidays when acting, football training, bar licences or building schedules were all put to one side. Mind you, I might easily have given up going on them after the first couple of times that Lee and I went abroad together. 'Bali, 1986' ended with a huge argument about who was winning at backgammon, which culminated in Lee tossing the board into the air and me storming out. I refused to come out of our room and in the end he sent a waiter up with a note saying, 'I love you. Please come out. We don't have to play backgammon any more.' A few years later we found ourselves on the Barbados equivalent of a motorway in a golf buggy after taking a wrong turning on the course. To be honest, it was more of a main road than a motorway, but nevertheless we ended up creeping down it wearing stupid hotel visors with clubs rattling in the back as cars beeped all around us. The sun went down and the light had faded by the time we made it to safety.

Luckily our holidays with the boys were more successful, but there were still a few classics. 'Virgin Gorda, 1996' started well with a visit to Richard Branson and his family on his private island, Necker, but the holiday ended with Lee being brought home covered in cuts by the police in the middle of the night. He'd been mugged and pushed into an overgrown ditch. The island was so small that the culprits were caught within a day, but I'd shuddered when I'd realised the ditch he'd been pushed into was feet away from a cliff edge. Or there was Jerez, a few years later, when Lee kept insisting he had terrible stomach pains and I told him he was being a drama queen. In the end I'd taken him to a medical centre on the way to the airport to have a morphine shot. So there was I – two kids, a husband on morphine and a flight to catch...Why me? But it turned out that poor Lee wasn't being overdramatic when a gallstone the size of a walnut was removed after getting home. Disasters aside, I loved our holidays together – at least we always had a laugh and the four of us were together. That was the most important thing.

'Well done, darling,' Mum said, as the music pounded around us. 'You did really well. I just can't believe it's all ended.'

'It might not have,' I replied. 'There could be Christmas specials or something. You never know.'

We were standing holding our vodka and tonics as the *Men Behaving Badly* crew got down and partied to mark the end of filming for series seven. Everyone was going for it – Vera in accounts getting off with John in props, that kind of thing. (By the way, these are only made-up names so I do apologise if there really was a Vera there because I don't know whether or not she did snog anyone.) What made this party even more special was the fact that it was the last – we'd just shot three 90-minute episodes to be shown over Christmas 1998 and that would be it for *Men Behaving Badly*. Apart from possible one-off stuff, we wouldn't be working together again – it was the end of an era. Earlier, we'd filmed the final shot of the final episode, in which we're all cooing at Gary and Dorothy's baby as a close-up of it flashes up on screen showing it's got its father's ears. I'd stood there feeling really sad and listening to the audience roar with laughter, knowing it would be the last time I'd hear that sound.

At the same time, I knew it was the right time for the show to end. The characters had all settled down together and the

STEVE ELLIS

ABOVE My bloodied hero: Lee Chapman in
action for Sheffield Wednesday around the time
I first met him.

RIGHT With Matthew Kelly, my co-star in
Of Mice and Men at the Sheffield Crucible, where
I was working when Lee popped the question in
November 1987.

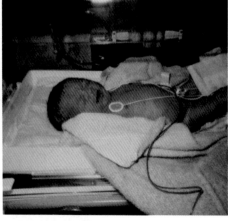

CLOCKWISE, FROM TOP Independence Day, 1988 – but not for me. Lee and I get married in St Mary's, Jersey; 30 January 1989, and the proud father holds baby son Joe; 1 June 1992, and Max lies in an incubator after being born with water on his lungs and jaundice.

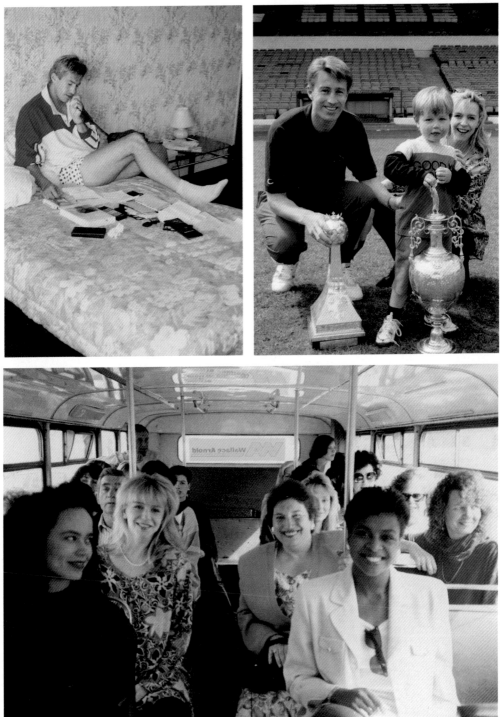

CLOCKWISE, FROM TOP The glamorous life of a footballer, 1988. Our first home together, in France, was awful, but fortunately Brian Clough came to the rescue and we were soon off to Nottingham Forest; Joe and the league trophy do a great job in hiding the large bump that was Max; Footballers' wives, 1992 style. The Leeds wives and mothers get ready for the celebrations after United won the league title.

One of the photo cards I had produced when I started to try to get back into work following the birth of Joe.

Neil Morrissey, me, Martin Clunes and Caroline Quentin pose for a publicity shot for *Men Behaving Badly*.

More from *Men Behaving Badly* – while it wasn't like that in real life, we had a huge amount of fun working on the show.

It wasn't just *MBB* during the
1990s. I also appeared in a few
other series.

ABOVE With Peter Bowles in
Perfect Scoundrels.

LEFT Next to Jaye Griffiths and
Craig McLachlan in *Bugs.*

ABOVE AND BELOW Panto can be a lot of fun, though it is hard work. Lionel Blair and me at the end of *Cinderella*; Marti Webb and I take on *Dick Whittington* in 1994.

My dad moved in interesting circles when he stayed out in Spain, getting to know Sean Connery among others. But we were able to give him a special seventieth birthday celebration in Teatro in 1998.

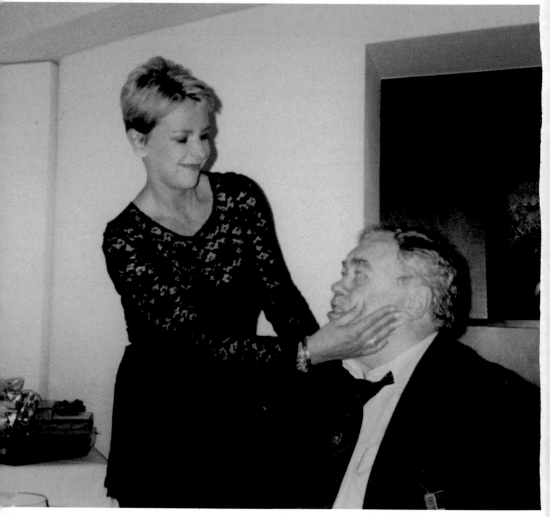

comedy that *Men Behaving Badly* relied on was disappearing. Simon was finding it harder and harder to write and I for one was getting too old to play the part! We were also getting other offers of work and everyone seemed keen to move into new areas. Even as we'd filmed the mini-series, the talk had all been about new things.

I think everyone agreed it was a good time for *Men Behaving Badly* to end – better to go out with a bang than a whimper and we were still on a real high. The previous year's Christmas special had got more than 15 million viewers and the number-one spot – it couldn't get much better than that – and I'd loved the thought of all those people settling down after a hard day's eating, drinking and present-opening to watch us. We'd all met up in the sticks somewhere to film the exterior scenes at an old Tudor house with beautiful lead-ed windows and a minstrel gallery. The idea of the episode was that it would flick between the real Christmas – Gary and Tony trying to buy presents just as all the shops are closing, that kind of thing – and the ideal one, where snow covers the ground and the four characters wear naff jumpers to sing carols together round a piano. It was really funny because we all looked so shiny and wholesome as we mimed our 'voices' over amazing opera-type ones. We kept laughing when they were played and so it took ages to film. The other scene that took a while to get right was one featuring the boys in the pub and a stripper. For some reason, Neil just kept getting his lines wrong and the girl kept having to pull off her top!

However sad part of me felt about *Men Behaving Badly*, I knew it was time for it to end – personally as much as professionally. Things on set just hadn't been the same since the night of the argument at Caroline's house and I found that hard. We'd filmed the Christmas special not long after, and while everyone was professional of course, I felt very much on the outside. To be honest, I always had done in a way – I was the straight girl who hadn't got the laughs like the others and over the years it had sometimes felt like I wasn't taken that seriously. I'd never really taken much notice of it, but I began to when Caroline and I grew distant. Maybe I was wrong to react like that, I don't know, but the situation definitely got worse. I'd known in the past that people could feel left out by the four of us, but now I was the one experiencing it. Having said that, I knew that whatever problems anyone had, you had to get on with the job as soon as you walked through the door of the rehearsal rooms and I wasn't the only one with personal dilemmas. I had a job to do and so I did it, but it wasn't a barrel of laughs.

'It won't be the last time we work together,' Beryl said, as she came up to give me a hug.

'I hope not, I really hope not,' I told her. She'd been so good to me – given me the part of Debs, kept believing in *Men Behaving Badly* when others didn't and looked after us all so well.

Beryl walked away into the dancing crowd.

I looked at Mum. 'Come on, let's go,' I said.

'I can't go out like this,' I said, as I stared in the mirror. I was wearing a red Cher-type wig with a blunt fringe and long bobbed sides, a tight bodice edged with fur, a miniskirt, massive heels and truckloads of make-up – I looked like a bloke in drag.

'Of course you can,' Lee said, laughing at the vision in front of him.

'I can't,' I insisted. 'It's all very well going to the party like this, because everyone will be in fancy dress, but I can't go out in public.'

'Well, we've got to,' Lee insisted. 'We've arranged to meet people. It's just a quick drink and then we'll go to Teatro. Anyway, I kind of like the new-look Les.'

'Ha fucking ha,' I said as I followed him through the front door.

There was no getting out of it. We had to stop for a quick drink at a really chic champagne bar called Bibendum on our way to one of Teatro's birthday parties. The theme was pimps and trannies, and it was all very well for Lee. He looked like David Soul out of *Starsky and Hutch* in a fantastic blond wig, silver glasses, neckerchief, shirt, fitted leather jacket and jeans. Meanwhile I looked like a hooker – and a really bad one at that.

Things didn't get any better when we arrived at Bibendum and sat down next to a table of American tourists. Lee, who'd taken off his glasses, neckerchief and wig, looked like he was on a normal evening out, while I looked as if I should be sitting under a red light with a mattress strapped to my back. The tourists couldn't believe what they were seeing. I decided things really had gone too far when we arrived at Teatro later and the doorman wouldn't let me in.

'Invite?' he boomed down at me.

'No, it's me,' I hissed, looking around for Lee, who was chatting to someone.

'I don't care who you are,' the doorman replied.

'It's me – Leslie,' I insisted.

Eventually I managed to convince him to let me into our bar! But it was all worth it. What a party! What a night! Dressed up and disguised, everyone went crazy. But then again there were so many great nights like that at Teatro. It was, after all, the place to be – packed with people, full of buzz and a guest list heaving with names.

It was as if the party hadn't stopped in the year since we'd opened, in January 1998. There had been a kick, bollock and scramble to get the place finished in time, but I had been overwhelmed when I'd walked in for the opening night. It looked so fantastic. What had once been an empty car park was now a sweeping corridor into a burgundy, cream and grey restaurant, with sparkling glasses, crisp tablecloths and a stunning members' bar, with a huge mural on one wall, deep blue leather sofas and a zinc bar. I was also really happy because I was wearing the most amazing dress I'd ever had. It was Dolce and Gabbana and Lee had bought it for me after I'd spied it when we were out shopping together. I'd had to scrape my face off the window when I'd seen it. Sky-blue silk with hundreds of hand-sewn flowers covering it and a black silk lining, it had a blue fox-fur collar and was the most beautiful thing I'd ever worn.

That night and so many after were happy times for Lee and me. Of course, we were never going to be Terry and June, and there were rows after Caroline's in which we each blamed the other for going so low – neither of us would back down and we'd both maintain we were right. Truth was, we were both right in our own ways, but we were still too stubborn to see that. Essentially, though, the whole thing had made me realise that even though our relationship could be complicated, we still had so much to hold on to. We had two children and a home, and if you love someone, you love everything – their good and bad points. Lee and I were human, but we loved each other, and while it would have been easy to walk away when the going got tough, we weren't going to. We'd had some bad times, but we also laughed and were still passionate – and I'd rather be like that than one of those couples sitting in a restaurant who are so bored with each other they've got nothing left to say.

Owning Teatro was like having a huge front room with a party in it every night and our promise to each other to cut down drinking soon got forgotten. Then again, it was so hard to be good when there was so much temptation, and I forgot about it amid all the nights out. It was at the weekends when we really let our hair down. Teatro was Lee's baby, so in the week he worked hard doing admin during the day and keeping an eye on things in the evenings, while I was at home with the boys. But it all changed at the weekends, when I went in as much as possible. We knew it was important that we were 'seen' at Teatro. We were the 'faces' of it and people expect their club owners to be visible, so that's what we were in the business of doing.

I loved it. After getting ready at home, I'd walk up the stairs to the club, swipe my card to open the door to the dark wood-panelled members' bar and order a 'sharpener', like a Martini, as I sat down. Then it was on to another longer cocktail, like a mai tai, while Lee and I chatted to people before going into the restaurant to meet friends. Usually there'd be six of us sitting at a round table to eat and people would come up to talk or drop in after doing a theatre show. Then, after a chat about how the night had been for the kitchen, we'd go back to the bar. Lee and I were both adamant about not playing loud music, so instead we'd got a piano and the pianist would do his thing. As the evening wore on, other people would start tinkling the ivories and by 3 a.m. we'd sometimes all be singing. Everyone from Jools Holland to Depeche Mode's Martin Gore had a go on that piano and I made one of my closest friends because of it.

Lee told me one night that a girl with an amazing voice had been singing. He pointed her out when she next came in.

'Will you sing something?' I asked as she walked by.

'Oh, no,' she said in an Irish brogue, looking all embarrassed. 'I couldn't do that.' But she whispered something to the piano player on her way to the loo and appeared in the doorway two minutes later.

'Summertiiiiiiiiiiiiiiiiime,' she belted out in a loud, throaty voice as the woman in front of me dropped her cocktail in surprise. Rose-Marie was one of the best friends to come out of that time.

Right in the middle of the West End, Teatro was popular with the celebrity crowd. Mick Jagger, George Michael, Kate Moss, Victoria Beckham, Robbie Williams, All Saints, Shirley

Bassey, Jon Bon Jovi, James Coburn, Charles Kennedy and Gordon Brown…the list went on. Some came in occasionally, others all the time, and it was fun being on the inside of all that. We got to learn the hidden habits of a lot of 'names'. For instance, Geri Halliwell always drank skimmed milk, Jerry Hall ordered pasta with tomato sauce for her party guests instead of something a bit more exciting, Kathleen Turner liked bourbon, and Van Morrison brought loads of friends and didn't want to pay a penny. Peter Mandelson also got caught out once. In the toilets, we had trendy metal troughs as sinks, but he thought they were urinals and promptly pissed in them. Imagine his embarrassment when he realised his mistake as a member of staff started washing his hands beside him!

I'll also never forget the day that Tom Jones came in accompanied by three security guards who stood with their back to him like a human shield to stop people coming over. When Lee and I went to welcome him and have a chat, I realised that poor old Tom must spend his whole time looking at his bodyguards' bums. Odd life, isn't it? He was lovely, but I couldn't help feeling a bit sorry for him: he obviously couldn't go anywhere for the ambience or the view because it would be ruined by those bruisers' buttocks.

There were just three things not allowed into the Teatro bar – mobile phones, cameras and journalists. After all that had happened to us in the past, we were wary of all three and wanted a place where people could relax without worrying about whether someone from the *Sun* was sitting next to them. Of course, journalists still came in with other members, but Lee and I didn't want them in all the time. We'd been burned and didn't want our customers feeling watched.

Teatro wasn't just a celebrity haunt – ad execs, music people and film-makers all came in – and the party didn't stop. We'd forever be on the way out and then bump into someone we hadn't seen for ages, go back to the bar for a quick drink and be in there until 4 a.m. During the summer months, it was always daylight by the time we got home and we were always passing cabbies having their breakfast at a roadside café on the way home. Admittedly, it sometimes got a bit out of hand, and after becoming one of the first bars to serve absinthe, Lee had to make a rule that no one could order any more than three glasses of the stuff, otherwise it would get messy. *Neighbours* star Mark Little even ended up getting his wife to drive into London from the country after a night on it because he'd lost his keys and didn't know where he was! On another famous occasion Kim Wilde's husband, Hal Fowler, came in after performing in *Les Misérables* and ended up staying with us at the end of a heavy night. He got home the next day to find the chicken Kim had roasted for his Sunday lunch speared to the front gate!

Then there were the girls who'd come in commando. I first became aware of it when Lee told me that he and *The Bourne Identity* actor Tim Dutton had nearly choked on their drinks one night when a girl had done a *Basic Instinct* and uncrossed her legs to reveal all.

'That's it,' I shouted. 'I'm banning girls who don't wear pants. They'll put people off. It's disgusting.'

I'd rather people wear knickers for the upholstery's sake if nothing else, so from then on a pair of Agent Provocateur knickers were kept behind the bar in case of emergencies.

The only other time I got territorial was when Lee was the focus of too much female attention, like one night when Cerys Matthews from Catatonia was in. She came in a lot and one evening I was sitting at the end of the bar with friends when she started talking to Lee. She was really animated, jumping up and down all over the place, while Lee sipped his drink. A few minutes later she sat down on a sofa, pulled him down with her and was soon pinning him down with her feet draped across him.

'I need a cigarette, give me a cigarette. Leslie, have you got a cigarette?' Cerys called, clicking her fingers.

I picked up my packet of fags and threw them at her head. 'There's your fucking cigarette,' I snarled.

Lee soon managed to break free and came back to join me.

Even though Teatro was popular with celebrities, there were still times when the staff got it all wrong. One night we were having dinner when someone told us Emma Bunton had left in a rage. Worried, we went to ask the receptionist, who was French, what had happened.

'I don't know,' she said. 'I asked 'er eef she was a member, eef she had a card, but she didn't so I couldn't let 'er in.'

'But she's one of the most famous pop stars in Britain,' Lee said in exasperation. 'How can you not know Baby Spice?'

A few months later I took the boys to Party in the Park, where I was introducing Julian Lennon on to the stage, and saw Emma.

'Now you'll always get in,' I said, as I handed her my swipe card to get into the bar. 'We'll see you there anytime you want to come in.'

Emma smiled, looked down at Max and gave him a kiss. He's never forgotten it. Maybe, just maybe, it made up a little bit for all the hassle in the supermarket.

There comes a point, though, when every party ends – the booze takes its toll, the fags catch in your throat, your feet ache, and you just want to go to bed. My Teatro party started ending in about September 1999, after it had been open for 20 months. Bit by bit the nights that were once so glamorous and fun began to get stale. I started noticing how much shit people talked after a few drinks, how nasty they could be when drunk and how many only said they were your friends when they were downing your free drinks. There were so many people whom I'd only seen in the dark – never in daylight doing something normal like having a coffee, but always at night, a few drinks in and talking for England. It's not that

I didn't have any fun any more – of course I did – it's just that I wanted a little less of it.

In addition to landing a big contract with Neil Morrissey to star in ads for Homebase, I was also about to go back on to the West End stage for a production of *The Pajama Game*, directed by the brilliant actor Simon Callow. Once again I felt really nervous about doing theatre work. Not the strongest vocalist anyway, I was singing out of my safety zone. Ulrika Jonsson had originally played the part, but had stopped doing it because it had been too much of a strain on her throat and so I got the job just two months before the play opened at the Victoria Palace Theatre. I'd learned lines during our summer holiday with the boys on a yacht in France, and then a voice coach had been flown to Morocco while Lee and I were there. I had to have daily singing lessons in the enormous ballroom of La Mamounia Hotel and I'm sure the other guests thought I was that evening's cabaret act. It was tough, and once the production had started, I used to sit in my dressing room listening to people's voices in the pub across the road celebrating the end of their working day, while mine was just beginning. I felt sick with fear, but as the weeks passed, I relaxed into the part and eventually realised it was great to do something so new.

I think it was then that my love affair with Teatro started to sour. Most nights I'd head there when the show finished, but by the time I'd got off stage at ten, taken off my wig and make-up and changed, I wouldn't get into the bar until at least 11. Everyone else would be a few drinks ahead of me, Lee would be settled with friends, and I'd feel on the edge, separated from him once again, like I had all those years before with the In Crowd. We still had some great times, but deep down I was beginning to feel uncomfortable with it all.

Increasingly I realised people were talking rubbish, finding bravery in being pissed that they'd never have elsewhere, and it bored me. Drink also made me more tetchy and I even managed to get upset once at the beloved football commentator John Motson. I'd been in a spoof of *Stars in Their Eyes* on *Hale and Pace*. They had asked me to do Rolf Harris and I'd seen Anthea Turner doing Shane MacGowan on a previous show so I had thought, What the heck! But when I was introduced to John, he turned round and said, 'Saw you on telly the other night. Bet you're really pleased you did Rolf Harris. That was a real career move.' Charming!

The biggest problem with all the partying was the guilt. As the months passed, I'd felt worse and worse about the effect drinking was having on me being a mum. I was permanently hungover at the weekends, my only real time with Joe and Max, and it just seemed to be getting worse. I can't remember how many times I pulled my head off the pillow when they appeared by my bed at 7 a.m. and, feeling dizzy and sick, went downstairs to get their breakfast.

It was all so different from those early, happy years when we'd lived a quiet life up North. Alcohol had come into my life even though I hadn't asked it in – it came with all the trappings of success and the jobs that both Lee and I did. A bottle of wine with a lunchtime meeting, another bit of networking over drinks, into Teatro to meet people, keep the profile up, promote the business – alcohol was everywhere. Even on a photo shoot they'd come in with bottles of champagne. Slowly but surely I'd gone from drinking occasionally in Leeds to regular but not too heavy drinking with the In Crowd to large sessions weekend in, weekend out. Our weekends now started on Thursdays, then it was another night out on Friday, sometimes again on Saturday and a boozy Sunday lunch. That meant you needed at least Monday to recover, which only left Tuesday and Wednesday. There were no two ways about it: I was regularly and heavily binge-drinking.

'You don't have to,' Lee would say when I talked to him about it.

I never confided my true fears to him. After all, why on earth would you want to go out if you weren't drinking? He would be drinking and so we'd be on different wavelengths if I was sober. Anyway, people just talked rubbish when they were drunk and you needed a drink to cope with it. Everyone seemed to want to have a chat when I walked into Teatro and a vodka and slimline or white wine always helped things along.

My guilt just got worse and worse as the months passed and the new millennium approached. Sometimes Lee would want to open a bottle of wine when we rolled in at 4 a.m. because he was finally not on show after a night at Teatro, but I'd refuse – knowing I had to get up with the boys in a few hours. Occasionally, that would cause a row and so I'd stay up – torn between Lee and the boys. I never knew what the right thing to do was, but it always amazed me that even if I was out until 5 a.m., my practical side was still sober enough to worry about things like how much milk there was in the fridge.

As I got more and more tired, though, I found myself getting bad-tempered, which only made me feel worse, and being pissed or hungover began to cause tension with Lee, who was also seeing a darker side to the sparkle of Teatro. His working relationship with Gordon Ramsay had ended on a sour note less than a year after it started when Lee had terminated Gordon's contract. A few months later they'd met up by chance. Lee was trying to hail a cab after leaving Teatro early one morning. It had all got a bit late as Steve Coogan and Rob Brydon entertained him with their spontaneous impressions and Lee had eventually left at the time most people were eating their breakfast.

'You're fucking pissed – you're a disgrace,' Gordon said, walking up to him.

'Yeah, but you're ugly and I'll be sober in few hours,' Lee replied.

That was it – Gordon wouldn't give it up and carried on shouting.

'I've had enough of this,' Lee suddenly exploded. 'You might be able to bully other people, but you're not going to bully me. Let's just sort this out man to man once and for all.'

At that moment a police car passed by.

'Is there a problem, gentlemen?' the officer asked as he got out of the car.

Lee took one look at Gordon and realised he just wasn't worth it.

'No, none at all,' Lee said, and walked away.

That was the last we heard from Gordon until several years later, when it seemed to me that he stuck the knife in as the press were trying to pull our marriage apart. I suppose his behaviour was hardly surprising for someone who became famous for bullying and swearing, so what did we expect?

Otherwise, Lee was still mostly enjoying the fun of Teatro, even though I felt more and more as if the only time I saw Joe and Max was when I tiptoed in to kiss them at whatever hour we got home. By the time I started work in *The Pajama Game*, Joe was at boarding school during the week and Max was a day boy and attending a lot of evening clubs, so the weekends were really important; but I kept ruining them by feeling so dreadful.

As I forced myself up and out with the boys, I knew I only had myself to blame. How many times did I walk across Wandsworth Common almost wanting to throw up? Or watch them do judo on a Saturday sitting on a bench and stinking of booze with a baseball cap pulled down on my head? And have you ever sat overlooking a swimming pool breathing in thick, hot, chlorinated air as you watch your kids jump around, hearing their screams echoing around you and feeling like you're going to pass out? But no matter what, my guilt forced me out of bed – bowling, ballpark or paint-balling, I was like Supermum.

Over time, though, I began to realise that I just couldn't carry on like I was and that I needed some control over my life. My stomach was knackered – I was throwing up some mornings after a heavy night, and I felt like shit. So I began going home early or not going out at all. At times it only made me feel worse because I'd wake up to find Lee still out and he'd come in at breakfast time while I sat there eating my toast. That, and the nights when I did go out and get pissed, added fuel to the fire of our drunken rows, but it was odd because we never argued on the days we weren't drinking and we were forever saying sorry. In a morbid kind of way, I think we got addicted to that – the closeness of those sober days and the fireworks of the weekends. It felt like we were on a rollercoaster ride centred on Teatro, and we had invested time and money into our business, so we couldn't just step off. Anyway, Lee got more out of it than I did. He was working hard, playing hard, and whenever he went for a medical, they'd tell him he was in better shape than most 21-year-olds, so there wasn't a reason for him to stop.

Gradually, the nights I stayed in became far more cherished than the big ones out. The best evenings ever were when Max, Joe and I lay in bed watching TV. I'd get under the duvet with a child under each arm, an action film on the telly, a pizza on my lap and a dog begging for scraps. The next morning I'd go to Battersea or Richmond Park with Mum, the boys, Charlie and a clear head. The problem wasn't solved, but it was a step in the right direction.

I was in the middle of the Yorkshire countryside, drizzle was coming down in a horizontal sheet, and the wind was freezing. What the hell kind of job was this?

'All right?' I said to Terry, the assistant costume designer, who was waiting with an umbrella outside the door of the mobile home to stop my costume from getting wet between takes.

I edged down the steps of the mobile home. I didn't want to leave its cosy warmth, but I forced myself to carry on as the door closed behind me – there would only be another hour or so of filming before the light went, so I just had to bite the bullet.

Thank heavens for all these clothes, I thought to myself, as I walked across the muddy grass towards the set, where lights shone on cherry-pickers, and cameramen stood around in wet-weather gear. I looked ridiculous and about 16 stone in thermal underwear, socks, jumper, scarf and duffel coat, plus an anorak and wellies. All I needed was a pair of gloves on elastic and I'd be five years old again.

'Can you lift up your foot?' Terry said, as I came to a stop and he moved towards me holding a rubber-soled 'sensible' shoe.

'I can do it,' I told him half-heartedly, looking around me.

'No, no, it's just as quick for me,' Terry replied. He bent down to take off my wellie boot. My God – I hadn't had my shoelaces tied since I was six.

'Can I have a fag?' I asked Jan, another wardrobe assistant, who was now holding the umbrella over my head as Terry tied my shoelaces and I stood there like Lady Muck.

It was February 2000 and I'd just joined the cast of *Where the Heart Is* as district nurse Karen Buckley – my first big TV job since *Men Behaving Badly*. *The Pajama Game* hadn't exactly gone to plan, having closed after just 11 weeks, but it was perfect timing because I was able to start *Where the Heart Is* almost immediately. I was really excited about it – a prime-time, Sunday-night family show in which I'd play a working mum of two – a character far more similar to me than Debs had ever been. I felt it was the perfect opportunity to start moving away from being 'something for the dads' to something a bit more serious.

Taking the part, though, meant spending six months a year shooting in Yorkshire and that had worried me. The producers said I'd have to work every other weekend, but I'd put my foot down and insisted I could only do it if I had weekends off, otherwise I'd hardly see Joe, Max and Lee at all. They'd agreed in the end, and while Lee wasn't exactly over the moon that I'd be away so much, he understood it was a good career move for me. Joe was at boarding school and home for the weekends, so that just left seven-year-old Max, who was being looked after by my mum. She'd started doing it while I was in *The Pajama Game* after the shop had finally closed. I'd been paying the rent on it for a while, but in the end she'd had to accept that her debts were just too big, even though she was worried she'd lose her home as well as her business.

'I'll always look after you,' I kept telling her. 'You mustn't worry.'

I'd bought her and Dad a new flat to live in, while Lee struck a deal with the shop freeholder – he kept the flat above and leased us the downstairs, where we were going to open another bar as well as a second Teatro in Leeds. Mum, though, was still worried she'd end up a burden and so I was pleased that by looking after Max she'd feel like she was contributing and be stopped from dwelling on things too much.

With everyone at home sorted out, I was good to go. Life on *Where the Heart Is* was certainly a change. On *Men Behaving Badly*, the four of us had all grown up with it as it became a hit and so there'd never been any luvvie stuff. Now, suddenly, I had top billing with Lesley Dunlop – I was a star! And, boy, was I treated like one. I was introduced to Ken on my first day on set. An ex-miner, he was a tall man in his sixties who chain-smoked and told some great tales about the miners' strike.

'I'm here to look after you. Whatever you need just let me know,' he told me in his broad Yorkshire accent. 'Do you prefer tea or coffee in the morning? And what would you like for breakfast? I'll bring it into make-up for you.'

He was as good as his word – nothing was too much trouble. In later years he'd even look after Max when he came to visit me on set. I still laugh about the time Ken took him to a mining museum and down into a former pit. They were both wearing helmets with lights on and Ken warned Max that miners never looked each other in the eye because the lights were blinding.

'What?' said Max, as he swung his head round, stared at Ken and directed his full beam at him.

'Nay, lad, look away, look away,' Ken shrieked, as if Max was Medusa.

He was fantastic. Lesley Dunlop also had a 'Ken', called Rob. Soon we started calling them our 'wives'.

'Every girl should have one,' we'd smile.

Ken and I became quite a double act and in the end were known as Ken and Barbie. I couldn't quite shake off the blonde tag!

So while everyone else shivered in caravans, Lesley and I lorded it up in our beautiful trailers. I even went on location in it, and if we'd had to shoot on a cliff edge, then I'm sure Ken would have got me and the trailer up there. In fact, the whole set seemed full of fairies with magical powers – someone who took your wardrobe at the end of each day and returned it clean and pressed, or conjured up the interior of a health centre with a few bits of wood and paint. It wasn't exactly Hollywood, but we were treated really well, and at the end of the day I'd go back to a lovely hotel in Leeds for my dinner, a bath and bed. I missed home, of course, but working away was much easier in some ways because instead of doing all the domestic stuff, like making dinner and getting a wash on, I could just concentrate on my job. After all the partying, I revelled in the boringness – I could watch what I wanted on telly, eat what I liked and put the light out whenever.

Having said that, it wasn't really as glamorous as it sounds – there was the time I had to get down to London after filming to present a BAFTA. There was no time to get ready, so I changed in the train loo, painted on a smile for the red carpet, went on to the stage to present the award, got into a taxi and back on the train, ditched the dress for the tracksuit again and arrived in Leeds in time for bed. That's what life was like on *Where the Heart Is* because the filming schedule was tough. Every day was pressured, and after learning your lines the previous evening, you'd be back in make-up by 7 a.m. and on set an hour later, knowing there were eight major scenes to get done that day. We were all up against it and had to be on the ball to work with the director to get scenes in the can as quickly as possible. But I was so glad to be back at work and, in some ways, was surprised by how easy I found the job. I'd suffered badly from nerves in the past, but this time I felt I knew my character and was comfortable with the work from my first day on set.

In fact, the only thing I wasn't comfortable with was the bloody weather. The exterior shots for *Where the Heart Is* were filmed in and around Holmfirth, where *Last of the Summer Wine* was also done, so while they got the summer bit of the year, we got the wind, rain, sleet and snow. The weather permanently seemed to sit on top of where we filmed, and there was always a big cloud with something freezing in it hanging overhead. That's why we wore so many clothes – good in one way, because I didn't have to worry about diets so much, but it also meant a constant battle against the cold. I remember one scene in which Lesley and I had to walk down the high street and into the supermarket. It was quite a long scene – walk down the road, talking, talking, into the shop, talking, talking – and we had to work fast because it was snowing and it would mess up the continuity if it stopped. Lesley and I started the scene at the top of the road, but by the time we had reached the bottom, everyone was laughing at us. We didn't know what was up until we looked at ourselves in a shop window and realised we had icecaps on the top of our heads shaped like little berets. The whole thing had to be reshot on another day when snow didn't stop play.

It wasn't much better even when we did the interior shots,

like those in the health centre, the pub and Karen and Anna's houses. All the sets were housed in an old mill, which wasn't weatherproof so there were forever buckets all over the place catching water when it rained. But it was really good fun, and Lesley and I became good friends. It's always the same – you spend so much time together that you get to know each other pretty well.

As the weeks turned into months, I threw myself into filming and concentrated on May when I would be home again. I missed Lee and the boys, of course, but I saw them each weekend and told myself it was only for a while. But even though they were all okay, there was one person I was very worried about. Not long after I started on *Where the Heart Is* I'd been phoned by our family GP, Dr Cantor, who'd asked me to go and see him.

'Your mother has serious heart problems,' he told me. 'If she does not receive treatment, then the consequences could be very serious.'

The doctor said that Mum's heart valves had furred up, and because of her age and the fact that she suffered from asthma, she was not suitable for surgery. Mum sat and waited for me outside and had no idea about the bombshell that was being dropped. We didn't think she should know because she wouldn't cope well with the news, so I made sure she started taking new medication and didn't make a big drama of it. Mum had already known that looking after Max was too much for her and so we'd found a new nanny who was just about to take over. However much I reassured her, though, she just couldn't stop worrying.

'What will happen to me?' she'd sobbed as she stood in the hallway at home. She'd worked all her life, looked after herself since she was a child and found it so hard that the shop had gone. She loved working there – the people popping in for a cup of tea, all the faces she knew in Clapham, something to get up for every morning.

Out of the Frying Pan

'Please, Mum, don't cry – I'll look after you whatever happens,' I told her as I hugged her.

It was 17 April 2000 and I'd just got back to my hotel room after watching a screening with the rest of the cast of Pam Ferris's last episode of *Where the Heart Is*. It was great, really emotional, but I was exhausted after a long day of filming. I picked up the phone and dialled Mum. I'd talked to her briefly earlier, but wanted to know how she was getting on handing over to the new nanny.

'So, how did it go today?' I asked.

'Oh, your bloody husband,' she replied in her familiar Canadian drawl. 'The new girl told Lee I had given Max chocolate before his tea and he told me off about it. I know I shouldn't have, but I couldn't say no to him. Stupid girl. If grannies can't give out chocolate, then who can?'

'Oh, don't worry about it, Mum,' I told her. 'Lee will be fine.'

'I know. So how are you, darling?'

'Knackered, but I'm not being picked up until ten thirty tomorrow, so I've got a lie-in.'

'Well, why don't I phone you in the morning and we'll have a chat then?'

'OK,' I said. 'Love you.'

'Love you too, darling.'

After a quick conversation with Lee, I turned off the light and went straight to sleep – waking up just once at about 1 a.m. The room was filled with a strange flashing red light and I rolled over to see the 'message' button blinking on my phone. I put a black top over it and went back to sleep.

The next morning I felt wide awake as I got up and started getting ready. I planned to phone Mum right before I left, but just then the phone started ringing. It was Lee.

'Les, I've got some bad news,' he said quietly. 'Your dad's just phoned and he can't wake your mother up. I'm going to go round there now, but it doesn't look good.'

My stomach turned over. I sat down on the edge of the bed.

'What do you mean?' I asked.

'The phone was ringing so he went into her bedroom to answer it and couldn't wake her up.'

'Has he called an ambulance?'

'It's on its way and I'm going over there now with Joe.'

'Well, I'll stay on the phone and you can tell me exactly what's happening.'

My mind went over it again and again during those long minutes as Lee drove to my parents' flat.

'No, no, no, please no, this can't be happening,' a voice kept repeating. I felt so panicked. What had happened? What was wrong with Mum?

Just look out of the window and stay calm, I kept telling myself. Everything will be fine.

Soon I heard Lee going into the flat and my dad's voice in the background.

'I'm going into her room,' Lee said.

Almost immediately I heard the voice of one of the paramedics. 'She's gone,' the voice said. 'She's been dead for hours. She probably had a heart attack in her sleep in the early hours of this morning.'

Later, I would learn that Mum had died at about 1 a.m. – the same time I had woken up to see the light flashing on my phone.

'I'm really sorry, Les, she's gone,' Lee said gently. 'There's nothing I can do and there was nothing your dad could have done.'

I sucked in my breath – unable to believe what was happening. How could she be dead? She was only 68. Too young to die. Mum couldn't be gone. What would we do without her?

'Touch her,' I told him. 'Make sure.'

There was a short silence before Lee's voice came back on the line.

'She's cold, darling. She's been gone a while.'

A cold fist closed round my heart as I sat in the hotel room and heard those words.

'What does she look like?' I whispered.

'She's lying on her side,' Lee told me. 'She looks peaceful, like she's sleeping. There's no pain on her face at all.'

The last time I saw my mum was on the morning of her cremation. She was lying in a coffin but still looked like she might wake up at any moment. My eyes returned again and again to her hand – the hand I'd clung on to as a small child, the hand that had stroked mine to comfort me as an adult, the hand that had picked me up time after time but wouldn't ever again. I never wanted to forget that hand.

CHAPTER 10

I'm Losing You

I opened my eyes and pulled the duvet around me. My back ached, and it was so warm in bed that I didn't want to get out, but I had to get moving because my car was due to pick me up soon.

'Damn,' I said as I reached for my watch on the bedside table and knocked over a glass. It fell to the floor, spilling the leftovers of a vodka and tonic from the night before.

I dragged myself out of bed and went into the bathroom to get a towel. Coming back, I knelt on the floor and wiped up the mess, then lifted my head to look at the miniatures on the bedside table. Silently I gathered up the tiny bottles and threw them into the bin.

'Come on, Leslie,' I said to myself out loud, and walked towards the shower. I had an hour to get ready. I'd worked late the night before and had to get back to London for my days off.

There were a few mornings like that in the winter of 2001. Nearly two years on, I was still struggling to come to terms with Mum's death, and all my promises to cut down on my drinking had been forgotten as I started to binge on alcohol again. I felt so lost without her. The anchor that had steadied me throughout my whole life had gone, and I hadn't been able to stop dreaming about her for the first few months.

'But I thought you were dead,' I'd say in my dream.

'No, darling, I'm fine,' she'd reply, and for those few precious moments it seemed as if she was.

But then I'd wake up crying and realise she wasn't ever coming back. I had no idea just how powerful my grief would be, and it wasn't any better during the day, when thoughts ran constantly through my mind. I even had some panic attacks when I thought about not seeing Mum again – my breath coming in gasps and my heart beating. I just couldn't seem to switch off my mind.

'No matter how much you love Joe and Max, you're going to die and leave them,' it would whir. 'You'll never see them again. Look how many years you've spent with them, they're the centre of your universe, and suddenly you'll leave and that will be it.'

For the first time I realised that people are speaking the truth when they say all you have are your memories. I could see Mum's hand when I closed my eyes, hear her laugh in a crowd, and sometimes I'd go into a department store just to smell her perfume and believe for a second that she was somewhere nearby. I didn't want to forget her. I never want to forget her.

Lee and the boys knew they were walking on eggshells with me, and as the nights when I couldn't sleep got worse and worse, I started drinking more.

Just a couple to make me drift off, I'd tell myself.

It wasn't really about getting to sleep, but blocking out my feelings. Whenever I was away filming, I'd head straight for the hotel minibar after work and sample its wares. I liked the fact that alcohol gave me forgetfulness at night and a feeling of punishment the next morning. As time passed, I might have carried on telling myself that I was drinking because I was depressed, but in fact I was depressed because I was drinking and so I only did it more.

Where once I'd enjoyed having time off from partying when I went up to Yorkshire to film *Where the Heart Is*, I now drank up there alone – something I'd never done before. I knew what I was doing was wrong – I even hid the hotel bills from Lee so he couldn't see how big my bar receipts were – but I enjoyed being in my own little world, thinking of Mum and feeling sorry for myself. It never affected my work – I was a professional and whatever was happening off set stayed there, so what harm was it doing?

Things didn't really improve when I went home. During the months when I filmed, I'd get on the train on a Friday night, arrive in London and go to Teatro on a bender before staying in on Saturday night and getting the train back on Sunday. Then, for the six months of the year that I was in London, I'd get back on the party rollercoaster and have a few big nights out every week.

Alcohol is a problem when it starts to change your character, and my character certainly changed. The more I drank, the more anxious and unreasonable I became. The reason why I was drinking soon got lost as the months went on and I became irrational. Night after night Lee and I would end up arguing as I demanded answers about where he'd been and who with, seeing things that weren't there and questioning his motives. There is no doubt that drink pushed Lee and me apart.

But it wasn't all about my mum. The time after her death was difficult in lots of other ways. Six months later my dad had a stroke and went from being pretty self-sufficient to needing a lot of help. I had been at home when I got a phone call from a friend of his.

'I've come to pick up your dad and he's not answering,' he had told me. 'I can hear him shouting, but he's not coming to the door.'

By the time I'd got there, his friend had broken the kitchen window to get into the flat and had found Dad lying on the floor by his bed. He'd been there for eight hours and his knees were raw from trying to get up. He'd had a stroke and it had affected him badly. He dragged his foot, was very unstable on his feet and walked with a stick, while mentally he'd all but given up. He was angry, stubborn and disbelieving that my mum could have left him on his own. After all those years of being looked after, I knew he was going to rely on me to pick up where she had left off and it scared me.

I couldn't refuse my own father, though, and so I started trying to please everyone. I set up Dad with some help from council carers during the week, but soon realised I needed more help so I got a housekeeper called Rita who came to me for two hours a day before going on to Dad's, where she'd make him a main meal, clean, wash and iron. But it was down to me at weekends and so I'd come home from Yorkshire on Friday night; party with Lee; spend Saturday morning taking the boys to their sports matches; take my dad his lunch; pick up the boys; feed and chat to them; go out again; get up on Sunday morning; start making lunch; drive to my dad's with his lunch if he didn't want to eat with us; go back to ours; serve and eat our lunch; and finally either drive the boys back to school or get back on the train, depending if I was working or not. I always seemed to be rushing and felt pulled in two between my dad on one side and the boys and Lee on the other. Of course, I'd always known what Dad was like, but it wasn't until I started caring for him that I realised just how selfish he could be.

'You're going already, are you?' he'd say when I went to go after bringing over his food. 'You've only just got here and now you're bloody leaving.'

It was strange, because he seemed to want people with him but would then watch telly and shout at them to be quiet when they made a noise. It tore my heart and I felt guilty about leaving him, but sometimes it seemed that whatever I did was never enough. I got him a walking frame, which he refused to use; I got him a neck alarm, but he wouldn't wear it; I took him to the golf club once a week to see his friends, but it wasn't often enough. Nothing was right. It was all so different from when my mum was alive – her main fear was of being a burden, while my dad thought the world owed him. Even so, I loved him and wanted to look after him as well as I could.

My relationship with Debbie had also gone downhill in the year since Mum's death. We'd been up and down for years because Debbie often seemed to need something – a shoulder to cry on, advice about business – and sometimes having to be the sensible one had annoyed me. But we always made up if we had a row. Gradually, though, as the months went by after Dad became ill, I began to feel very angry that so much of the looking after seemed to be down to me. Eventually, on her birthday, we'd well and truly fallen out.

Lee and I had taken her to Souk – the bar we'd opened six months before in my parents' old shop in Clapham – because both of us wanted to cheer her up. Debbie's then husband was in prison and her kids were away, so she wasn't going to have a great night alone. We'd had a really nice time, drinking champagne all night and having a laugh, until the bar closed. Lee had stopped to talk to the bar manager, while Debbie and I got into a waiting cab. We'd sat there for ages until she went to see what he was doing.

'He'll get another one,' Debbie said as she climbed into the cab, and we drove off.

We'd only just got through the front door and into the kitchen when Lee appeared behind us.

'Where did you go?' he asked angrily, obviously really annoyed.

'Debbie said you were following us and so we left,' I told him.

'But I never said that,' he shouted. 'I said I'd be right out. Why couldn't you have just waited? You knew I was coming.'

He was really mad.

'Oh, stop shouting, Lee. It was only a mistake,' Debbie chipped in.

'Actually, Debbie, it's got nothing to do with you,' he barked back.

'I don't care. I'm telling you. It was only a mistake. We didn't realise you wanted us to wait,' she went on.

'Well, you shouldn't have left me, anyway,' Lee yelled. 'You should have checked.'

Suddenly a three-way screaming match broke out. I could see Lee was furious as he started poking a fork into a pan of cold leftover spaghetti on the cooker. He'd long felt that Debbie had been relying on him too much – asking him for advice about starting up a dance studio, inviting him to give her away at her wedding ceremony conducted at Her Majesty's pleasure, that sort of stuff – so Lee had always felt he couldn't speak out. This time, though, I could see he was finding it hard to bite his tongue.

'Don't you shout at my sister. How dare you shout at my sister?' Debbie shouted.

'You know what? You're really fucking ungrateful,' Lee replied.

I grabbed Debbie's arm to try and drag her out of the kitchen. I just wanted her to shut up before Lee really let rip about all the issues in the past and things between us all became too messed up.

'Just go to bed,' I demanded. 'Go upstairs, stop arguing.'

'No,' she snapped. 'He might talk to you like that, but he won't talk to me like that.'

Lee stared at her. 'You know what? I can't be bothered with this,' he said in a low voice. Then he grabbed the saucepan, threw it to the floor and stormed out. The pan bounced up against the fridge door – my beloved fridge that I used to polish like a car – and dented it. The kitchen was covered in sauce – the ceiling, the walls, everything. Great.

But even though I could see why Lee was angry after plying us with champagne all night and getting left behind, Debbie wasn't giving up so easily.

'Come back and talk about it,' she called after him. 'Come back.'

'Debbie, just stop it,' I cut in. 'You'll only wind him up more. Just let him calm down.'

But she was like a dog nipping at someone's ankle – it was almost as if she wanted to wind up Lee to prove she could stand up to him. He wasn't over the top, just pissed off, but she couldn't let it go.

'He might speak to you like that, but he won't to me,' she insisted.

I'd had enough of this.

'Look, Debbie, you'll have to go if you can't calm down,' I told her, and my threat made her back off as quickly as she'd attacked.

Everything seemed fine the next day – we had a barbecue for lunch, Debbie chatted to Lee about exercises to tone her stomach, and the kids played together – but the whole thing had left a sour taste in my mouth. It had changed things between us and soon we only really spoke about Dad. Debbie wasn't as involved with him as I was because she lived further away, but it felt as if all the work Mum had put in to keep our family together had started to fall apart as soon as she'd gone.

Meanwhile, life for Lee was also very full. I was busy with work, Dad, grief and the boys, while he was caught up with Teatro London, Teatro Leeds and Souk. The London places did really well, and Lee and I spent some time together in Leeds, which was good. He came up to oversee the new business while I was filming, and I enjoyed those nights. Once again Lee did a great job and Teatro Leeds looked amazing. It was ahead of its time, but because of that, it suffered and you can't survive on being packed out for just two nights a week instead of seven. We'd had bad advice, been let down by fellow investors and had tried to run before we could walk, so in the end we had to cut our losses and let Teatro Leeds go. It closed after just a year, in July 2001, and it was a difficult time for us. Business worries, heaped on top of all the personal ones, meant Lee and I had little time for each other.

I also broke my pelvis during that time. It happened one Sunday night when I drove up outside the house after taking the boys back to school. A friend had parked in my place on the drive, so I pulled up on the other side of the road, while our friend came out of the house to move his car. I saw Charlie follow him out and knew she would run across the busy road as soon as she saw me.

'Hold the dog,' I screamed, jumping out of the car.

Just like all those years before in Sheffield, however, I'd forgotten to put the bloody handbrake on and my Range Rover started rolling towards our neighbour's brand-new Audi. Thinking I was a) Wonder Woman and b) could stop a moving vehicle, I dived in between the two cars. Of course, the car kept going and a big pop echoed around the street as I was pinned between two bumpers. I screamed as our friend pulled the car off me and I tried to straighten up but couldn't.

Lee came running out of the house. 'What's happened?' he asked.

'Get an ambulance,' I screamed.

When the ambulance hadn't arrived after waiting for 15 minutes, Lee and our friend lifted me across the road and into the house – still bent over. Finally the ambulance arrived and took me to St George's in Tooting. It took six weeks for the bone to heal.

All in all, those two years after my mum's death were pretty lousy.

So there I was, 42 and with high hopes for 2002. I was leaving *Where the Heart Is* after three series because executive producer Mal Young had offered me a role in BBC1's *Merseybeat* and it seemed like a good career move. *Where the Heart Is* wanted me to do both, but I knew I'd never be at home if I did. I was sad, of course, to leave Yorkshire for Liverpool, but I'd played Karen Buckley for a while and wanted a new challenge. *Merseybeat* seemed like the perfect opportunity – from a gentle Sunday-night show to a grittier mid-week cop drama. It meant being away from home again, but soon it was all decided: I'd film *Merseybeat* from August to October 2002 and then do my final episodes of *Where the Heart Is* from November to January 2003 before Karen left for good.

A few weeks before taking on my new role on *Merseybeat*, I looked at myself in the mirror and wasn't entirely happy with what I saw. Let's face it, everything starts drooping the older you get, and I'd already helped turn back a few of Mother Nature's reality checks with a bit of filler to smooth out some creases and a breast-lift after Joe and Max were born. I didn't go around shouting about it, because while plastic surgery is fairly acceptable today – thanks to programmes like *Extreme Makeover* – it was far more of a dirty secret a few years ago. I was working in an industry where there's huge pressure to look good and it had as much of an effect on me as anyone else. It's a no-win situation: if you look old, a magazine will slate you, but if you do something, you'll be in the 'she's had something done' pictures. You're damned if you do, damned if you don't. But I think women like Sharon Osbourne who've had work done look amazing and they're just the tip of the iceberg. People in my business have been doing it for years – I've heard about parties where you get a quick dose of face-freezer – and loads of people I know have had wrinkles filled, injections to smooth out their forehead and their breasts pumped up.

As I stared in the mirror, I remembered some lip work I'd had done two years before. They were injections to make my lips appear plumper: the combination of being a smoker and hitting my forties had made my top lip disappear. I'd finally taken the plunge after talking to a friend about it. I'll call her Sarah.

'You should let my mother do it,' she said to me, as if a plastic-surgeon mum was the most natural thing in the world.

'You what?' I replied.

'My mother was a top plastic surgeon in Venezuela,' Sarah said. 'She does my lips and it lasts for a couple of years – unlike collagen, which only lasts a few weeks.'

I stared closely at her and I must say she looked great.

'So where do I go to get it done?' I asked. I didn't think my lips required a trip to South America to get sorted out.

'Come to my flat,' Sarah told me.

So, a few weeks later, I arrived at her home feeling really excited. Sarah's lips looked great and I trusted her so I trusted her mum. Perfect. I was going to have a pout like Bridget Bardot.

I was a bit surprised when Sarah's mum came into the lounge looking not too dissimilar to Peter Lorre. She was small with thick specs perched on her nose. The only thing missing was the cigarette, and that was only because Sarah wouldn't allow smoking in the flat. I told myself to relax as I lay down in a bedroom and Momma came towards me shining a light into my eyes. Then came a series of small, annoying pricks...and there wasn't a bloke in sight. All done.

I needn't have worried, because the outcome was great. When the swelling went down, my lips looked plumper and refreshed, and as Sarah predicted, the effects were long-lasting. Two years on, as I looked at myself in the mirror in the run-up to *Merseybeat*, I thought a touch-up was in order. Got to keep up with the Joneses, not let myself fall behind the field, etc. I called Sarah, who said her mum was coming to town, so once again I went to the flat and once again there were a few annoying little pricks. I then said goodbye and went home.

Over the next couple of days I noticed the swelling wasn't disappearing as quickly as it had before. I didn't worry too much, though. It would go down eventually, I told myself and didn't think twice when, a few days later, Lee and I were snapped by a photographer on our way into a 40th birthday party at the V&A Museum. We stopped – always happy to pose together – and thought nothing more of it.

'What's the secret of Leslie's new smile?' a headline asked the next day, while another said, 'Leslie's big night pout'. I felt angry it had got into the papers, but thought the excitement over my lips would disappear as soon as the swelling went down. Instead, it was just the beginning.

The puffiness disappeared over the next month, but little by little I began to notice that my lips were hardening. They and the area around my filtrum – the dip between your nose and lip – felt solid. The skin wasn't elastic but tight, immoveable and swollen. It was quite painful at times, especially in the mornings, when my mouth felt stretched. I didn't understand what was happening, but I'd had the procedure done before, so there shouldn't suddenly be any problems, should there? I couldn't over-react, ring Sarah and start firing questions at her, so I kept telling myself it just would take time to settle down, like it had before.

It was brought home to me that I might be getting it wrong when we went on holiday to Majorca with the boys a few weeks after the 40th-birthday-party pictures appeared in the papers. We'd got lost after picking up the hire car and I'd eventually got sick of going round in circles trying to find the bloody hotel while Lee refused to ask for directions. What is it with men? They'd rather struggle and argue than admit defeat by asking a stranger which way is up. So in the end I did.

'I've had enough; the boys are tired, hot and smelly,' I announced. 'I'm going to ask.'

I stopped the car and went into a nondescript building, where a man gave us directions to the hotel.

The next morning I was enjoying a swim with the boys,

messing around with them and throwing Max into the water, when someone called the hotel and asked to speak to me.

'Hello, Miss Ash,' a voice said.

'Who is this?' I asked, immediately suspicious because I was always Mrs Chapman on holiday.

'You came into our office yesterday asking for directions to your hotel. We are the local British newspaper and we'd love to do a piece with you in Majorca.'

Oh, shit. Of all the places to ask, I chose the offices of the only British newspaper in Majorca. Now I understood why men didn't ask for directions.

'Well, thank you,' I replied. 'But I'd really like to keep it quiet that I'm here. I hope you understand.'

There was no way that was going to happen, though, and sure enough a very unflattering picture of me blowing out in the swimming pool was printed. I was upset about it of course, but the people who knew me told me not to worry and I was also too busy to really think about it. When I wasn't filming, I was looking after Dad, being a mum to the boys and socialising as madly as ever. On top of that, we were moving out of our house on Balham Park Road just before Christmas 2002 and I had loads to sort out because we were leaving our huge house for a penthouse apartment. It was still being built so we were going to rent for a while, which meant everything was going into storage. All the packing would, however, be worth it because Lee and I had been rattling around in our big house ever since Max had joined Joe at boarding school, and I was convinced that we were making a new start in a new home so, like magic, everything would be fine. I'm stupid at times.

I now know that silicone had been injected directly into my lips – which you shouldn't do – but back then only one thing was certain: an allergic reaction had made them harden. I started seeing a cosmetic physician, who gave me injections to bring down the swelling and also told me to massage my lips to reduce the hardness. It helped but didn't solve the problem.

Always remember that nice photos don't sell well to the newspapers but horrible ones – like Jerry Hall with cellulite or something – do. The paparazzi went mad when pictures from a photo shoot I'd done for *Woman* magazine were printed in early 2003. Smiling at the camera, my lips were slicked with bright-red lip gloss and looked huge. I wondered if they'd been altered to make me look worse, but it sparked a whole new level of attention because photographers knew bad pictures would sell to the papers. Soon it seemed as if there were paparazzi everywhere and I couldn't leave the house without hearing camera shutters click. One night, for instance, I went out for dinner with Lee and some friends. It was a last-minute thing. I was in jeans, not much make-up and a leather jacket with a huge zip-up collar. As we left, the restaurant manager warned us there were photographers outside and I knew I couldn't face another shitty picture.

'Come on, we'll make a run for it,' Lee said, as I zipped up my jacket and put my glasses on. They weren't going to get a picture of me tonight.

When we walked outside, cameras started flashing bright white in the darkness. It was blinding and I could hardly see where I was going. Lee walked in front to try and protect me. I heard the camera shutters closing as I rushed towards the car park, desperate to get away, but suddenly there was a chain in front of me. Not knowing whether to go over or under it, I got caught up trying to get away. I was shaking by the time I got to the car and shut the door on the photographers.

At the time I found all the attention unbearable and, to escape it, started spending less time at Teatro. In some ways Lee and I drew closer during those months because I leaned on him for reassurance, but in others we drifted apart as I withdrew from the world. As usual, we didn't talk too much about what was happening. I didn't really go there with anyone and Lee wasn't the exception to the rule.

I walked into the hospital ward. It looked old and tired with a nurses' station in the middle and beds around the sides.

'Hi, Dad,' I said, and bent down to give him a kiss. It was summer 2003 and my dad had had another stroke. 'How are you feeling?'

'I want to go to the loo,' he said as I sat down. His voice was small and sad.

'Well, I'll get someone to help you,' I replied.

Soon a male nurse was standing beside us. 'What does he want?' he shouted, his voice filling the entire room. 'Number one or number two?'

Anger filled me. Now the whole ward knew about my dad's toilet troubles.

'Can he do it in the bottle? Does he need assistance?' the nurse boomed.

Embarrassment flooded over me. Dad shouldn't have to put up with this. He looked pathetic lying there in the narrow bed. 'He just wants to go to the loo,' I hissed back. 'Can't you help him?'

'Get me out of here,' he said, looking up at me.

'I will,' I replied. There was a pause. 'But you know you won't be able to go home, Dad?'

'Anything,' he said. 'I'll go anywhere. Just get me out of here.'

We'd talked about this day before. Dad had been getting increasingly unsteady on his feet but had been so set against leaving his flat. Meanwhile, I'd felt at the end of my tether as I waited for the next phone call telling me he'd hurt himself. The tension between Debbie and me had been building.

'I can't do this on my own,' I'd say to her during horrible phone calls from Liverpool, where I was filming *Merseybeat* that summer. 'I need some help. You've got to agree to do some days – he's your dad too.'

'But I can't,' she'd reply.

'But you're going to have to, just like I'm having to.'

It wasn't that Debbie hadn't done anything at all – for a while she'd agreed to look after Dad every other Saturday and it had worked, but eventually the arrangement had fallen apart and I'd got sick of the uncertainty. It just seemed easier to organise it myself. We'd recently had yet more cross words when she'd asked me for money. It wasn't the first time

'Leslie, it's me,' she said one day, when I picked up the phone. 'I need nine thousand pounds urgently and I was hoping you could help me out.'

'I can't, Debbie,' I replied. 'I've got a massive tax bill to pay and everything's going into that.'

'Well, do you know anyone who can?'

'You can't start asking people you haven't seen for years to lend you money. I'm sorry, but you're going to have to sort this out on your own.'

Dad's latest stroke made us start communicating again because we had to find somewhere for him to live. From now on he'd have to use a wheelchair, but even so Social Services had said he wasn't ill enough to go into a nursing home when they'd assessed him. It was obvious that neither he nor I could cope with him living in his flat alone, however much help he had, and we both knew he couldn't move in with us. I was working, we were buying the new flat, and we would all be miserable. I phoned Debbie and we started looking at residential homes on a list the council had sent me. We didn't even go inside some of them. I only had to drive up outside to know I wouldn't put Charlie in there, let alone my father.

Eventually, though, I found a lovely place about a mile from us and felt happy as Dad left hospital after a two-week stay. He'd be near his friends and me, getting 24-hour care, medication and regular meals. There had been times since Mum's death when he'd just lain in bed, refusing to wash, not bothering to eat, and now he was going to be looked after properly.

It was going to cost, though – £600 a week after the council had put in their £300 – and while I was happy to foot the bill, we'd all agreed that some of Mum and Dad's things would be sold to put into a fund to help pay the bills. Dad didn't have any money, but he wanted to contribute what he could. On the day he left hospital, he was transferred by private ambulance to his new home because the NHS didn't do journeys to private places. I tell you what, you spend your life saying you can't take it with you, but all I can say is keep it all because you're gonna need it.

As he settled himself into his new room, I went over to the flat to pick up some stuff he particularly wanted, such as Mum's picture, her ashes and a print of the *Mona Lisa* he'd brought all the way back from Spain on his knee.

'I need a fan,' he said as soon as I got through the door. 'It's bloody hot in here. Can you get mine from the flat for me?'

I headed back to the flat to get it – maybe that would be it once I'd done this trip – but I couldn't believe what I found when I opened the front door. It was as if the heart had been ripped out of my parents' home. Pictures, silver, china, figurines and vases had all gone.

I stood in the living room and burst into tears. There was only one person who could have done this. Debbie had said she wanted a few things, but she must have come with her car while I was out, filled it up and gone. My heart was beating like mad as I realised that all my mum's stuff had gone, everything.

'What have you done?' I screamed when Debbie answered the phone.

'I don't want to sell all this stuff,' she shouted back. 'I want Candy and Holly to have it as memories.'

'But you've taken everything. How can you have taken everything?'

'Because otherwise you'd sell it all.'

'Of course I wouldn't. We could have talked; you could have told me what you wanted. But you've taken everything. How could you do that?'

I was so upset. My dad was hardly gone and his home looked empty. I didn't want to sell the stuff either, but Dad had insisted because he wanted to contribute.

He was furious when I took the fan back to the nursing home and told him what had happened.

'I'm going to phone her,' he said, and he did.

'If that stuff isn't put back by eleven tomorrow morning, then I'll phone the police,' Dad told Debbie.

He might have been unsteady on his feet, but his tongue was still working fine.

I was in the flat the next day when Debbie came back and we said nothing to each other as she carried in boxes. As she turned to leave, I knew I had to do something.

'Debbie, look, this is stupid,' I said.

'Leslie, I have nothing to say to you,' my sister snapped as she walked out.

In that moment I knew my family had finally fallen apart.

In early 2004 I found out that *Merseybeat* was finishing and the news upset me. I'd been on a bit of a high only a few months before, after filming my second series and playing a murderess in an episode of the legal drama *Judge John Deed*. It had been the most unglamorous but challenging role I'd ever done and I'd really enjoyed it. But then came the news that *Merseybeat* was coming to an end, and although I was one of Britain's top-earning actresses and work offers were coming in all the time, it was hard to be level-headed about it when I felt so alone.

The press interest in my lips had started a cycle of retreating into myself, and even though things were dying down, I was still withdrawn and it had left Lee and me increasingly distant with each other. I was drinking less, not going out as much, and night after night I thought about how far we'd come since meeting each other. We'd been so young and irresponsible back then, but gradually our life had become a conveyor belt of work and family responsibilities. What had kept us together were the big nights out and the shared love of partying. But when I decided to cut down drinking, we'd started leading different lives and it felt as if we were on two train tracks that rarely intersected. Lee would come home from a day at Teatro, put down his bag and the administrative part of his working life was finished, but then he'd shower, change and eat dinner with me before leaving again to become a club owner. He spent most Thursday, Friday and Saturday nights at Teatro, while I stayed at home, and I felt more and more as if I was in competition with a members' club – Teatro was the 'other woman' and she was winning.

I knew Lee had to work in order for us to maintain our lifestyle. The West End is the most competitive bar environment there is and he could never relax if he wanted to keep Teatro successful. Besides, whenever I worried about it all too much, I just went on another bender and tried to kid myself that everything was OK. My mind played tricks on me, though, and I convinced myself Lee was looking for ways to get away from me. Outwardly we went through the motions – going out for meals or to Souk when I did agree to go out – but inside it felt like we were coming unstuck. I thought we'd put all the bad times behind us, but once again there were holes showing in what had once felt like the perfect marriage.

I kept on going, but every so often something reached in, hit my rawest nerve and reminded me of how much things had changed. There was one particular line in U2's 'The Sweetest Thing' which always did that: 'I'm losing you,' Bono sang. 'I'm losing you.'

CHAPTER 11

A Night to Remember

Martini stirred with a twist, ice-cold sake to wash down Japanese food, chilled white wine, champagne, vodka tonic and finally green, syrupy absinthe – it had been a long, long night. On the day of my accident – Friday, 23 April 2004 – Lee and I didn't stop partying until around 7 a.m. and by that time we were so drunk we could hardly stand.

We'd been for dinner with my mate Nathalie Dufresne-Smith and some other friends at the Japanese restaurant Nobu in Mayfair, and yet again none of us had been ready to be tucked up by 10 p.m. It had been a great evening – really busy in the restaurant – and I'd soaked up the atmosphere. It had been one of the first nights out I'd enjoyed for months and I had been determined to make the most of it. A few days before, I'd presented a BAFTA to Beryl Vertue with Neil Morrissey and it had felt as if the whole lip saga might be on the way out at last.

'Why don't we go back to the flat?' Lee suggested to everyone, as we walked out on to Park Lane after dinner.

Usually we'd have headed for Teatro, but that night we wanted to go home. After all those months of renting, we'd finally moved into our penthouse flat with huge windows overlooking the river, dark wooden floors and a New York feel. We'd been busy christening the place with bottle after bottle of champagne and now was another chance.

We all piled into taxis, went back to the flat and got settled on the huge sofas in our living room. We had a drink, chatted, laughed, had another drink, then another and another, and of course one for the road, and it was after 7 a.m. by the time we'd decided enough was enough. Time went so quickly on nights like those, but I was looking forward to lying down by the time we closed the door on our final guests.

Lee and I headed for bed, and fuelled by the cocktail of alcohol inside us, we started making love. Too much information, I know, but it's important for everyone to understand exactly what happened on that night and this was a vital part of it. Despite the distance between us, the fall-outs, the responsibilities and the busy schedules, our sex life was the one area of our relationship that had never suffered. And I mean never – in all the years we'd known each other. It's part of the way we were and are, like sleeping and eating, and we'd never stopped fancying each other. Emotional distance doesn't necessarily mean physical distance, so if you're passionate in one area of life – whether it's work, having an argument or about each other – then you're physically passionate too. Just as we'd always found each other interesting enough to argue with, we'd also found each other interesting enough to be turned on by.

Drunk and in the half-light of the bedroom, I didn't notice how close I'd got to the edge of the bed as Lee moved behind me and I knelt in front of him. Suddenly my leg splayed out from underneath me, my knee gave way to thin air and I felt myself fall. Putting out my hand, I tried to grab the bedside table to stop myself, but Lee was falling with me and all 6 foot 4 inches and 14 stone of him was propelling me forward. I fell half on, half off the bed with him on top of me and felt a sharp pain as my upper body crashed into the bedside table. Its corner dug into my right side about halfway between my waist and armpit.

'Get up, get off,' I panted, as adrenaline sliced through the alcohol in my bloodstream. 'Fucking get off me.'

Lee pulled himself back on to the bed.

I knew I must have hurt myself because I'd crashed into the cabinet with such force. Getting slowly to my feet, I expected to feel a stab of pain during every tiny movement, but I couldn't feel a thing. I straightened up. Nothing. I felt a crack and inhaled. Nothing. As I breathed out, however, pain suddenly stabbed through my side and I realised with a rush of shock that there was no air going back into my lungs. Even as I was breathing in, there just didn't seem to be anything going inside me.

'I can't breathe, I can't breathe,' I gasped to Lee, taking tiny, short, rasping breaths.

'You'll be all right – you've just winded yourself,' he replied. He didn't have a clue.

'No I bloody haven't. I can't breathe.'

I turned towards the door. It suddenly seemed so dark and close in the bedroom. Maybe I'd get my breath back in a bigger space with more air. Maybe I really was just winded. I'd only banged the bedside table, for God's sake. But it was obvious I wasn't winded when I took a few steps out into the corridor and nothing changed. I was still gasping for air and had to crouch over.

I had to call an ambulance.

Going back into the bedroom, I went to grab the phone. Where was it? It must be in the living room, where we'd used it to call cabs for people. Knowing the gardener was due any minute, I pulled on some tracksuit bottoms and a big T-shirt before turning to leave.

'I'm going to phone an ambulance,' I hissed over my shoulder.

Lee got off the bed. 'Come on, Les,' he kept saying, as he pulled on some shorts. 'I've seen this before. Straighten up and let the air get in. Give it a minute and you'll be fine.'

But I just wanted to stay crouched as I walked into the living room hunched over like a little old lady. Forcing myself to stay calm, I picked up the receiver and started dialling 999.

'What are you doing?' Lee said as he walked in behind me.

'Dialling a bloody ambulance,' I snapped, frustrated by the fact that he didn't seem bothered by what had happened.

'Come on, Les,' he repeated. 'You don't need to do that. You're just winded. Give it a minute. You'll get your breath back.'

Doubt flickered in my mind. Maybe he was right after all. Still drunk, Lee was convinced I was fine, but he also now admits that fear flashed into his mind when he saw me lift the phone and remembered what had happened the last time someone had dialled 999, at Caroline's. I had a lucrative advertising contract that could be null and void if we got splashed across the tabloids again in a blaze of bad publicity, and after the year we'd just had, he panicked. I hung up the phone.

'Straighten up, Leslie, straighten up,' Lee said, walking towards me.

Still crouched over to try and lessen the pain that was stabbing at me every time I breathed, I could see he wanted to get me standing upright.

'No, don't touch me, get away from me,' I shrieked, and moved to the other side of the room.

He was going to really annoy me if he didn't leave me alone. I didn't want to straighten up, to make things worse. I just wanted to get my breath back.

'Leave me alone,' I screamed, still bent double. 'Get away from me.'

Charlie started barking as I shouted and suddenly I heard knocking at the door. Now the bloody gardener must have arrived.

'Well, answer it,' I hissed to Lee, who went to open it.

'Is everything all right, Mrs Chapman?' an Australian voice suddenly said.

I lifted my head to see the gardener standing in the kitchen door.

'I've hurt myself,' I groaned. 'I fell. I'm having trouble breathing. I need an ambulance.'

I'd had enough of all this waiting around. I still couldn't breathe properly and it was beginning to scare me.

'Look, mate, she's fine,' Lee said hurriedly. 'She'll be OK in a minute. She fell. She hurt herself. I'll look after her.'

'OK, Mr Chapman, OK,' the Australian replied, before looking at me. 'What do you want me to do?'

'Just get me an ambulance,' I pleaded.

The gardener went on to the balcony to make the call.

As Charlie carried on barking at the sound of our raised voices, the message finally got through to Lee that I wasn't winded, I wasn't getting my breath back, and I wasn't over-reacting.

'Come on, Les,' he reassured me. 'Just try and breathe. You've got to stay calm.'

Unfortunately, there was no way that was going to happen because just then I turned to the door to see four police officers piling into our flat. What the hell was going on? I didn't know it then, but apparently the 999 call I'd dropped had been registered and had triggered an automatic response, which was why our flat was now crawling with coppers.

'Where's the ambulance?' I shouted. 'I don't want the fucking police. I want an ambulance. I can't breathe properly.'

As a woman officer put her arm round me, her male colleagues ushered Lee into the hallway and the paramedics arrived. It was chaos.

'What's going on?' one of the policemen demanded.

Lee looked at him in disbelief. 'She had an accident. I don't want to go into detail,' he replied.

The policemen stared at him.

'It's private,' he insisted. Ever since Caroline's, he'd never felt quite the same about the police because so much information had got into the papers, but the officers just carried on staring.

'We were making love,' Lee sighed. 'Just ask my wife.'

'We will in due course,' came the reply. 'But in the meantime we'll need you to come with us.'

'What?' he exploded. 'You're kidding, aren't you? Just ask her. This is ridiculous. It was an accident. She's over there. Ask her.'

But no one did and I heard none of this.

'We're not happy with your version of events, Mr Chapman,' an officer told Lee. 'We would like you to come down to the station for questioning.'

As the police took Lee into our bedroom to get properly dressed, I was walked slowly out of the flat and into the lift. I thought he was following behind. Still breathing in shallow, laboured gulps, I was ushered into the ambulance with the policewoman.

'I just want to have a quick chat, Mrs Chapman,' she said softly as I sat down. 'Did he attack you?'

I looked at her, almost feeling annoyed at the ridiculous question she was asking. I couldn't breathe properly and I was still half pissed – what was she talking about?

'No, no,' I said hurriedly.

'You're absolutely sure?' she replied.

'Yes, of course I'm absolutely sure,' I said with what little breath I had. 'No, he didn't attack me, and can we please go to the hospital now?'

All I could think was that I might be breathing my last and she was wasting time. As the doors slammed and we finally started moving, I willed the ambulance to drive the half-mile to our local hospital in record-quick time.

'Would you like your husband to join you at the hospital?' the policewoman asked.

'Yes, of course,' I told her. Was she stupid or something? 'Why? Where is he?'

'He's been taken to Fulham Police Station for questioning,' she replied.

'What?' I said disbelievingly. 'Why have you done that?'

What on earth was going on? Oh, shit. Lee had been right. It was a mistake to dial 999. What a mess. I should have got him to drop me off, or got a cab, I thought, as anger and fear filled me. He was right. I've done it again. The police have got involved. What a fuck-up.

Still only breathing in shallow gasps, I turned to the police officer.

'Please get him out of there,' I told her desperately. 'I want him with me. He's done nothing wrong.'

Even as I pleaded with her, Lee was being arrested and driven to a police station.

'Which hospital is my wife going to?' he'd asked as a police officer stood over him while he got dressed. 'This is ridiculous. I'll come along, but this is stupid. Just talk to my wife.'

The officers, though, insisted that Lee was going to be taken for questioning at the nearest police station. Once there, he was taken into a reception area, where a duty sergeant was waiting.

'Can you tell me what I'm doing here?' Lee asked as he sat down, hopeful that someone in charge would be able to put things straight.

'That's a good question, boys,' the duty sergeant said. 'Why is he here? Has any complaint been made?'

'No,' one of them replied.

'Hold on, sir,' the sergeant told Lee. 'I'll try and sort this out as quickly as possible.'

He disappeared through a door as Lee sat there wondering when they were going to let him go and where I was being taken. He couldn't believe this was happening again.

'I'm sorry, sir,' the sergeant said, when he reappeared about five minutes later. 'There seems to have been a mistake and I apologise for the inconvenience. You're free to go. Can we give you a lift?'

'Well, yes,' Lee replied. 'I'd like to be taken to wherever my wife has gone, please.'

All we can assume is that the duty sergeant had contacted the woman officer, who'd told him what I'd said. Anyway, it meant that Lee was free to go and soon two of the officers who'd arrested him were driving him to the Chelsea and Westminster Hospital, chatting about his football career as if nothing had happened. The drama was over almost as soon as it started, and he was out of the police station within just 20 minutes.

But of course it wasn't that simple. In fact, we had no idea how dearly we'd pay for what was now our third brush with the police.

I was still having trouble breathing by the time I reached hospital and was sick within moments of getting through the doors.

Please don't let things get out of hand, I thought to myself, and wondered when the police would let Lee go.

Soon I was taken in for an X-ray, which showed I had cracked two ribs. A doctor gave me morphine to dull the pain. Lee arrived and told me what had happened to him at the police station.

'This is going to get out,' he said worriedly. 'There's no way the papers won't find out about this. And because the police jumped to conclusions, then everybody else will too.'

'Let's hope not,' I said woozily.

I knew he was right, but the morphine meant that nothing was really worrying me any more and now it was my turn to be the one who kept calm. Everything washed over me as the drug kicked in and my breathing eased. Soon I was taken off for another X-ray, which showed that one of my broken ribs had nicked my right lung, causing it to partially collapse and fill with fluid. That was why I'd had difficulty breathing.

With X-rays and waiting, chats with doctors and various

examinations, it must have been about lunchtime by the time I was finally put into a private room courtesy of my health insurance. Sadly it wasn't quite the plush hotel room I'd expected – a bit like getting to the airport and being invited to be upgraded to first class (yeah!) only to find the plane is in bad need of renovation (boo!). I didn't think too much about it, however. I felt knackered and wanted to rest.

No chance, though, because the phone rang within minutes. It was Neil Reading, a guy who'd done PR for Teatro and now did press stuff for us whenever a story appeared or we were asked to do an interview. He told us *Mirror* editor Piers Morgan had been in touch, after getting a tip-off about Lee's arrest. It's unbelievable how fast supposedly bad news travels and you'd be amazed how many coppers there are out there with journalist friends.

Lee knew Piers Morgan of old. They'd known each other a bit from being out and about in London, and Piers had always said he wouldn't use any stories about Lee. But he did, of course, when he was the editor of the *News of the World* and got the story about the night in Ibiza. Later Lee confronted him about it.

'I do feel bad,' Piers had replied. 'But look at it this way – I could have put it on the front page.'

All in all, we didn't really want to speak to him on the phone, but we knew that with or without a chat with us he'd print the story and we thought it would be better to explain things. We wanted to nip the whole thing in the bud – explain what had happened and stop it running out of control.

'It's just really embarrassing,' I told him. 'I can't go into too many details, but we were having a good time and I slid off the bed and put my hand out to save myself and ended up between the bedside table and the bed.'

Piers made soothing noises down the phone.

'It's new and very springy,' I quipped, and we chatted a bit more.

'It must have looked really awful,' I went on, when he asked about the police. 'They all got the wrong idea. It was like a Brian Rix farce or something. They were asking me all these questions and I couldn't talk. I was in agony.'

So there I was: on morphine, on the phone to a flipping tabloid newspaper from a hospital bed and on a mission to try to stop them printing crap the next day.

'I've had X-rays,' I told Piers. 'It's OK. I just hope people don't make a meal out of it. I don't think I could go through any more.'

That was the bottom line. As I'd picked up the phone to Piers, the thought of another press feeding frenzy had made me go cold. After I'd done my bit and Lee had had a chat with him, all we could do was hope we'd done enough to stop the storm that would definitely be brewing in a teacup. It wasn't too long, though, before other papers got hold of the story and my agent, Michele, called to say her phone was ringing off the hook. I told her what had happened and asked her to explain it for Lee and me. I don't know what I was expecting – probably nice stories taking the piss out of us 'behaving bedly' or something. Silly girl.

Last but not least came a visit from the man in charge of my case – a consultant vascular surgeon called Mr Nott, who said he wanted to wait until the next morning to assess whether my lung was inflating by itself. I agreed – he was the professional, after all. After he left, Lee also went, because he had to pick up Max from school.

Finally, my room was quiet and I closed my eyes – I felt so tired and hadn't had a chance to sort out things in my mind. I couldn't believe what had happened. Last night Nobu, today the Chelsea and Westminster Hospital. One minute I was in bed making whoopy, the next I'd cracked a bloody rib. I'd never realised how easy it was to do.

Time slid by until the door opened sometime in the late afternoon and I looked up, thinking it was Lee bringing Max to see me. Instead, it was Debbie. How strange. I hadn't seen my sister since our row at Dad's. So how did she know I was in hospital? I felt so tired and sore. I didn't need this as well.

'What happened? How are you?' Debbie asked, as she edged into the room.

'Fine,' I replied. 'Well, not fine, really. I've broken some ribs, but I'm OK.'

'But what happened, Leslie?'

'What do you mean?' I asked.

'Well, what happened?' Debbie replied.

I told her – hoping to get the conversation over with as soon as possible. It felt awkward seeing her like this, but I couldn't be bothered to get annoyed.

'Well, if there's anything I can do – if Lee needs any help with ferrying the boys around or something – then just let me know,' Debbie said, as she got up and turned towards the door.

I felt really uncomfortable. I hadn't seen her for months and now she'd quizzed me before leaving soon after she'd arrived. We all knew there were people who thought Lee had been violent towards me that night at Caroline's all those years ago and I wondered if Debbie thought likewise.

Lee and I weren't stupid; we'd been aware of the whispers after the door-kicking thing. I'd taken out an injunction, after all, and in some people's minds there's no smoke without fire. Nobody ever actually came out and said anything, but it was implied and I found it hard both for Lee's sake and mine – I didn't want him to be portrayed as a monster, or for me to be made out to be a victim. I had always been the happy-go-lucky girl-next-door who was married to a footballer, and suddenly there was this image of me I didn't recognise. Lee's card was marked after the injunction was taken out and that, plus the fact that we were really bad at keeping some of our noisier rows behind closed doors, had only added more ammunition. We just ignored it and got on with our lives because we both knew the truth. Life's not like an episode of *EastEnders* where everything has to be discussed and so we didn't go there. In fact, the only person I had really talked to about it had been Mum.

'Look, Leslie, just throw the paper away and ignore it,' she'd tell me.

She was a big believer in there being no such thing as bad publicity, but with two broken ribs, I was feeling really sore and needed some more morphine. In those circumstances, I felt Debbie was just being irritating.

My lung still hadn't improved by the following morning and Mr Nott told me I'd need a tube inserted to reinflate it. He then introduced me to an anaesthetist called Dr Cox, who told me I could have the procedure done under local or general anaesthetic or I could have an epidural.

'It will serve as a pain-block,' he told me. 'Do you have any problems with that?'

'No, not at all,' I replied. 'I've had two epidurals for the births of our sons so I know what to expect.'

Later that day I was taken into theatre and the epidural needle was inserted into my spine between my shoulder blades. It felt like a pin piercing an orange because the needle was so thick, and numbness crept over my ribs and torso until all I could feel was tugging as the chest drain was put in. Job done, I was taken back to my room in a wheelchair, where two nurses carefully put me back into bed. They had to be gentle because I had one tube coming out of my arm for a drip, one under my armpit for the drain and one between my shoulder blades for the epidural. They were going to keep me numb for a while to control the pain and then they'd disconnect the epidural but leave the needle in place, just in case they needed to use it again to do something to the drain.

I lay back in bed and tried to relax. I wasn't in any pain, but felt weak. Earlier I'd read the *Mirror*'s article headlined 'It's a new bed and it's very springy'. It was fair enough but I had no idea what the other headlines were screaming. It wasn't until later that I found out – 'Beaten up? No, I broke a rib while making love,' one paper reported, while another said, 'Call me an ambulance,' because according to them, I'd staggered to a window pleading for help (presumably to a passing bird as we're on the ninth floor). Far from putting the record straight, I'd just fed the frenzy. Eventually my explanation about a 'good time' would be turned into 'making love' and then into 'rough sex' in the newspapers and I'd want to die of embarrassment – my sons, my dad, my friends, what were people going to think?

As I lay in my hospital bubble, I had no idea about the storm that had blown up. While I tried to get comfortable and sleep, there were journalists and photographers waiting outside the entrance to our flat, hiding in the underground car park, ringing on the doorbell every few minutes and staking out all the entrances to the hospital. It was the beginning of a terrible time for Lee and everyone I loved – including my elderly dad, my mother-in-law and even 15-year-old Joe – as journalists desperate for information approached them all for a story.

Lee didn't want me to know what was happening and didn't say anything about it all when he came to see me. He just wanted me to rest and so that's what I did as I lay in bed trying not to disturb the tubes attached to me.

I was getting a bit bored after two days in bed, though. My Teatro friend Rose-Marie and agent, Michele, had popped in, but the only other people I had to talk to were the cleaners and I wasn't that impressed by them. The room didn't look nearly as spotless as they did on old films in which scary matrons shouted at mousey nurses. Rather than hot soapy water, the cleaners had a spray they used over all the surfaces like a polish, and even the nurses didn't seem to wash their hands but wore latex gloves instead. All very modern.

The next day was pretty much the same, as they monitored my lung and I continued to rest. The only differences were that I woke up to feel a burning sensation between my shoulder blades at the site of the epidural needle and I noticed my pillow was damp. I pushed the button for a nurse, but she didn't seem that concerned when she had a look. She simply changed my pillowcase and put another dressing over the original one.

'I don't want to take it off in case it dislodges the needle,' she said. 'Everything seems fine.'

'Can you turn on to your side?' the doctor asked me.

It was early evening on my fourth day in hospital and a male doctor had arrived with a pretty Nordic-looking woman to take out the epidural needle. Earlier in the day I'd held my breath as Mr Nott had removed the tube for the lung drain because everything was back to normal. All I had to do now was rest and let my ribs mend. But no one had warned me just how bloody painful it would be to remove the drain – Mr Nott had taken hold of two threads he called 'purse strings' on either side of the cut where the drain had been inserted and given them a quick pull to close the gap. Ouch! But at least it meant I would be going home the next day, so it was worth it. I was so looking forward to getting out of hospital. What a palaver for a cracked rib – I thought rugby players just bandaged them up and carried on playing.

Now all that was left to do was take out the epidural needle. I tensed up as the doctor bent down and pulled back the dressing.

'The needle's not even in,' he said behind me. 'It's already fallen out. But you've been left with a nasty lump where it was inserted.'

That must explain why I'd woken up that morning on a wet pillow again. The lump must have been weeping in the night, but no one seemed worried about it, or about the fact that my nightclothes were stained. At least the needle was out now and I was finally free of all the drains and drips. Job done, the doctor and his glamorous assistant left my room.

'Have a look at this lump, will you?' I said to Lee, who'd just arrived. 'How big is it? What does it look like?'

I stayed on my side as he looked at the spot between my shoulder blades where the needle had been inserted.

'It looks pretty bad,' he said. 'It's a lump about two inches wide and about an inch proud, like an enormous boil. There's a big head on it, too.'

'Well, it must have been the dressing or something,' I replied. 'The nurse I spoke to about it just put another one on. If there was a problem, then they'd have done something about it, wouldn't they? It must be a reaction to something.'

'Oh, OK, then,' Lee said, then bent down to kiss me. 'I'm sure it's nothing. After all, the doctor's just seen it.'

I didn't go home the next morning because I woke up feeling really sick and Mr Nott advised me to stay in another night to be on the safe side.

Bollocks, I thought, as I lay back in bed. Lee was on his way to pick me up and I knew he'd be upset. I was also getting really sick of hospital food and just wanted to get home.

'Make sure everyone washes their hands,' Michele told me later in the day when she saw the lump on my back.

She had reason to be so cautious. Her husband, Nigel Smith, a top-drawer comedy writer, had contracted MRSA after having a brain lesion and it had paralysed most of his nervous system. Nigel couldn't blink, swallow or move his limbs and it was really touch and go for a while whether he'd make it at all. Michele was there for him every step of the way and never took no for an answer as she questioned every doctor and specialist while heavily pregnant. She even found the time to carry on looking after a bunch of actors, including me.

'I will,' I told her. 'But no one seems that bothered about it.'

Another day, another 12 hours lying in bed staring at the TV until the following morning came and I got up, determined to go home. I still didn't feel great, but knew I'd feel much better in my own bed. There was just one thing left to do before I left – Lee and I had agreed to release a picture to the media. Although I didn't know everything about what was happening, I still knew something had got into the papers and agreed it would be a good idea to do a photo because otherwise we'd be followed for weeks. We'd done the same kind of thing before when we were on holiday and photographers had started staking out the beach. It had worked well because everyone had got what they wanted – the photographers their pictures, and Lee and I our peace. Loads of the pictures in celebrity magazines are like that – it looks as if the person doesn't know they're being photographed, but they do. If they look crap, then they probably don't, but if they're wearing jewellery and their hair looks great, then you can pretty much bet they know they're about to be snapped. Looking back, I wish we'd never decided to do that photo. Once again we played right into the newspapers' hands because it looked really cheesy. We wanted to show that things were all quiet on the Western Front, but in the end it seemed too staged and I really did look like a victim – all weak and frail, insisting I was OK and still with Lee. It was a bit naff.

That morning, of course, I didn't know that's how it would turn out as I lay in bed waiting for my friend Katie Limmer, the make-up artist on the Homebase ads, to come in. I really didn't feel great and she was going to have her work cut out getting me ready for the camera.

'What's that?' she asked, after she'd arrived and my

hospital gown fell open at the back to reveal the lump on my spine as I sat on the edge of the bed.

'Just a spot or something,' I replied. 'I've mentioned it a couple of times. A nurse had a look after I had a shower this morning and squeezed it for me. It's a reaction, I think.'

Photo done, I was pleased when it was finally time to go home. We left by the back door at about 2 p.m. It was strange going outside after days in the stuffy hospital and I felt pretty rough as I walked into the fresh air. Despite having done the picture, there were still photographers waiting for us and I could hear their cameras click as I shuffled towards the car. I looked awful in those pictures and only now do I know why. If only, if only, if only – those words have rung constantly in my ears ever since that day. If only I had been more aware of superbugs, if only the nurses had reported my discomfort, if only I'd been given antibiotics, if only the hospital had been clean and free from infection, then life today would be so different. Back then I knew nothing of this and closed the car doors on the lenses as I got into the car. I was going home.

'Come upstairs and have a look,' Lee said, as I lay under the duvet.

It was the day after I'd got back from hospital and so far I hadn't moved out of bed. I felt absolutely dreadful – pounding head, stiff neck and really sick. In fact, I'd felt worse and worse ever since coming home. Charlie had rushed up to see me, bottom wiggling and barking with excitement, and our housekeeper, Rita, had also been there after getting the place spick and span for me. But I'd gone straight to bed and not got up since. Having been told to rest for a week, I'd decided that a couple of days under the duvet wouldn't hurt.

Maybe this is just how everyone feels, I thought, as I downed painkillers. Or it could be the flu.

Whatever it was, I wasn't feeling any better when I woke up the next morning – worse, in fact. I had a splitting headache, my neck was stiff, my body aching, and I felt hot. Lee had brought me a cup of tea that morning, but I hadn't drunk it or got up like I'd usually have done. Instead, I just lay in bed all day watching TV and napping.

Now he wanted me to go upstairs to see a huge shelving unit we had had designed in our lounge. The TV was going into it, books, ornaments, that kind of thing, and he was really keen for me to see the progress.

'But I feel shit,' I told him. 'Can't I just stay here?'

'Come on, Les,' he said. 'Just have a quick look.'

I forced myself out of bed – the boys were coming home tomorrow so I had to be up and about for that – and pulled on my dad's old silk dressing gown he'd given me. My ribs still felt sore and I moved carefully as I shuffled upstairs to the living room.

'You don't look very well,' Tim, the furniture-maker, said as I walked in.

'Oh, thanks,' I replied, trying to smile at him in spite of my pounding head. 'I think I must be getting a migraine or something. I don't know what it is. Or maybe it's the painkillers the hospital gave me.'

I managed to admire the shelves for about a minute before heading straight back to bed. I just wanted to get out of the room – I felt like I was going to throw up. I rubbed my neck to try and stretch it out as I lay back down. Soon I fell asleep. All I needed to do was rest and I'd be back to normal. The boys would be home for the weekend soon and I needed to be ready to see them.

'I'm going to get a takeaway,' Lee said, as he walked into the darkened bedroom at around 7 p.m. 'Do you want anything?'

'Just some Chinese,' I replied sleepily. I felt so rough, so sorry for myself.

Later I heard Lee's voice calling to me from down the corridor.

'It's here, Les. Do you want me to bring it in, or are you going to get up?'

'I can't eat anything,' I shouted back. 'I'm going to stay in bed.'

I just wanted to be left alone. I felt terrible. Earlier I'd tried to go to the loo but hadn't been able to pee. It felt like my bladder was full, but I couldn't release anything. Maybe it was because of the catheter I'd had put in briefly after the epidural. Maybe it was a urine infection. I didn't know anything except that I felt awful. I curled up into a ball once again and pulled the duvet over me. All I wanted was to sleep.

I opened my eyes. It was about 2 a.m. and the bedroom was half lit. Beside me, Lee was reading with his bedside lamp on and its light bathed his side of the room in a soft golden glow. My head felt heavy and painful. I felt sick and needed to go to the loo again, so I shifted on to my side and moved to get out of bed. As I flung off the bedclothes, I realised my legs felt numb. Nothing. Signals rushed from my brain to my nerves for action, but there was no response. It felt as if a lead weight was trapping my legs...

CHAPTER 12

Back to Life

Bright light.
Voices.

Freezing.
'I'm so cold.'
'OK, Leslie. We'll get you nice and warm in just a minute.'

'Is she OK? Is she awake?'
Lee.
Moving. On a trolley. Bright lights.

'One, two, three.'
Hands slide under the top of my back.
I am lifted on to a bed.
Cold water drips down my spine.
Blackness.

I'm looking down on a waiting room, a doctor's waiting room, where a woman sits. She looks up. Mum.

She doesn't notice me. She looks anxious, fretful. I know she is waiting for me and I am in another room with Dr Cantor, who is telling me about her heart condition.

Mum looks so sad as she sits and waits. I want to reach her, to hold her, but I can't. I need her with me. She's so close I can almost smell her.

She is so alone, so trusting, and I never told her what the doctor said about her heart. She sits and waits for me, but soon she will die.

I start to cry.

My eyes open and slide around the room where I am lying. Bright lights shine above me, and I can see a window high up on my left. I am lying on a bed in the middle of a large room with a door to the right. I look downwards to see tubes covering me – drips and needles running in and out of both hands. All I can hear is the hiss of an oxygen mask covering my mouth. I do not move a muscle.

'Where's Lee?' I whisper. My mouth feels dry, my voice cracked and thick.

'He's on his way.'

Soon his face appears above. Looking down at me, I can see how tired and worried he looks.

'Les?' Lee says as he bends down.

I remember the last time I saw his face – just before the operation. I've woken up. I have pulled through. I am alive.

My eyes flicker shut again.

A hand pulls back the mask covering my mouth and I can feel water trickling on to my tongue. I am so thirsty.

'Everything went well, Leslie. You've just got to rest now.'

I feel so drowsy. I can't keep my eyes open.

Finally the bustling in the room stopped and I woke up. It was quiet. Just Lee and me. Looking down at my legs, I remembered what had happened before the darkness came. I tried to move. Nothing. I was still dead from the chest down. The memory of how it had felt when the nurses lifted me – like ice-cold water trickling over my skin wherever their hands had touched me – hovered in the back of my mind.

'Hey,' Lee said, as his face appeared in the air above me. 'How are you feeling?'

I looked back at him. My mouth was so dry I could hardly swallow. I needed water and tried moving my hands to my mouth. A nurse moved my oxygen mask aside before dabbing a pink sponge on my lips. As Lee bent down to kiss me, all I could think was how bad my breath must smell.

It was two days since I had woken up at home unable to move and the neurosurgeon Professor van Dellen had operated on me to save my life. I'd been kept sedated on an intensive-care ward with other patients, but had now been transferred to a single room. Saline was keeping me hydrated, morphine was deadening the pain, and a massive intravenous dose of antibiotics was attacking the infection that had nearly killed me. I felt disorientated, spaced out, confused.

Soon Professor van Dellen walked into the room and stopped at the foot of my bed.

'Good afternoon, Mrs Chapman,' he said. 'I've heard you're waking up and I'd just like to take a look at you. Now, can you move your toes for me?'

I looked down at my feet, concentrating as hard as I could, asking them to move, to make a sign that I could control my limbs once more.

The big toe on my right foot flexed. Nothing else.

'I still feel numb,' I said, fear pinching inside me. 'Somewhere I can feel pins and needles, but that's all.'

'Well, you've undergone major surgery, Mrs Chapman,' the professor replied. 'An abscess had developed on your back and the infection from it entered your spinal column. I had to cut through two vertebrae to reach and drain it in order to stop the infection spreading further.

'The operation went well, but I'm afraid we believe the abscess caused some damage from the pressure it put on your nerves. At the moment we are unsure of its extent, but that is why you feel so numb.'

During a four-hour operation Professor van Dellen had made a 20-centimetre incision in my back to reach the abscess. Twenty-seven staples were needed to close up the incision, and I'd have died within two hours if I hadn't got to hospital because the infection would have reached my brain.

Now I was suffering from a condition called paraesthesia. Most people suffer from temporary paraesthesia at some time or another – it's more commonly known as pins and needles – and it's caused when pressure is put on a nerve by sleeping or sitting awkwardly. In those cases, it disappears as soon as the pressure is relieved. But I had chronic paraesthesia, caused by the nerve damage done to my spinal column as a result of the abscess, which was why the numbness wasn't going away.

I started crying.

'But how long will it be before I'm back to normal?'

The professor looked at me through his glasses. 'I don't want to get your hopes up,' he replied gravely. 'It's difficult to say. We don't know the extent of the damage yet. Only time will tell.'

I couldn't think. I felt woozy, and as the morphine pumped through my body, I could hardly concentrate on where I was, let alone how I'd come to be there.

Lee reached out to take my hand.

The nights were the worst. During the day I could hear the constant sound of voices and people moving in the corridor outside my room, but everything went silent at night. I couldn't understand how it could be so quiet when there were still the same number of patients and nurses.

It was really difficult to sleep. I could hear the constant hiss of the oxygen mask and had an ache deep in my tummy, like period pain. You can still feel even when you can't, if that makes sense. Jolts like electric currents ran up and down my legs, and occasionally one would jerk as if in response to some command I could never give it. I felt terrified. All I could do was lie there until I finally drifted off to sleep.

'I'm just going to do your obs, Leslie,' a nurse would say every so often when she came in to check me.

I would hear the beep of a blood-pressure machine or something.

'Would you like me to change your mask for a little tube that sits just inside your nose?'

'Yes,' I replied. Anything was better than that bloody hissing noise.

The nurse left and I lay there. From time to time I would hear a distant groan from another patient, but other than that it was quiet. I felt so alone, like the loneliness you experience in the middle of a winter's night when you're feeding your baby and the world is so still you feel as if you're the only two people in it. Except now I didn't have the comfort of Joe or Max lying against me.

Again and again my mind kept returning to my numb body and legs. I wanted to move my hips, twist my waist, lift my foot, anything, but however hard I thought about it, I couldn't. All my thoughts would rush to one spot, silently screaming at my ankle, my knee, my thigh to move, but nothing would happen.

The nurse came back to change my mask. Once again the light in the room dimmed, but I couldn't get comfortable. I was lying in a cot bed with bars at the sides and pillows all around me, but one was out of place and putting pressure on my back.

Eventually I drifted off again and into a dream coloured black, red and grey. Ravens were flying above me, and I could see a stone castle, blood, suits of armour with no one in them and rows of bracken standing in my way. I didn't know where I was going.

'I'm just having another look at you,' a voice said, and once again the light went on above me.

It was the same all night and I dozed on and off until it got lighter. Slowly the room went from black to grey and I looked around. I was already familiar with everything. The machines around my bed, the green walls, the sink that dripped and the door that stuck on the floor every time someone came in or out.

'Good morning,' a nurse said brightly, as she stood beside me with a colleague. 'It's time for your wash.'

The women turned me carefully on to my left side and started washing me. I stared out through the bars of the cot. My eyes drifted over the floor to a spot on the lino, a reddish-brown circle about 5 centimetres wide. Blood. It wasn't mine, and even though I watched them mop that spot every day for a week, it never disappeared. Soon I was turned on to the other side to face the sink – drip, drip, dripping – with a sign above saying, 'Now wash your hands,' and a set of diagrams about how to do it. I started crying.

'Thank you,' I said automatically when the nurses turned to leave.

Later Lee came in to see me with some things he thought I might need, but I felt too tired to talk much. All I could think about was moving. When you can't do it, you get obsessed by trying to and I kept pulling on the cot sides with all my strength until I finally managed to wedge my body with pillows to stop myself rolling back. It was exhausting, and as the hours passed, the small amount of energy I had left sapped away.

It must have been sometime in the afternoon when the door opened and I turned my head to see a nurse come in with my sister. Lee had gone by this time and we were alone as Debbie sat down on a chair at the foot of the bed. What was she doing here again?

'I've just taken about twenty minutes to get comfy,' I said

weakly, looking at her over my shoulder, 'so I won't move, if you don't mind.'

But she didn't say a word – just looked at me before suddenly getting up and rushing out of the room, muttering something under her breath. I could hear her sigh in frustration – almost as if she was annoyed. I didn't understand. What had I done wrong now? I felt too ill to care.

Later that day Lee returned with Joe and Max.

'Hello,' I said, trying to smile and make myself sound strong and happy as I lay looking up at them.

'Hi, Mum,' the boys said, staring down.

I've never been so glad of anything as when they bent down and I put my arms round them – thankful that I still had enough feeling to do it. I never wanted to let them go. I could see Joe was crying as he stood up and a lump rose in my throat. I hadn't seen him in tears for such a long time. Joe was 15, a young man, and he never cried in front of his mum any more.

I started crying too. I couldn't bear to see him like that. What was happening to me? My chest felt tight and sore, tears filled my eyes, and Joe, Max and Lee swam and flickered in front of me. We'd never seemed so far apart.

'Hello, Mrs Chapman,' a voice said. The faces of Mr Nott and Dr Cox – the surgeon and anaesthetist who'd treated my broken ribs the week before at Chelsea and Westminster Hospital – appeared beside me.

'We've come to talk to you about the infection you contracted,' Mr Nott said.

I stared up at him.

'A culture was taken when Professor van Dellen operated on you,' Mr Nott continued. 'It has now been tested and has shown that you have contracted MSSA – methicillin-sensitive staphylococcus aureus.'

I had no idea what he was talking about.

'Staphylococcus aureus is a very common bug. You may have heard of MRSA, which is an infection that can be very dangerous because it is resistant to antibiotics,' Mr Nott continued. 'But you're lucky because MSSA *is* sensitive to antibiotics, which you are now being given to fight it.'

'How long will it be before I'm back to normal?' I asked. It was the only question that had gone round and round in my mind since Professor van Dellen told me my spine had been damaged. What did that mean? How long would it take to heal? I'd kept asking, but everyone seemed to be hedging their bets and no one would give me a straight answer.

'I think you'll be here for a while, but I'd say you will be up in between eight to nine weeks,' Mr Nott said as he looked at me.

Eight weeks? I thought, panic filling me. Eight weeks? But what about the boys? What about work? I'm supposed to be going to perform at the Edinburgh Festival. I can't lie here for eight whole weeks.

Once again I started crying.

The information meant nothing to me. I couldn't make sense of anything. Lee could explain it to me. What was MSSA? I didn't really care, to be honest – all I could think was that it would be weeks before I was back to normal.

I woke from another dream. I'd been walking through the corridors of the London Underground with Joe, who was really little, about five. Something had happened, a fire had broken out, and everyone was panicking as they rushed to escape. I realised the escalators weren't working as the crowds ran towards them and so pulled Joe with me towards a lift. The doors opened and people ran inside. I knew we both wouldn't fit, so I pushed Joe in, wedging his tiny body among the legs. Then the doors closed and I stood standing in the crowd as panic filled me again. Joe was alone. He was only tiny. I'd left him with strangers. He'd walk outside and I'd lose him. I threw myself at the doors, trying to open them, to get inside the lift and reach my son, but however hard I pulled or pushed, they stayed shut. Using all my strength, I tried again and again to pull the huge metal doors apart, but they wouldn't move. I had to get to Joe. I had to reach my son.

I woke up. My heart was beating. All around me was silent. Staring up at the ceiling, I realised the dull ache I'd had in my stomach for a couple of days was getting painful. I pressed the call button beside my bed and the night nurse came in. She smelt of cigarettes.

'I'm in real pain,' I said. 'I think it's wind. It really hurts.'

'Right,' she replied. 'Well, I'll have to get the on-call doctor to come and see you.'

I'd been having problems with trapped wind for a couple of days and couldn't do anything about it. It made the boys laugh when it finally released itself in a most unladylike fashion, but almost upset me because I had no idea when it was coming and there was nothing I could do to stop it. I couldn't feel a thing, and it was yet another reminder of what had happened. I couldn't even tell what was happening inside my own body any more – let alone move it. Hooked up to drips and catheters, I felt like a useless shell.

Soon a large lady doctor appeared in the room.

'Somehow I knew I wasn't going to get any sleep,' she sighed to the nurse, as she walked over to the bed.

I felt awful. I'd woken her up because of bloody wind. She felt my stomach before telling me she was going to put a pipe down my nose into my throat. I lay still as the nurse started helping her thread it inside. It was really painful – I could feel the tube crawling up my nose before it hit the back of my throat and made me gag. I spat it back up.

'We'll have to have another go,' the doctor said, and the whole process started again.

I told myself to stay calm as once again I felt the tube running up my nose. All I really wanted to do was get off the bed, run, be able to just sodding fart without all this. Panic rose up inside me and I gagged once more. The process started for a third time. Maybe this was it. My organs were giving up. If I couldn't feel anything on the outside, then how could everything be working as normal on the inside? I felt my pulse racing.

'We'll give her an anti-spasmodic,' the doctor said after the third unsuccessful attempt to get the tube inside me.

'OK,' the nurse replied, and soon returned to give me an injection.

I looked up at her, trying not to panic but still fearful about what was happening. What is it about the middle of the night that allows the bogeymen you've shut in the closet all day to jump out and scare you? It's like all your good work at keeping fears at bay is undone.

'I don't want to die,' I blurted out, trying not to cry.

'Of course you're not going to,' the nurse snapped, before turning to leave.

I was alone again.

Time gets broken when you're on morphine – hours pass in minutes, days in hours, as your mind wanders from one thing to another. It's like being a goldfish because your memory span is reduced to about 30 seconds. Again and again, I would wander off into the corners of my mind, only to find myself wondering what I'd just been thinking about. Snatches of information whirred around my brain. I slept fitfully, unable to keep my eyes open for any length of time and dipping in and out of dreams – convinced the ravens I was seeing in them meant death. The only thing clear in my mind was the fear about not being able to move. Already I could see differences in my body – in just a few days my muscles had started to waste and I'd lost a stone in weight. With no food, only water to drink and absolutely no movement, it's scary how quickly your body deteriorates.

As I woke up to each new day, I found myself willing it to end from the moment my eyes opened. All I could think was that in eight weeks I'd be OK again so each day that passed brought me closer to being well. Time was only broken by a visit from Lee or Professor van Dellen. The neurosurgeon came like clockwork to see if my movement had improved. Could I flex my ankle? Move my knee? Feel a scratch on the sole of my foot? The answer was always no and I cried each time I saw him. There were tiny improvements as the days went by – I was beginning to be able to flex my feet a few centimetres, for instance – but we both knew that centimetres don't make a step, a walk or a run, and it seemed like every day it was bad news. However gently the professor tried to break it, his delivery was necessarily matter-of-fact.

The clock seemed to slow down as everything that had happened began to hit me and I started crying all the time. Worries crowded into my brain. When would my feeling start coming back? Would I recognise the signs that it was? How would the boys and Lee cope without me for two months?

There were so many reasons for those tears. Firstly, I felt sorry for myself – sorry I had to lie in bed and couldn't be at home doing what I wanted to do. There was so much to sort out at the flat, and the boys would be home for the summer holidays soon. I needed to be there. Then there was the part of me that cried because I knew how lucky I was to be alive. I'd come so close to dying and the thought scared me. What would the boys have done without me? How could I be so fragile? Who'd have looked after Dad? And finally I cried because I'd lost control not just of my body but my life – even if it was for just a few weeks. I'd always been in charge, the one who ran the ship, and now I was unable to move while nurses checked tubes, doctors inspected reflexes, and cleaners mopped around the blood spot on the floor. It felt at times as if all anyone did was prod me like a piece of meat or stick needles into me. In fact, they took so much blood that my veins eventually collapsed – I felt like a pincushion and soon started dreading the arrival of the little Chinese phlebotomist who came to 'spear' me again and again.

He was just one of the people who pissed me off – the start of a long list as my temper ran short and anger pushed up inside me. I'd lie in bed seething while they rushed in and out of my room so quickly that I'd hardly be able to make them out, or talked to me from a place where I couldn't see them. Stupid things could make me furious, like not turning off the tap properly, leaving the door to stick on the floor where it always did or throwing a paper towel halfway into the pedal bin. All I wanted to do was jump out of bed and turn off the tap, close the door or sort out the bin, and I couldn't.

Underneath all the tears, frustration and anger, there was one feeling that remained – fear. How would I get out if there was a fire? Would everyone leave and forget me? What would I do if someone came into the room and attacked me? As anxiety built up, my heart would beat and I'd reach down to touch my legs. They were still so numb and dead – like your fingers on a cold day when you're trying to undo your buttons but can't make them work properly. On some distant level, you know they're there, but you can't control them. That's how my lower body and legs felt, and it was almost as if they weren't mine any more.

'I think you're ready to go up,' the professor finally told me, after seven long days in that horrible room. I was going to be moved up to Charing Cross's private wing on the 15th floor to carry on recuperating. 'We're happy with the way you're responding to the antibiotics.'

I looked at him. The professor's straight-talking might really get me down if I wasn't careful, but I wouldn't let it. Eight weeks. That's all it would be. That's what Mr Nott had told me and that's what it would take.

CHAPTER 13

Reality Bites

'Here you are – your new home,' the porter said.

All I could see were huge windows and blue sky – the first I'd seen since arriving at Charing Cross – as I was lifted off a trolley and on to a bed.

'Hello, Leslie,' a cheery voice said, and a nurse stepped into view. 'I'm Cherry.'

I almost gasped. She looked so like my mum – same tight, curly hair, same glasses. Maybe it was a sign.

Looking up, I saw a metal bar above me, and when I was finally propped up on pillows, a few more inches of the view out of the windows at the foot of my bed. The River Thames snaked away in front of me and I could just make out some treetops and the domes of the Harrods' depository in the distance. After the room downstairs, it was like I'd stepped into the Ritz.

'I'm going to leave you to settle in a bit,' Cherry said, as she put the phone and call button next to me.

I lay back my head and looked at the TV in the corner. A girl with red hair and pale skin, looking beautiful but scared as she stood in a tutu, was on the screen. *The Red Shoes*. I'd loved the film as a kid and had dreamed of being a ballerina when I watched Moira Shearer dance. But I'd also never forgotten the terrible ending, when her red ballet shoes had thrown her under the path of a train. She would never dance again.

I pushed the sadness out of my mind. I'd left the frightening room downstairs at last and was going to enjoy feeling far more comfortable in my new one. Warm and light, there was a carpet on the floor, nice curtains, a mirror and a wardrobe – just like a hotel room.

When a little man in a bowtie and waistcoat appeared with a chicken sandwich, I thought I'd hit the jackpot. It was the first thing I'd eaten in a week and it tasted delicious. The intensive-care diet might be a good way to lose weight, but I wouldn't recommend it.

Professor van Dellen could see the change when he came to visit that afternoon. 'You seem a lot more comfortable,' he said.

'I am, thank you,' I replied chirpily.

'Well, let's have a look at you. Can you move your toes for me?'

I stared down at my feet and flexed my right big toe. I had no idea why, but it always went first and then the left would follow. I willed my toes to separate and they flickered with movement but no more.

'Good, good,' the professor told me, then put his hand over the top of my feet. 'Now, can you resist against my hands?'

I couldn't feel anything, had no idea what was up, down or sideways, but slowly, slowly, my feet flexed upwards a few centimetres. It's odd, because you never think about how you actually move when you can do it – it just happens – but you think about it all the time when you can't, and however much your brain screams, your body simply ignores you.

The professor went through all the usual questions before fixing me with a serious look. 'Leslie, I wanted to speak properly to you now that you are more lucid,' he said. 'I feel it is important for you to understand how serious your condition is and I'm not going to get anyone's hopes up.'

'All right, then,' I replied slowly. Here we go.

'As you know, you've had a very serious operation on your

spine,' the professor continued, 'but I want to explain how serious.

'The spine is made up of vertebrae and a spinal cord. The vertebrae are the bones that protect your spinal cord, which is an extension of the central nervous system from your brain responsible for sending messages to the rest of your body.

'The abscess you had was on your spinal cord, so to reach it, I had to drill through two vertebrae and remove bone. After I had drained the abscess, I pulled muscle back over your spinal cord to protect it in the future. That was a very serious procedure and will take some time to recover from.

'In addition to all that, the abscess also caused nerve damage because of the pressure it created. In that area, there is a twenty-five per cent compression of your spine. In time we will be able to do a scan which will tell us how permanent that damage is.

'In the meantime, it is important you understand that your injury will take considerable time to heal and your recovery will involve a lot of physiotherapy and rehabilitation.'

I stared up at the professor. What was he talking about?

'But what about eight weeks? I was told I'd be OK again in eight weeks,' I said, feeling panic tighten my chest.

'Leslie, I have to tell you that your recovery is going to take a lot longer than that,' the professor replied. 'You have significant spinal damage and that is very serious.'

I didn't understand what he was saying. All I cared about was when I'd be well again.

'But how long will it take?' I asked, feeling like I was going to start crying yet again.

'Well, that is up to you and how your body recovers,' the professor said. 'But your nerves have been seriously damaged and they will have to grow back. Nerve regeneration is very slow.'

'What do you mean?' I asked. 'Months?'

The professor said nothing.

'Years?'

'Yes,' he replied bluntly.

'But Mr Nott told me I'd be OK again in eight weeks,' I gasped, as I started sobbing.

I couldn't believe what I was hearing. How could this be?

'Well, I'm afraid your condition is very serious and I think your recovery will need a lot more time than that.'

I couldn't say a word. Tears ran down my face and the professor silently left the room. Cherry came in.

'Leslie, I know that's not the news you wanted to hear, but people do amazing things,' she said quietly as she took my hand. 'I've seen it many times during my years as a nurse, and you have to think positively. You've got to believe, stay strong. You can take two patients and the one with belief will do amazing things. I've seen it happen.'

I stared numbly at her. I couldn't believe what I was hearing. Years? How could I be like this for years?

Trembling, I picked up the phone to Lee. He would explain this to me. I was going to be fine in a few weeks. He'd sort it out.

'Professor van Dellen's been in,' I sobbed, the words rushing out of my mouth. 'He said my recovery is going to take longer than eight weeks. It might take years. I don't understand. What am I going to do?'

'I'm on my way in. I'm nearly at the hospital,' Lee replied. 'Just wait for me.'

He arrived within minutes and I could see how angry he was when he walked in.

'That's the last thing you needed to hear,' he said. 'They should have talked to me first before getting you all upset. I'm going to speak to Professor van Dellen.'

'No, don't do that,' I told him. 'He was just doing his job, being upfront. But what does he mean, years?'

Lee sat down on the bed and started hugging me. 'You're going to do this – we're going to do this,' he said quietly. Then he moved away and looked at me. 'Don't worry about any-thing at home, Les. You've just got to concentrate on getting focused and getting better, because you are going to get better.'

Crying, I gulped in air.

'But years? How can he say that it will take years?'

'Look at me, Leslie,' Lee said. 'Look at me.'

I turned my head and met his eyes.

'You must listen to me. This is really important. You are going to get better and you must believe that. We are going to do this together. All we need is each other.'

Lee reached forward and cuddled me again. I held on to him, never wanting him to let me go. This wasn't just a tem-porary thing. It might take for ever, and who could say if he'd be able to wait that long?

What is it about bad things? They're a bit like buses – they never arrive alone. Within a couple of days of seeing Professor van Dellen, Lee arrived in my room once again with a serious look on his face.

'What's wrong?' I asked.

'Your sister, that's what's wrong,' he exploded. 'She's sold a fucking story about us to a Sunday newspaper. I've just heard.'

'But about what?'

'I don't know, but we'll find out. She's sworn an affidavit and it's being printed tomorrow.'

I felt sick as I picked up the phone to Dad – maybe he would know more. I hadn't seen him, but we'd spoken on the phone now that I was upstairs.

'We've just got some weird news,' I told him in a rush. 'Has Debbie been in touch?'

'No,' he replied.

'Well, apparently she's doing a story on us. You've got to phone her, Dad. Tell her to stop. Why is she doing this?

You've got to call her. I don't understand why she's doing this. I haven't seen her properly for months.'

'Oh, Leslie, you know your sister.'

'But you don't understand, Dad,' I persisted. 'It must be bad, otherwise they wouldn't print it. She came in last week and left without saying much at all. I don't know what she's up to, but whatever it is won't be good.'

That turned out to be the understatement of the century. The next day an article appeared headlined 'Why I fear for my sister Leslie Ash's life unless she leaves Lee' in which Debbie described the 'denial' I was in about supposed violence in my marriage. She also talked about the row she'd had with Lee after her birthday night out – adding in few small extra 'details', such as him throwing her across the table, hitting me about the head and face, and spitting at her.

On the same day a former head of security at Teatro called Roland Ball did a story in another Sunday newspaper. It was more of the same and the rival papers had obviously worked together to maximise the impact. Apparently he'd seen Lee, who's 6 foot 4 inches, punch 5 foot 5 inch me in the face so hard in the Teatro loos that I'd fallen to the floor. Funny that no one else in a bar packed with people had seen anything out of the ordinary when I came out of the loo, or that I hadn't been injured by a huge smack in the face. A photo of that would surely have made the newspapers at the time.

In fact, Lee did hit someone that night, but it wasn't me – it was Roland himself. I'd been chatting in the loos with a friend when Lee had come in annoyed about something and we'd started having an argument.

'Come on, mate, come back and have a drink,' Roland said as he walked in on our row.

He was on a night off and had been drinking in the bar. Suddenly he grabbed Lee from behind round the waist before pushing him towards the basins. Instinctively Lee shoved Roland away to free himself from his grip and that should have been it – Lee and I would have carried on our noisy row and Roland would have backed off. Unfortunately Roland lost his footing and smashed his head on the door frame of the toilet as he fell. It was awful. Blood was pouring from a gash on his forehead and we had to get an ambulance. Lee felt terrible that he'd hurt him – even if it was by mistake.

The West End is a small place though, things get twisted as they're passed on from one person to another, and word eventually got round that Lee had supposedly taken on Roland and won, rather than it being an accident. A few months later he left Teatro and Lee didn't see him until just before the article came out.

What's the truth behind those articles? Lee and I have tempers, we argue, we fall out, we've had some really bad times, we are far from perfect and neither is our relationship. We break up, make up and break up again, but just three words sum up those stories: load of bollocks.

I couldn't stop crying. During the first week in hospital I'd been too out of it, too ill, too disorientated to really understand what was happening, but I suddenly gave up after Debbie's story. How could she have done it? She might have said she'd sold the story out of concern for me, but I believed it was for her own benefit. She'd never said a word that suggested she thought Lee could hurt me, so where had all this come from? The more I thought about it, the more anxious I became. What was wrong with her? What else was she going to do? On some level, I'd been able to understand all the stories about my lips because I'd taken the decision to have them done. But I just couldn't take the fact that my marriage was again being dragged through the papers.

I got more and more worried about the effect it was having on Lee, the boys and my dad. I could see that Lee wasn't only furious but also really upset. He couldn't settle down when he came to see me, was up and down, on and off his phone to lawyers like a yo-yo, and I didn't know what I was going to say to Joe and Max. What would be happening at school? How could they possibly understand what their aunt had done?

'Why is she doing this, Mum?' Joe said to me on his next visit. 'I remember that night because I could hear Debbie shouting when I was in bed and the next morning she was talking to Dad like normal.'

'I don't understand it either, Joe. I'm just so sorry it's happened.'

'But it's like me doing a story on Max.'

'I know, but I don't want you to worry about it,' I told him. 'Maybe I've done something to really upset her. I don't know, but all that's important to me is that nothing like this ever happens between you and Max.'

'Of course it won't,' he said.

I couldn't stop the tears. I sobbed and sobbed in those first few days upstairs at Charing Cross. Lee decided not to tell me anything else about what was going on in the papers. In the months that followed he remained silent as story after story attacked him. But, even so, when he and the boys arrived, when he and the boys left, during all the long hours while I was lying alone in bed, I cried and cried. Debbie and the chat I'd had with Professor van Dellen had taken all the fight out of me and I felt too weak to even try to stop my tears.

Again and again my mind returned to my sister. I thought back through our life together – our childhood in Streatham, the bedroom we'd shared in Clapham. As I searched through the years, I gradually realised how little I'd actually known her. Debbie had left home the first chance she got, worked away a lot, kept her cards close to her chest – I'd spent my whole life assuming we had a bond and it shocked me to realise that the relationship I believed had existed never actually had.

I asked myself how many others were like that and felt fear rise up inside me as I thought of Lee. Did he really not mind me being like this? He'd done nothing but be there for me since the accident, but I couldn't forget how distant we'd been at times before it. Was our love strong enough to survive? What if I never walked again? Could Lee push me around in a wheelchair for the rest of my life?

I got increasingly anxious as I kept thinking about what Professor van Dellen had told me. Was he really right, or was he just being negative? How could I be like this for years? What about the boys? What about Lee? What about work? When the worries got too much, I tried to push them down, but my body wouldn't let me forget and my heart would pound as irrational thoughts once again flooded into my head. Even the tiniest thing could end up scaring me – like the night I decided to visualise the damage the abscess had done to my spine. I thought it might help calm me down because I'd heard how beneficial visualisation could be to healing. But the moment I started thinking about my nerves, I started thinking about my central nervous system and then wondered whether anything else could be affected.

In a panic, I pressed my call button and the night nurse arrived.

'Could I go blind?' I cried. 'I can't go blind. I'd never see Joe and Max again.'

'What?' she replied gently, switching on the light over my bed. 'Get your breath back, Leslie. What's wrong?'

'Well, I've had an injury which has damaged my nerves, so does that mean the damage could reach my brain and I could go blind?' I said in a rush.

'No,' she replied softly. 'The damage is in your back. Nothing to do with your eyes. You'll be fine. Talk to Professor van Dellen in the morning and he'll explain.'

The nurse stayed and talked to me until the sleeping tablet kicked in and I became drowsy. It turned out her other job was catering at the studio where we did the Homebase ads. Small world, isn't it? Finally I dropped off.

The professor didn't say anything about the previous night

when he came to see me the next morning and ran his usual examinations – toes up, toes down, knees up, knees down – but he turned towards me with a smile just as he was leaving.

'By the way, you're not going to go blind,' he said with a chuckle.

I couldn't see the funny side at all and still the tears carried on falling. When I was visited a few days later by our family GP, Dr Cantor, I don't think he was prepared for the change in me.

'You can't keep crying like this,' he told me. 'I'm going to talk to your neurologist and get you put on to antidepressants. I think they'll help.'

Soon I was started on the medication and blackness washed over me.

Every bodily function you can think of was controlled by muscles that I now couldn't feel. I was 44 and someone had to clean me. The first time this happened, Lee was visiting and I was so embarrassed.

'Do you want to go out?' I asked, looking up at him. Was this how it was going to be for us from now on?

'No, I'll stay,' he replied.

'But I don't want you to see me like this.'

'Les, it's fine. Really it is. It's absolutely fine.'

He didn't leave the room that day or in the future. After that I started wearing an oversized nappy and tried to hold on to what little dignity I had left. I looked like a massive baby, but I felt more comfortable. Even so, it's amazing how low you can go.

Now the emergency was over and life was beginning again, I was starting to realise why Professor van Dellen had said what he had and to understand the grim details of what my condition really involved. Until then I'd been lying still – not testing my body in any way – and being unable to move was like an abstract thought rather than a real thing. When my physiotherapy started, though, it really hit me just what it all meant. My physio, Ruth, was in her mid-twenties and had long, red hair and a bright smile.

'We'll start you off very gently,' she said as she stood beside my bed for the first time. 'The idea is to start getting you moving and try to help build up your muscles again.

'Muscle wastage happens very quickly and it can take a long time to rebuild, so we need to start work as soon as possible. I'm going to show you exercises you can do any time to keep your legs moving because there is a danger that blood clots could form. It's things like wiggling your toes, trying to separate them, rotating your ankle.'

Fear filled me. I couldn't even scrunch up my toes. I had to be pulled and pushed into position like a dead weight while nurses changed my nappy, checked my catheter, topped up my morphine. How was I going to do all those things? I calmed down when she told me we'd start slowly. We did start slowly, but we progressed very swiftly. Ruth came to see me every day without fail and soon announced I wasn't just going to wiggle my toes a bit – it was time for me to sit up.

She propped me up with pillows and, with her arms holding me, moved my legs over the edge of the bed. Then she raised me into a sitting position, supporting my back, and handed me the monkey bar that I'd seen hanging above my bed on my first day upstairs. One hand gripping the cold metal, the other on the bed, and with Ruth still holding me, I was upright. As soon as she let go, however, my body slumped down. I felt like a Weeble who was about to wobble and then fall over. Just like a baby, I was unable to control myself and weaved around unsteadily. My core muscles – the ones that keep you upright – were completely asleep, and because I couldn't feel my bottom, there was no connection between me and the bed. If I hadn't been able to see that I was sitting, I'd have said I was floating.

I gasped as pain flooded into my body. 'No, no, stop,' I pleaded with Ruth.

I couldn't do it, couldn't stay up alone. I was in agony. Until then morphine had kept everything nicely blurred while I lay in bed, but now I could feel tugging in the muscles round the incision in my back, aching in my ribs, which hadn't yet healed, and pain like an iron grip round my ribcage where the paraesthesia began. It was like a vice squeezing so hard it would break me in two.

'Please stop,' I cried, as I started sobbing.

'Just a little longer, Leslie,' Ruth told me. 'You're doing so well.'

I felt dizzy and sick as I sat on the edge of the bed, willing her to let me lie down again. All I wanted was to stop. I must have managed about 30 seconds, although every one seemed like an hour.

There was no chance of any let up, though, and Ruth was back the next day to get me sitting up again. It was no better, but still she persevered and arrived within a couple of days with Cherry and a canvas hoist.

'Today we're going to get you into a chair,' Ruth said. 'We've got to get the strength back into your muscles and the only way we can do that is by using them. Your muscles have a memory and you've got to remind them of how to work by using them.'

The hoist was a triangle of fabric that went under my bottom before the three sides were hooked on to a lever overhead. It was attached to a mini crane, which was going to pull me up and move me across to a chair positioned next to the window a couple of metres away.

Slowly, slowly, Cherry and Ruth slipped the canvas under my bottom as I lay on the bed – checking all the time that I wasn't uncomfortable or hurting anything – looped the sides of the fabric on to the crane and started elevating me. Slumped down and hooked up to morphine, antibiotics and a catheter, I looked like a critically ill sack of potatoes and crumpled the moment the hoist slackened when I touched the chair. I felt like you do when you get off a boat that's been rocking, as if the room was weaving around me and the chair was made of Plasticine. But they weren't. It was me who was unstable, me who was rocking, me who was unable to hold myself either straight or still. The vice closed round my ribcage and I felt sick as Ruth and Cherry continued to smile encouragingly.

'Well done, Leslie, well done,' Cherry said softly.

She'd better watch out. Any second now I was going to vomit on her shoes from pain. What kind of sadists were these people? The good kind, of course, but at that moment I wasn't so sure.

'Put me back into bed,' I moaned, and eventually they gave in.

Every step into my new life was a painful one because my sleeping body just didn't listen. There were tiny improvements as the days passed – for instance, I was starting to feel pins and needles in the bottom of my legs where once there was only numbness – but it was hard making myself put my fingers back into the fire every day during physio when I knew how painful it would be. A shot of painkiller might have helped me get out of bed, but there was also a big part of me that just didn't understand why it was all so difficult. Nothing could have prepared me for it. Deep down, I still believed that I wouldn't have to do much and one morning I'd just wake up and – pop! – everything would be back to normal. Ruth seemed determined to reintroduce normal life, but I didn't want to be forced to do stuff that hurt so much. Life wasn't normal. Someone must have made a mistake. My recovery wasn't going to take years. All these people just needed to leave me alone and my body would wake up on its own.

'We are soon going to have to do another MRI scan on you so I can have a look at exactly what is happening to your spine,' my neurologist, Dr Shakir, told me during his visit one day. 'But what we do know at the moment is that you have a compression on the spine, which means it is bruised. We also know that your nerves have been damaged in the area governing proprioception. Do you know what that is?'

Apparently, we have more than just the five senses we all know of. For instance, we also have thermoception, which governs our sense of heat, and proprioception. It's the sense that tells you where your body is in relation to the space around you and how much effort you need to use to move it. For instance, it is because of proprioception that we can walk in complete darkness without losing our balance, or stay steady if we close our eyes when standing up. It's what tells us internally – and instinctively – where we are and helps us keep upright.

'But when are my nerves going to get better – how long will they take to regrow?' I replied, after I'd listened to Dr Shakir.

'Mrs Chapman, nerves regenerate at the rate of a millimetre a day and that is why your recovery will take time,' he told me, then paused. 'But I also believe that some of the damage to your spine will be permanent.'

I looked at Dr Shakir – first weeks, then years and now permanent? Every time I thought I understood what was happening, someone gave me a new bit of information that blew it all apart. What was he talking about?

'You must remember that the body has an amazing way of compensating,' Dr Shakir continued. 'One part will start working harder to make up for another that has been damaged.'

My head certainly was – it felt like it was going to explode.

'Essentially, Leslie, we don't know how much you will be affected, because things are still at an early stage and nothing is certain.'

His voice blended into the background. All I wanted was a fact, a full stop.

'Until you show more signs of improvement, then we really are in the first stages of your recovery. We just need to wait for your body to start repairing itself and go from there. But you must be aware that it is very possible you could end up being in a wheelchair or having to use crutches for the rest of your life.'

I looked out at the sunny world beyond my hospital windows, unable to take in what he was saying. I'd never even considered not getting back to 100 per cent. It hadn't even crossed my mind. Fine, I knew it might take a while, but I'd be back to the old Leslie in time, wouldn't I?

Ever since waking up I'd been asking people to tell me where the finishing line of all this was and now I knew why they hadn't. I had so far to go they couldn't even tell me where that line was – let alone when I'd reach it. I couldn't even sit up on my own, let alone walk, and it wasn't going to take weeks or months to get better, but years and maybe never. I could end up in a wheelchair. That's what Dr Shakir had said. As I looked out of the window, I remembered the scene in *The Secret Garden* where the little boy gets up from his wheelchair and everyone gasps in amazement. Such a fucking lie.

CHAPTER 14

The Hard Work Starts

All I remember are hot, sunny days as May got underway and I lay in bed listening to the sounds of traffic, voices, building work and sirens filter up from the street below. Life was so close I could hear it going on at breakneck speed, but the silence in my room at Charing Cross Hospital was broken only by the sound of an electric fan. I could see it all in my head – Lee walking Charlie, the boys standing on a cricket pitch, the gardeners on nearby Royal Hospital Road getting ready for the Chelsea Flower Show – and I longed for the busy, messy days I could hear other people having when someone shouted or a horn blared. Instead, my life had slowed down to the kind of predictable routine it hadn't had since Joe and Max were babies.

My day started at 7 a.m. with pain medication, before a cup of tea and a bowl of cereal arrived. Then the slow process of getting dressed started. Lee popped in at around 9.30 a.m., and I did physio at 11 a.m. For lunch, I'd eat something light like fish because it's hard to digest heavy foods when you're on morphine, and Lee would arrive for another visit. Afterwards the long afternoon stretched ahead of me – sometimes I'd watch TV or see a visitor, but mostly I just lay there. I didn't want to pick up a book or magazine, be in anyone else's world. I was so far from fashion, and, anyway, the morphine made it hard to concentrate. Then, at around 6 p.m., I'd have a sandwich and Lee would come in for his third and final visit of the day. Three hours later the night staff would offer me tea, cocoa or biscuits before handing me my sleeping tablet – that ever-loving pill which brought each day to an end.

I felt more and more lonely as I lay in bed listening to the sounds of life carrying on without me. With the news that the damage to my back might be permanent, I felt as if mine had suddenly stopped. I felt trapped like an insect in amber, while everyone else's life hurtled along. People even seemed to move more quickly than usual and Lee would arrive like a whirlwind, smelling of the outdoors, pacing up and down with his mobile constantly bleeping as he chatted about his news, the people who sent their love, the latest happening at Teatro. I was always pleased to see him, of course, just as I welcomed a visit from Marti or another friend, the boys or Michele, but it was sometimes almost too much.

'How was physio today?' Lee would ask brightly.

I'd describe the 2 millimetres of progress I'd made.

'That's great, Les, that's great,' he'd reply cheerfully. 'You're doing so well. You've just got to keep going. You've come so far already. Just keep focused.'

Mostly I agreed with him, but when doubt crept into my voice, he'd sit down on the edge of the bed and look at me.

'You will get better, you know,' he'd say. 'I know you will.'

I lost count of the mornings when I woke up thinking that I just couldn't do it that day. Then the nurses would arrive and I'd tell myself they had other people to see, other patients to get out of bed and so I'd better get a move on.

Coming off morphine during my second week upstairs, though, only made things worse. In one way, it was good because the powerful drug deadens both your brain and body and I'd kept wondering where I'd ever find the strength to keep going. But it also meant I was in pretty much constant pain as thoughts tumbled through my mind about what the doctors had told me.

'You'll recover,' they whirred. 'You'll walk again. They've got it wrong. You've got to stay strong, keep going. You'll prove the doctors wrong.'

'That can't be right,' another voice said. 'They know what they're saying, and look at how far you've got to go. Will you ever make love again? Ever step on to a stage? I don't think so. You'll be useless for ever. Just give up. You'll never dance, wear high heels or run again.'

Even the flowers and cards that filled my room got me thinking. Everyone – from school friends like Tracey Ullman and acting friends like Joanna Taylor and Beryl Vertue to members of the public I'd never met – had been so kind. They'd all thought about me, were wishing me good things, and I'd been so forgetful with so many of them. I'd always moved on – from school to school, job to job, left friends behind and made new ones – ignoring the fact that it only takes two minutes to pick up the phone and telling myself I only needed my family. Look how that had turned out. It was small-minded of me and I felt humbled by how kind so many people were.

Cherry and the other lovely nurses were very good to me and constantly there to stop me from dwelling on things too much, while Ruth was also determined to help me meet the tiny goals she set during our half-hour sessions each day. For instance, lying in bed being washed by nurses isn't exactly my thing and the next big hurdle was getting me into the bath. Until then, even my hair had been washed by slipping a plastic tray under my head and rinsing it with water, which then drained into a bucket below. Now it was time for me to start washing myself. After being hoisted on to a commode and wheeled into the bathroom, I was lifted into a metal chair, which lowered me into the bath to waist level.

It felt so strange. You know how your hands feel when they

go numb from cold and you put them into hot water? That's what it felt like from my chest down. On some level, I could feel the water's heat, but it was like I was wearing trousers. I had no idea if it was too hot or cold, and I could once again feel little electric currents throbbing in my legs as my whole body twisted with pain. It was like a huge Chinese burn and each movement hurt me – lifting my arms to wash myself, clasping my hands round my thigh and pulling up my leg to wash my feet. The muscles pulled across my scar, the vertebrae that had been cut into ached, and the damaged nerves tore around my ribcage. It was exhausting. Each time physio had ended, I'd feel weak and tearful as the tiny bits of energy left in my body drained away. The bath, though, was something else and I kept having to stop to recover. I'd lather myself, sit for a while, take the soap off, sit for a while and start on another job. The minutes crawled by as I washed and shampooed my hair. Something so simple, that I'd once been able to do in a few minutes, now took about three-quarters of an hour.

Eventually I was lifted out of the bath and covered in towels by the nurses before being taken back to my room, where I was put on to another towel on the bed. I started moisturising my skin for the first time since my accident. My body looked so strange – pale, weak, skinny, lifeless – and everything was hairy – my legs and armpits were covered in thick stubble that I'd never in a million years have allowed to grow before the accident. But I felt too ill to even think about it. Make-up and shaving seemed so far away, and I hadn't even bothered to ask Lee to get me some of my own nightclothes. I just wanted to be in a hospital gown. I didn't want to wear pyjamas, for everything to be normal, because it wasn't.

I was exhausted by the time I was finally put back into bed an hour and a half after getting out. But I also felt relieved to be clean again and happy that for the first time I'd done something for myself without the help of the nurses. Maybe somewhere there was a spark of hope. Maybe it wasn't all doom and gloom. If I was able to have a bath within a week, then who knows what I could achieve. I felt like a child who'd got a gold star at school.

'Guess what I've done?' I told Professor van Dellen excitedly when he arrived to see me – if I'd been able to ask for a drum roll and an 'Aaaah' from the crowd, then I would have. 'I've had a bath.' I looked at him expectantly.

'That's good news, Leslie,' he replied. 'Every bit of progress you make is part of your recovery. But you must remember there's still a long way to go.'

I felt crushed and disappointment filled me. Why wasn't he praising me? Encouraging me? Why was he always so negative? Deep down, I still wondered if the doctors were just being too pessimistic.

I was still numb from the chest down, but tiny areas of feeling were starting to appear as the days turned into weeks. By 'feeling', I mean lots of jerking, little patchy areas of sensitivity – a thumbnail-size area on my thigh, for instance – and pins and needles. I could trace the feeling via the goose bumps because wherever they were meant my nerves were still working on some level and where the skin was smooth meant there was no sensation.

Ruth continued to work with me every day: pulling in my turned-out feet to straighten them; flexing and pointing my toes; sliding my lifeless legs up the bed; bending my knees before my feet slipped down the second she let go because I had no grip in them. After she left, I'd swear at my lifeless body as I pulled myself up again and again on the monkey bars. But I didn't put my heart into the exercises. Either the doctors were right and I was going to end up in a wheelchair or they were wrong, my feeling would return and I'd be fine again. Either way, what was the point? Each day Professor van Dellen came to see me and it seemed as if

I'd never be able to pass the tests he set.

Even so, Ruth wouldn't let me give up, however much I wanted to, and gradually I gained enough upper-body strength to sit for longer in the chair and was soon having lunch in it every day. I couldn't feel the muscles, but had now strengthened them enough by using them to be able to support myself a little better. It was painful, though, because I was still very unsteady and all my effort went through my arms and intercostal muscles when I pulled up on the monkey bar or used my hands to hold myself up. Your intercostals are the muscles that run between your ribs and under your shoulder blades. They run parallel with the site of the damage to my spine and so it was painful to use them, but I had to. After about a week upstairs, Ruth decided that it was time to start putting some weight on my lower body – even if I couldn't feel it.

'I'm going to teach you how to use a banana board,' she said one day, as she held up what looked like an oversized yellow boomerang. 'You use it to transfer between your bed and whatever you want to move to, like a wheelchair or the commode. Learning to use it will be very important for you.'

Ruth put the chair next to my bed and wedged the banana board between them.

'Let's get you sitting up,' she said.

She supported my back and I shuffled across the bed until my bottom was resting on the edge of the board.

'Now, you should aim to move from bed to chair in three goes: one, on to the banana board; two, slide into the middle; and, three, slide on to the chair.'

Using my arms to take my weight, I gradually inched on to the board. I couldn't tell when I was on it or not – I just had to look and touch with my hands to let myself know where my lower body was going – and I wobbled around as I sat there. This wasn't going to take three goes – try 3,000 – and fear rushed into my stomach. What would I do if I fell? I couldn't put a leg out to stop myself. I didn't want to hurt myself again. Look what had happened the last time I hurt myself. I felt as if I was dangling thousands of feet in the air and there was nothing I could do to save myself.

Eventually I made it to the chair, but I hated the banana board until I learned to master it and then it became my friend because it opened up my world a tiny bit. I didn't just have to lie in bed or be hoisted into a chair any more. Now I could move myself into a wheelchair or on to a commode. Again and again my mind kept returning to Dr Shakir's words – he'd said some of my spinal damage would be permanent – surely this would show him he was wrong?

My world closed down to that two-foot gap between bed and chair as I practised transferring again and again. But however cut off I was from real life, it could still sometimes break into my closed-off world. Although I had no idea just how many stories were appearing in the papers about my 'violent' marriage or how difficult life was for Lee, there were some things he couldn't keep from me and one was what my sister had done. We both agreed we should contact a lawyer, who sent letters to the Sunday newspapers involved. About the same time, our solicitor, Peter Cadman, also suggested we explore the possibility of legal action against the Chelsea and Westminster. I was surprised, but I felt it might be a way of answering all the questions I had. I'd been so frightened of saying anything, fearful of questioning what had happened to me because I didn't want to look stupid, but I wanted to know how I had come to be infected with MSSA because if that hadn't happened, then I wouldn't be lying in a bed now. I couldn't stop thinking about it. I'd broken a rib, caught the infection and woken up unable to move; I'd been discharged from hospital supposedly well and had now been told I might never walk again. How could that have happened? How in this day and age could a person go into hospital and come out with such a serious infection? Peter put us in touch with a colleague of his, Janice Gardner, who specialised in medical negligence.

'I think it is likely you acquired the MSSA infection in hospital and that is what caused the abscess,' Janice told Lee and me. 'You were not ill before you were admitted and the abscess only appeared after you were.

'I think we will also be able to explore the possibility that the infection entered your body via the epidural needle because that is the only thing that gave direct access into your spinal column.

'There is something else we should consider,' she said, as she looked at Lee before turning to me. 'And that is the fact that no one treated the abscess. If you had been given antibiotics immediately, then you may not have been in this position and the outcome may have been very different. We will have to ask medical experts, of course, but I think this issue will be central to any case.'

I sucked in my breath as pictures flashed through my mind. My damp pillow, the livid red lump on my spine, the faces passing in front of me who said there was nothing wrong.

'Do you mean I'm like this because I picked up an infection in a dirty hospital?' I whispered. I couldn't believe what I was hearing.

'Well, we don't know yet, but I think it is a strong possibility,' the lawyer replied.

It soon became clear that we faced a choice: to issue a libel action against the newspapers or start legal proceedings against the Chelsea and Westminster NHS Trust. Financially and, more importantly, emotionally, we were not in a position to do both, and while we knew that the stories were potentially damaging, we also knew none of our family and friends took the slightest bit of notice of them and that was the most important thing. With this in mind, we decided that suing the Chelsea and Westminster was more important, partly because of my financial future – it looked as if I might be off work for a long time – but also because by asking questions we might help prevent something similar happening to other people in the future. I didn't know much about it, but I was sure that questions needed to be answered.

Strange as it sounds, I didn't feel angry – that came later. I was just scared as I tried to take in what I'd been told. All I could think was that if something so awful had happened so easily in the very place I'd gone to get better, then why shouldn't it again? I felt anxious, life suddenly seemed so fragile, and like people who refuse to walk under ladders, I created rituals to keep myself safe. My pillows had to be arranged in a certain way and things put in the same places on my bedside table every night – a picture of Joe and Max that I kissed before I went to sleep, my glasses on the side, my watch next to my glasses – before I could sleep. I was trying to make myself feel safe again, but I just couldn't stop thinking as I lay in the dark.

'Please help me,' I'd ask God. 'Make me strong enough to accept what has happened to me. Help my nerves recover. Let my proprioception come back. Please, God, let me walk again with Lee, the boys and Charlie. Keep them all safe when I'm not there. Let my feeling come back.'

I don't know where my prayers came from – I'd stopped going to church when I was a kid. But even though I'd never believed in a bearded man in the sky, I'd always privately had faith in a god – the goodness inside us all that keeps us focused and motivated. Now I started praying every night as Cherry told me to find something to believe in and ask for help. For me, it was God. If other people found strength in their faith, then I should look for it too.

'Please help me walk again, keep Lee and the boys safe, look after them while I'm not there,' I'd repeat again and again.

However much I asked for help, though, I couldn't stop guilt twisting inside me that I didn't deserve it. Abscesses, MSSA, nerve damage, proprioception, wheelchairs...it all led back to the night when I'd broken my ribs because I was drunk.

'You were so pissed you couldn't even see the edge of your own bed,' my head screamed. 'What kind of person are you? How many years have you wasted getting drunk? It's the one thing you can rely on, isn't it? Leslie's a good-time girl, she likes a drink. It's pathetic. What a waste. Why's God going to help you?'

It was true. Pissed, sozzled, bladdered – whatever you want to call it – I was it when I fell off the bed, and everything led back to that moment. If I hadn't been drunk, then I wouldn't have broken my ribs, caught the infection or developed the abscess. I'd still be able to walk, be a mother to Joe and Max, a proper wife to Lee and an actress. And it wasn't even a one-off. All those evenings of throwing vodka down my neck to keep up with the party came back to haunt me as I lay in the dark. Look where it had all got me. A cripple unable to walk, that's what.

It was the first time I'd really thought about alcohol in all the 26 years I'd been drinking. I remembered my teen years, when I'd hardly ever touched it, and my early married life up North, when Lee and I had only had the occasional boozy lunch. How had I gone from that to the party monster I'd become? I'd been on a rollercoaster of binge-drinking ever since coming to London, and everything bad that had happened to me was connected to it – Ibiza, the door-kicking incident and my accident had all happened after big nights out. Alcohol was the devil inside me and I'd used it to abuse myself for years. It was the blue spark that lit the touch paper between Lee and me; it was the poison that kept me lying in bed when I should have been looking after my children; it was the drug that allowed me to push all my worries below the surface where they couldn't scare me; it was the demon that made me scream about my problems rather than talk about them. I'd wasted so much time suffering from hangovers, arguing, not liking myself.

For the first time in years, there was no place to run – no job to throw myself into, no party to go to, no children to look after. As I lay trapped in my hospital bed, I realised I should have known better. Memories returned that I'd long tried to forget. My mum's father had been a drinker, and when Debbie and I were growing up, I knew there were a few times when Mum had had a bit too much after another long day working in the shop and would start arguing with us when we got home from school.

'Tidy up your room, clear up your homework, wash up your tea things, sort out your school uniform,' she'd snap.

There were enough of those times for me to know that the kind, caring and funny woman I knew could change completely with drink inside her. Now guilt flooded through me when I thought about my kids. I'd been like that: alcohol had made me less of a mother than I'd wanted to be at times. What about all the mornings when I'd been short with Joe and Max because of a hangover, snapping at them and being impatient when they were just kids? How many times can children hear 'Mummy doesn't feel very well today'?

It whirled round my head and I hated myself more and more for allowing drink to take control of my life at times. Finally I was forced to admit something to myself that I'd never even considered before: I had a drink problem. Away from my real life, away from the parties and the binges, I realised it had been there for a long time. Not hiding-bottles-in-cupboards alcoholism, but a problem with drink because it affected my life – and not in a good way – and it was only going to go on and on, get worse and worse, unless I stopped. I felt so angry with myself, so frustrated. I'd had warnings in the past – throwing up, arguments that should never have

CLOCKWISE, FROM TOP Joe cools off in a bucket; Preparing for Santa: a carrot, a minced pie and a glass of something a little stronger; I can guarantee the glass was emptied. Getting ready to celebrate my fortieth birthday at Teatro.

The racier side of life.
Stirling Moss gives
Gina Campbell and me
some tips on tank
driving during *Driving
Force*.

I get ready to speed
round Silverstone.

Freddie Foreman holds court at Souk, our Clapham bar.

A lovely photo of my mum, whose death at just 68 in April 2000 was an unbearable loss.

ABOVE With Philip
Middlemiss in *Where The
Heart Is*.

RIGHT as Karen Buckley.
It was during this period,
particularly after my
mother died, that I began
drinking heavily on my
own for the first – and
last – time.

RIGHT The cast of
Merseybeat line up.

BELOW With Paul
Venables, who played my
fiancé in the series.

THIS PAGE, LEFT Visiting a gallery in April 2003. In the aftermath of the injections on my lips, we couldn't go anywhere without the paparazzi wanting a picture of me.

BELOW Posing in front of one of the Playtex images shot for an ad campaign in September 2004, just after I came out of hospital having contracted MSSA.

OPPOSITE PAGE, LEFT A helping hand at home, just after I came out of hospital. It was great to be back with Lee, Joe and Max after so long.

RIGHT Joe, looking lovely in his uniform, kisses Max goodbye on his first day of school.

BELOW On holiday with Lee in Zermatt, after the injury.

PA

Still behaving badly!

happened – but I'd ignored them all. Now, with most of my body numb and lifeless, I finally knew what I had to do.

I think most people who have a drink problem don't know they do, and it's not like a neon light spontaneously goes on and they see the truth. I'd always managed to ignore mine because drink had never affected my work and was kept to weekends and days off. What harm is a little headache and a bit of sickness after a great party if you haven't got to work the next day?

My accident was like a huge great stop sign being put in my path, and if it hadn't been, then I don't think I'd have ever given up booze. But the fact was, the sign was there – life was telling me to stop because if I carried on, then I would become seriously ill.

I spent days lying in bed going over it all – the accident, drink, the future – and kept repeating the same questions as I got increasingly down, until one morning I couldn't see a way forward any more. If I didn't want to end up in a wheelchair, then I had to work harder than I'd ever done before to get myself better, but I felt the weakest I ever had in my life.

'Dear Lord, if You are there, then give me the strength to walk again, give me the determination, give Lee the will to help me, look after the boys,' I prayed, as I stared out of the window.

What had I done to myself? How could I keep going when I knew I was to blame for all this? I felt so ashamed.

'Give me a sign,' I silently prayed. 'I'm so unsure. But if You can give me the strength and determination to walk, then I'll never touch a drink again. I need to know You're listening so that I can do this, get well and be sober. I know You're there to help me, but please give me a sign. Please.'

I know it might sound like a scene from *The Life of Brian*, but I swear that as I looked up into the fluffy clouds, I saw the word 'yes' etched in one at that moment. Maybe it was a gust of wind, maybe the sun was dazzling me, maybe I just made it up, but, whatever it was, I took it as a sign that my prayers would be answered. I have never touched alcohol again. I made a deal with God and I've stuck to it.

Everything was moving so fast around me – the shiny floor speeding away under the wheels of my chair, people rushing past, lights disappearing overhead, even the lift doors seemed to slam shut in a second. It was the first time I'd been further than the bathroom since arriving at the Charing Cross and Ruth was taking me downstairs in a wheelchair. She'd suggested that we go to the hospital gym for some physio, but I didn't want to get stared at, so instead she wheeled me into what looked like an office with a desk in one corner and a set of parallel bars with a full-length mirror at the end in the other.

Ruth wheeled me to the end of the bars and put the brakes on the chair before sitting in front of me on a box.

'We're going to try to get you standing today,' she told me. 'I know it's going to be hard, but I want you to try and pull your body into an upright position using the parallel bars.'

'I don't think I can,' I replied. My heart pounded. 'I know I've improved, but I don't think I can do it.'

It was true. By now I was able to bridge by pushing my feet on to the bed and lifting my bottom in the air. But standing up? I'd never be able to.

'Well, let's just give it a go, Leslie, and see how you get on,' Ruth replied gently as she wedged her knees against mine to stabilise me.

I put my hands on the parallel bars just above my shoulders and gripped as hard as I could. I knew I wouldn't have the strength or feeling to push off on my numb feet, so I'd have to pull myself up with my arms if I was ever going to get there. I shuffled forward on the seat, looked down to check that Ruth was still holding my knees, then pulled with all my strength. Immediately the vice closed round my chest and I wanted to pant with pain. I pulled and pulled myself up out of the seat. It was one thing using my arms to lift my upper body, but it was so much harder pulling the weight of my legs as well.

It seemed like for ever until I looked down to see I was standing – my knees locked tight back and my bottom pushed out. Shock rushed through me. I couldn't feel a thing. I had no sensation of standing up at all. If I closed my eyes, I knew I'd have no idea whether I was up, down or sideways. I didn't know how I had got up, but I had. I tensed my arms – they were the only thing keeping me up, keeping me safe. I felt separated from the floor by stilts, or like a puppet being worked by strings. I lifted my head to look in the mirror ahead of me.

'Oh, my God,' I whispered.

'Take a bit of weight off your hands,' Ruth urged me. 'Try and use your legs, Leslie. Just release your grip a tiny bit. I'm here. I'll look after you.'

I heard the words, but all I could focus on was the reflection in the mirror in front of me.

'Use your memory of taking a step,' Ruth said, taking hold of my right leg. 'Remember how you shift your weight, lift your leg, bring it through to the floor. That's what you've got to do now, remember.'

She lifted my right foot and pulled my leg forward, then put it down again on the floor. But my first 'step' wasn't a step. It was a nothing. Still I stared at the mirror in front of me as Ruth took my other leg and moved it forward. I couldn't think about that joke of a walk. It was the first time I'd seen my whole body since the accident and I couldn't take my eyes off my reflection. Until then, all I'd seen was my face in the dressing-table mirror as I sat in my chair, but now there was a woman in front of me wearing a baggy white hospital gown, surgical stockings and trainers, with a catheter bag strapped to her ankle. She looked like a ghost – pale white, her face shrunken, her legs like tiny sticks as they dragged along the ground. I wanted to scream.

It took 15 minutes to get to the end of those bars and every 'step' was a joke. I was so exhausted when I got back to my room that all I could do was cry. I couldn't believe what I'd seen, what I'd realised in that first moment of standing up. Whatever help God was going to give me, I literally had a mountain to climb and I had to do it alone. Only now did I truly understand what had happened to me.

'I think you are now strong enough to be transferred to the Wellington Hospital,' Professor van Dellen told me on his visit one day. 'You've reached all the goals needed in order to move there, such as transferring from bed to chair, and we don't have the facilities required for the kind of intensive rehab you are now ready for. So I'm going to ask the Wellington to come and have a look at you to see what they think.'

Tears pricked behind my eyes as I looked at him. Even though I'd only been upstairs at Charing Cross for just over two weeks, I relied on everyone and was full of gratitude to them all: Ruth, patient and hard-working; Cherry, caring and supportive; and I'd even got used to Professor van Dellen's straight-talking. I was deeply thankful to him – he'd saved my life, come without fail to see me every single day and was constantly caring and interested, jollying me along and making me laugh. It was obvious how much the staff respected him, and I did too. I didn't want to leave. I felt safe with them all.

But if Professor van Dellen said it was time to move on, then I had to, and within a few days the Wellington's head physiotherapist, Alison, and administrator, Eileen, had come to see me. To be suitable for admission, I had to show them I could dress myself on the bed by bridging – pulling on my clothes while pushing my bottom into the air – as well as being able to transfer from bed to chair.

'Well, Mrs Chapman, we're happy that you're ready to move to us,' Alison told me after I'd done my little performance. 'But you will need to work on your endurance before you come. You'll be undergoing intense physiotherapy at the Wellington, building up to three or four 45 minute sessions every day.

'We will sort out an intensive schedule for you and you will be supported by Team Leslie – a whole group of people dedicated to working with you, including physiotherapists, an occupational therapist, a neurologist and psychologist – but you must understand that this is where the hard work will really start.

'We will give you goals to meet every two weeks and there will be meetings with heads of department to review your progress. We'll want you into the hydrotherapy pool as soon as possible, walking on crutches in the near future and making real advances with your recovery.'

I thought of the woman I'd seen in the mirror – that thin, pathetic figure with no life in her eyes. How was she going to do any of this? But I knew I had a choice. Give in and become that woman or do something. I was being given the chance of the most extreme makeover imaginable and I couldn't believe what they were offering, what they hoped I'd be able to do. It sounded like a different person from the Leslie-in-a-wheelchair I'd been getting used to. All I wanted was to be able to tie my own shoelaces, have a little independence, and now I felt almost excited by how sure they sounded about what I could achieve at the Wellington.

Later Dr Shakir came to see me and, as always, took hold of my big toe.

'Close your eyes,' he said. 'Now, tell me if I am moving your toe up or down.'

I hadn't got a bloody clue. Couldn't feel a thing.

'Now, can you feel this?' he asked, after he'd tested my knee reflexes with a hammer, then dragged its scratchy handle along the sole of my foot.

No again.

I couldn't stop thinking of what Alison and Eileen had told me.

'What quality of life do you think I will eventually have?' I asked in a rush. I wanted to know where all the hard work might get me, the best-case scenario if I applied myself like a good girl and really went for it.

'Well, as you know, you may have to use a wheelchair,' Dr Shakir replied.

Good old Dr Shakir. Blunt as ever. These guys really needed some lessons at charm school.

'But if not,' he continued, 'I think your movement will always be affected – for instance, you will probably shuffle your feet and have a hump on your back.'

Hump? I thought, as I stared up at him. A fucking *hump*?

For the first time since waking up, I felt defiance rise up in me. Sod them all with their doubting Thomas ways.

They can stick their hump, I thought angrily, as Dr Shakir left the room. I'm going to strut into Dolce and Gabbana wearing my Jimmy Choos. Just see if I don't.

CHAPTER 15

Step by Step

I tried not to cry as I felt warm sunshine on my skin for the first time in weeks. To avoid the paparazzi, I was being taken out of the back door of the Charing Cross to start my journey to the Wellington. It was the first time I'd breathed fresh air for weeks, but I didn't feel excited – just scared.

'Good luck, Leslie,' Cherry said as she hugged me.

I hugged her back and couldn't stop myself sobbing. I didn't want to leave Cherry, the place I knew and all the other staff I liked. I felt like Eliza Doolittle as she pleaded, 'I'm a good girl I am.' Now what was going to become of me?

We pulled away in the ambulance and soon London was rushing past the back windows – Hammersmith, the Westway, Lord's Cricket Ground and then the Wellington. I'd seen the hospital so many times on all those journeys North up the M1 but had never imagined I'd be in there one day. All I knew was that it was a very expensive, exclusive hospital full of sheikhs and princes.

The smell of new carpets filled the air as I was wheeled inside and taken up to a freshly decorated room on the sixth floor. It was clean and light with a noticeboard on the wall opposite, a TV, a big window and of course a bed. I could also see an en-suite bathroom through an open door and there was even a security guard outside. Apparently, he was there to protect me from photographers and I'd even been admitted under a false name – Mrs Plume. It all seemed a bit much, but I didn't have time to think about it as Team Leslie started arriving to introduce themselves. First came a nurse called Agnes, who was going to be my new Cherry, then Eileen, the Wellington's administrator, who'd assessed me at the Charing Cross, and Alison, the head of physiotherapy, whom I'd also met. Then came Rachel, my physiotherapist, and Catherine, my occupational therapist, plus nurses called Pam, Helen, Annaleesa, Joycent, Merlin and finally Jennifer, the sister in charge of the floor where I was.

I tried not to feel too scared. There were so many people and so much to do. The next morning I was starting a new routine of two 45-minute physio sessions a day, building up to three, or even four, in time, plus visits with the occupational therapist. There would also be routine stuff like X-rays and blood tests. It sounded so much. I'd been used to just 30 minutes of physio each day, not two and a quarter hours or more, and I felt scared as person after person came in to see me. I just wanted to be left alone. I didn't like the new smells, the new sheets, the new room, the new faces, when I'd only just got used to the Charing Cross. I'd felt so determined to prove Dr Shakir wrong when he'd predicted I'd end up like the Hunchback of Notre-Dame or something, but now I just felt overwhelmed. All I wanted to do was lie in bed and watch TV – not be reminded all the time of how useless my body was.

I gazed out of the window. Instead of the view down the Thames, all I could see were apartments – a bit like the film *Rear Window* – with people going about their business, making tea, working at their computers. My eyes wandered down and rested on a woman who seemed to be staring straight back at me. She had wild hair and eyes like a zombie and I couldn't stop looking at her. Surely she couldn't see me? Here we go again. I don't know why, but I've always acted like a magnet to slightly odd people – mostly on trains, thanks to all the travelling to film in Yorkshire and Liverpool. On one occasion, I sat opposite a woman who paid £180 in cash to upgrade her standard ticket to first class, ordered a bottle of white wine and two cheese and ham toasties, before pouring the wine to the rim of two glasses and not touching a drop. She then started telling Space Control the time in a loud voice. She seemed perfectly nice, but it was a bit worrying. On another occasion, I was travelling from Runcorn to London with a soldier who shouted down his mobile in graphic detail about his sexual exploits with this poor girl at the weekend. Everyone had no choice but to listen, although thankfully it was so boring that I fell asleep.

'No one can see in,' Agnes told me when I asked her about it. 'The windows are tinted and have reflected glass, so people can only see in at night when the lights are on.'

That was good, then.

Soon Eileen came back and started filling out all the forms needed to go into hospital courtesy of BUPA. I felt sick as she told me my room cost £1,600 a night and my insurance company would only cover the bill for up to six weeks.

After she left, I panicked: 'What happens if I'm not better by then?' I might not even be back on my feet in that time, let alone ready to go home. How was I going to do all this work they were talking about? Where would I go if I wasn't ready?

'How are you?' Lee said later, when he walked in. 'Are you settled in OK? This all looks nice. I've brought you some stuff.'

'Oh, you know,' I replied moodily.

He sat down on the bed and started unpacking a bag, handing me new photos to put beside my bed and pulling out some gym clothes.

'What the fuck are they for?' I snapped. I was wearing a nappy and gown as usual; I didn't need all that.

'I don't know. They told me to bring them,' Lee replied

patiently, then put everything into the wardrobe.

He'd even brought my trainers – or 'diddy shoes' as he likes to call them because they're so small. I felt scared and anxious. I hadn't worn my own clothes since going into hospital and was dreading putting them on the next day. Then the work would start and everyone would see I'd never be able to do it. Tears burned hot behind my eyes. I couldn't believe how far I had to go in so little time. The Wellington wasn't a hospital, it was a boot camp, and I was going to have to start pushing myself. I'd always been one of those who liked having a chat in the gym, but that was really going to have to change now.

'This is nice,' Lee said, as he studied the room-service menu. 'It's like a hotel – they've even got a wine list.'

I didn't say anything; I just lay and stared at the TV screen. Silently, Lee sat down on the bed, then lay down next to my numb little body and put his arms round me.

'Everything's going to be fine,' he said, and pulled me to him.

Trying to learn to walk again is a bit like building a house – you've got to have strong foundations – and the basis of that is the core muscles. They're what help us put one foot in front of the other and hold ourselves straight. All the mothers out there will know about them because they're what can go to pot after childbirth. But while most people use them naturally, it was going to take me months. The work started on my second day at the Wellington, when I was taken to the gym, where Rachel, the physio, showed me some exercises to engage the core muscles.

'I want you to put your hands on your hipbones, then put your fingers five centimetres inwards on your stomach and tighten and relax, tighten and relax,' Rachel told me.

I looked up at her. I couldn't feel the muscles, so how the hell was I going to tighten them?

'You'll know when the pelvic muscles engage because you'll feel your stomach tighten underneath your fingers,' she explained.

I stared down as I put my hands on my hips. How on earth was I going to do this? I couldn't feel my feet, knees, hips or bottom, so there was no chance I'd be able to flex a muscle deep inside me. I concentrated.

'Good, Leslie, good,' Rachel said encouragingly.

But it wasn't. It was pathetic.

That was the start of the intensive regime. It centred on physiotherapy, which is all about strengthening your body, and occupational therapy – basically teaching you to live in an able-bodied world. My first goals were learning how to stand up from a sitting position and standing unaided. I literally had to get moving because the more I used my muscles, the more they'd remember how to move. The paraesthesia meant my body was 'asleep' and now I had to wake it up. No one could predict how far my recovery would go, but the more I moved my body, the more chance I had of not ending up in a wheelchair.

'Where once you moved without consciously thinking about it, you are now going to have to concentrate on every single movement you make, until one by one they flow with some sort of normality,' Rachel told me.

'Use your eyes to see what is happening, your hands to feel and your mind to visualise moving your muscles. You will literally have to picture a movement in your mind and your body will follow.

'Remember that your muscles are all connected, so strengthening one will set off a chain reaction in the others – flexing your foot will work your calf, for instance. So the more you work, the more muscles you'll be waking up.'

Day after day I went back to the gym to practise the sitting to standing movement with Rachel, who sat in front of me with her knees against mine and my hands on her shoulders to stabilise me. Each time, I would get halfway out of the seat before falling back into the chair. The problem was the critical balancing point when I had to throw my weight forward to get up: I'd bottle it for fear of falling. I felt like a one-woman rollercoaster – out of control and about to crash – because I'd lost all trust in my body and how to use it.

Meanwhile, back in my room, I started learning how to put weight through my numb legs using a standing frame, which looked like a big Zimmer frame. Sounds easy, I know, but even something so simple had to be broken down into parts which I could then learn to put together. Standing included the following: feet hip distance apart; pull in pelvic floor; engage stomach muscles; bend forward to bring weight directly over knees; press down on heels; tuck in arse; steady body with hands on the frame. It's amazing just how complicated something so simple can be!

All I can say is thank goodness for Alan Titchmarsh. My first few days at the Wellington coincided with the Chelsea Flower Show and I used the TV coverage to reward myself after I'd been to the gym. I'd never been a huge gardener, but flowers and plants had always been associated with my mum and childhood, so I loved them. The flower show was the one summer event I never missed and I loved wandering round with Lee for a couple of hours before he said the same thing every year.

'Well, I think that's enough, isn't it?' he'd announce, when his patience had run out, and we'd go to our favourite French restaurant, Le Poule au Pot, nearby for a long, leisurely lunch outside.

I thought back to last year – me walking by Lee's side and never for a moment realising how lucky I was as we looked at the show gardens. Now I was standing in a hospital room. It was still great seeing the gardens – even if it was just on TV – and I felt comforted as I watched the coverage and remembered, as a child, watching Mum while she patiently dug, watered and weeded. It was a time when I'd felt happy and safe, and I clung on to those feelings now as I thought about how much things had changed. I'd gone from speeding round in cop cars on *Merseybeat* to trying to lift my pelvis 3 inches into the air instead of 2 inches. All I could see was that pathetic figure in the mirror at the Charing Cross, and looking down, I knew I was still the same person. How was I ever going to get from that to walking around?

Sometimes it felt like a massive wheelchair had moved into my brain and I couldn't get it out – it was all I could see or think about. How would I manage at home? How would I watch the boys play football? How would I take my dad out? All I knew about disability was ramps and handles on everything, machines to lower you into the bath, mobilised scooters, flat shoes – I'd have a permanent bloody crick in my neck if I couldn't wear heels, because Lee is so tall. I know it sounds stupid, but back then I knew so little about disability, the positive and fulfilled lives people lead, and believed mine would close down to nothing if that was my future. All I knew was that I couldn't end up in that wheelchair. I had to get up, on to my feet: using a stick, limping, crawling...anything was better than not being able to walk at all.

The medication and endless medical tests associated with spinal damage don't just affect your movement. Drugs make your mouth dry, blood tests leave your arms looking like join-the-dots, and remember your mum saying don't eat lying down? Well, I learned what that really meant when I was told my tooth enamel was being destroyed by gastric reflux as acid tracked up my oesophagus into my mouth. Usually people know they have it because it causes heartburn, but I couldn't feel anything, so of course I didn't know. Later my dentist would tell me I had the teeth of a bulimic because the problem had gone on for so long that my teeth had started rotting.

I began discovering such hidden side effects of my

paraesthesia during those first few weeks at the Wellington and they were probably the most difficult weeks. Everyone kept telling me what I had to do, but I didn't really understand what they meant; I kept asking my body to do things, but it wouldn't listen; and gradually all the different levels of my condition – such as the fact that my menstrual cycle had shut down for the first time in my life – became clear. Despite all the hard work in the gym, it still took me 15 minutes to do up my shoelaces and the pain kicked in after every gym session as my ribs went into spasm and the band of steel closed round me. It was such an uphill struggle, and however hard I worked, nothing much was happening in the sensation, movement or morale department.

I swear it was like the opening bars of the theme from *2001: A Space Odyssey* were playing in my head when I got out of bed each morning. 'Daaa, daaa, daaa, da-da,' went the trumpets. 'Boom-boom, boom-boom, boom-boom,' went the kettledrums.

'Her eyes are open...She's sitting up...She's here for another day,' a deep voice shouted, as the crowd roared, 'Hurraaaaaay!'

Most of the time I just wanted to switch it all off and go back to sleep, but then Agnes would come in and I knew it was time to start the day. Just as Cherry had been, she was the person who kept me going, and from the day I arrived she encouraged me, supported me, wiped away my tears and soothed my fears. Agnes was a shoulder to cry on, a warm hug when Lee or the boys weren't there and, with her strong religious faith, a constant believer that I would recover. Most importantly, she laughed at all my jokes! She was wonderful, just like all the nurses, and it's a shame all hospitals can't be like the Wellington. I know it's not possible, it's about money, and I was very lucky to have private health insurance, but you can't put a price on well-being or lives.

When Agnes wasn't there or I wasn't working in the gym,

my mind was as full as ever. Lee was being brilliant – visiting three times a day without fail, being a dad and running Teatro – but I knew he was worried because the police had announced an investigation into Debbie's allegations. I kept thinking of him and the boys at home. I like everything tidy, clean, in its place and kept imagining the dining table covered in Lee's business papers, teacups and dirty plates left out and pizza stains on the sofas. What was happening to our beautiful new flat that I hadn't even had time to enjoy? It would be ruined by the time I went home. But then I'd think of Rita and tell myself to calm down – she'd never allow that to happen – before my mind drifted off again. Had Joe and Max got their summer sports stuff together? Did Rita know where I'd put it away last year? Were they both revising properly for their end-of-term exams? How were they really feeling about everything that was happening? It was like getting a winkle out of its shell when I tried to ask them.

They were so sweet, though. It must have been really boring for them to visit every weekend, but they still came at about 6 p.m. on the Friday and again on the Saturday evening. I so looked forward to seeing them, and they'd tumble into the room in a rush of words and energy. They'd come in holding a salt-beef sandwich from the deli round the corner, raid my fridge for chocolate, eat all my grapes, take over the whole room, flick around the TV channels, talk noisily and then leave. I'd always try to stop myself from crying when I said goodbye, but normally I didn't manage it and they'd give me a big hug before backing out of the door looking uneasy about leaving. I tried not to let them see me upset, but I just didn't want to let them go, and no matter how hard I tried, my tear ducts would always let me down. I worried about how everything was affecting them, but told myself we were a strong unit, they'd be OK.

Then there was my dad and I also ended up crying whenever I spoke to him on the phone.

'Come on, girl, chin up,' he'd say.

'I'm sorry, Dad,' I'd sob. 'I've let you down.'

There I was, unable to walk or do anything for him when he needed looking after. I thought I couldn't rely on Debbie to do it and I felt so guilty. If only, if only, if only...All I could do was remind myself of the deal I'd made with God, but there were many times when it just didn't seem enough.

It seemed like weeks since I'd started crying and I was still doing it. As ever, the worst time was the evening and I was at my lowest when Dr Shakir visited somewhere between six and seven, just after I'd had a painful blood-thinning injection. I'd got used to injections by now, but this one was bloody awful. After a long day, I couldn't wait for the sleeping tablet that would end it, but then Dr Shakir would arrive, stand at the end of my bed and tell me to close my eyes.

'Am I lifting your toes up or down?' he'd ask.

No idea.

'Can you feel a scratch on your arm?'

Yes.

'How about on your waist?'

No.

'And now on your thigh?'

No.

'Your calf?'

No.

'Your foot?'

No. No. No.

Every evening he'd scratch the sole of my foot and my toes would flex upwards – apparently, it wasn't what he hoped they'd do – and then he'd hit a tuning fork on the bed, hold it at the top of my back and gradually move downwards. Night after night I could feel the vibrations at the top of my spine until the tuning fork drew level with my scar. Then nothing.

Don't get me wrong. Dr Shakir wasn't nasty or unpleasant. He was just like all the doctors – reluctant to be too positive and give me false hope.

'So, how do you think I'm getting on?' I'd ask him every night.

'Well, you've got a long way to go,' he'd reply. 'You know you'll never be back to a hundred per cent because of the damage to your spine. You will never be back to how you were before, never be able to run up and down stairs or walk in a dark room without falling over. You will always have to look at your feet to place them because the damage to your proprioception means you will not instinctively be able to do it. But you must work hard and keep focused.'

Then he'd leave and I'd lie there waiting for my sleeping tablet to arrive, dreading the beginning of the next day, when it would all start again. If only something was certain. If only someone could say to me, 'This is it, this is the end point,' and then I'd have something to start coming to terms with. But they couldn't and I'd wonder when the time would come for me to stop recovering and start accepting that I was disabled. I was so scared I wouldn't work again. My job had been my life. I'd never been out of work or even considered not acting because it was something I could do until the day I dropped. But would I be forced to retire because people wouldn't want to hire an actress in a wheelchair?

Trying to calm myself down, I'd say my prayers as I held my Angel of Courage stone a friend had given me and looked at the pictures on my bedside table of Mother Teresa, Jesus, Joe and Max.

'Bless Joe, Max and Lee, help them to be strong through this difficult time and let me be able to walk with them and Charlie again by the river,' I'd pray. Would this be the prayer I'd say for the rest of my life?

Please, please let there be peace...and finally it would

come in the form of a tiny sleeping pill, which sent me falling into dreams.

Although I didn't really see the people I shared the gym with each day during physio sessions, I could certainly hear them. Each day we went to the different corners of the room we always used during the same time slot, and while no one ever talked and old-fashioned screens separated us, we'd catch sight of each other's scared faces on the way in and out.

First, there were two brothers, aged about 15 and 17, who'd been in a car accident back home in the Middle East. One, like me, was learning to balance and walk again, while the other had brain damage and, sadly, was significantly worse. Then there was their father, who attended every physio session and drove the therapist a bit mad, I think, and finally there was a little Greek man. It could get a bit confusing at times with all the different languages being shouted as we each hit our pain threshold.

'*Ockey, ockey, ockey!*' exclaimed the little Greek man.

'*Zen, zen, zen!*' cried the boys.

'Fuuuuuuuuuuuuuuck!' I'd shout.

However much it hurt, we were all there every day – you've got to turn up, after all, because you're in hospital, it's an institution, and there's nothing else to do.

'The more you put in, the more you'll get out,' Rachel would keep telling me, and I tried to listen, but there were some days when I just wanted to tell her to shove it.

Standing unaided, without leaning on anything, without any help at all, was still my most important goal, because if I could do that, then I could balance, and if I could balance, then I might be able to walk again one day.

Maybe today, I'd tell myself, as I stood at the sink brushing my teeth, or in the frame looking out of the window, and would lift my hands for a split second to let my legs take the strain before starting to fall.

At last, two long weeks after I'd moved to the Wellington, came the moment I'd been waiting for. Staring down at my hands, I eased them off the sides of the frame and let go. There I was, on my own, no one holding me – unlocked knees, bum in, tummy in, shoulders away from my ears – what a breakthrough. It only lasted a few seconds – the blink of an eye for most people – but I knew it was the cornerstone of my future recovery. Maybe I would walk again.

'Keep looking at your feet, Leslie,' Rachel urged me. 'And, remember, tighten your pelvic floor, lift your right foot from the hip, up straight on the left, bum in and shift your weight.'

Rachel stood in front of me at the parallel bars with her arms outstretched as I locked mine on top of hers. It was a few days since I'd first stood up and Rachel had immediately got me using the bars because if I was ever going to walk, that was where I'd learn.

'I want you to remember how it feels, Leslie,' she told me. 'Hold on to me and use your arms to feel the movement in mine and create a mental blueprint of walking.'

Rachel's arms rose as she pulled her foot back to take a step. Leaning heavily on her, I could feel the movement – like a wave crashing on to the beach in one smooth roll.

How was I ever going to manage that?

I'd been so excited when I first tried out the bars and had been impatient to feel what it would be like to try and walk again. Pushing the memory of the woman in the mirror at the Charing Cross out of my mind, I stared ahead. My legs might as well have been a couple of kippers that day, but things were different now. I could stand and I felt like a giant after all those weeks of staring at everyone's waistlines.

Once again, though, it was the balancing bit I found hardest, and when it came to walking, that was the moment when I had to push my weight forward on to my front leg as I lifted up the back to take a step. I felt like a skittle about to tip over. It was all about sensing when the time was right and placing your foot – difficult to do when you can't feel a bloody thing.

'Tummy strong,' Rachel reminded me. 'Pelvic floor engaged. Now place your front leg on the floor, Leslie.'

I stared down at the white, withered stick jerking in front of me. The nerve damage had caused spasticity in my legs and I might as well have been attempting to hit a golf ball into a hole from a mile away as I tried to lower my leg.

'Tuck your bottom in,' Rachel said. 'Think about your posture during every step you take. You can't get into bad habits.'

I focused on my leg as it twitched forward – weaving around as it tried to meet the floor. I thought of the feeling I'd had when Rachel moved, of the wave – if she was a Bentley, then I was more like a Metro bunny-hopping at the lights.

'Nearly there,' Rachel said. 'Heel to toe. Bottom in. Tummy strong.'

'For fuck's sake!' I wanted to shout. 'Have you ever tried to walk when there's a bloody shopping list being shouted at you?' But I stayed silent and felt myself get breathless with effort as pain tightened round my chest and I stared at my feet. Nowadays I had to wear shorts or rolled-up tracksuit bottoms to gym sessions so that I could see my legs during every step because that was the only way I knew if they were going the right way.

'Get on the floor, you bastard,' I wanted to shout as my foot carried on moving downwards with the speed of a geriatric snail. It seemed to take for ever until we finally had touchdown.

'Now, lift up your back foot,' Rachel said.

Off we went again.

Day after day we went back to the gym – me holding on to Rachel like some kind of weird ballroom dancer as we edged down the bars. Back in my room, I'd carry on practising by using my legs to move my chair around, rather than the wheels. The main thing I'd had to get used to was the falling over. Because I had no sensation that I was about to fall, I'd hit the ground like a sack of potatoes. I had to find new reserves of patience. Having children had taught me something about that, but having to be patient with myself was a whole different story. I was so slow and clumsy. For instance, occupational therapy sessions nearly drove me mad when I'd go into a little galley kitchen with Catherine, she'd ask me to put in a load of washing and it would take for ever as I shuffled around like ET. I couldn't let myself think about what it would be like if I was still the same when I got home.

'Les, you're doing really well. I know it's hard, but you've just got to keep working at it.'

Lee sat on the edge of the bed beside me. Two weeks into walking on the parallel bars, I'd had enough. My legs were jerky, I moved slowly, my feet pointed outwards, my arches fell in, and my shoulders were hunched...I wasn't walking, just shuffling in a forward direction.

'It's going to take time,' Lee said. He started to smile. 'And if the worst comes to the worst, we can always fit you with castors and I can pull you along.'

'Very funny,' I snapped. 'I know I've got to keep going. I keep going every day when I wake up. But how long will it take? I've been doing this for weeks now and it's not getting better. It's not getting easier. I'm sick of it. I'm just so tired.'

Coming to terms with disability is a bit like peeling an onion – there's layer after layer of tears and I'd reached another. Just as it had hit me when I had first started trying to move, now I wanted to give up once again after realising how difficult walking was going to be. How were things ever going to be right again? I felt like I was on the edge, hanging on to keep myself together mentally, but knowing I'd fall if I went too deeply into my thoughts.

It was the first of many plateaus in my recovery. None of the hard work seemed to be paying off; there'd been no improvement, however slight, for ages. I'd had enough. I'd felt so excited after learning to stand – it seemed like a door had opened and I just had to step through. But now I realised it was the first of a thousand to be unlocked. All I could see were my jerking legs, my snail speed, my bum stuck out like a duck as I took two steps before stopping.

Lee was always encouraging and congratulating me, but if ever there was a day when I felt like I wasn't improving, I'd take it out on him; if ever there was a day when I felt grumpy for no good reason, I'd snap at him; and if ever there was a day when I felt like I wasn't getting his full concentration, I'd have a go at him. You become very selfish when you live in a hospital bubble because people are at your beck and call and you don't appreciate what's going on outside. I felt people should leave their world behind when they came into mine and sometimes I'd get really pissed off if I could see Lee's mind wandering. Nothing was enough.

'Don't worry so much, Les,' he told me, as I stared grumpily out of the window. 'It will all be OK.'

'No it won't,' I whined back. 'Stop saying that, will you? It's not all fucking OK, Lee, and I've had enough of you saying it is. Just stop.'

'All right, then – give up if you really want to,' he said curtly, and turned to watch the telly.

Tears welled up inside me. How could he be so nasty when I was the one lying in bed?

Then guilt crept over me. 'I'm sorry,' I sobbed. 'I'm so sorry.'

'That's OK,' Lee replied as he turned to me. 'But you can't give up, Leslie. That's all I can say.'

Deep down, I'd always assumed I'd be off once I started walking, so why all this hard work? I just wanted to get to a stage where people wouldn't notice I was damaged. I was an actress, for God's sake, so surely I'd be able to fake it, and even if I still couldn't feel properly, the audience would never know.

Now I was scared it was never going to be like that. All those nights of dreaming about walking with Charlie and the boys by the river, wearing my high heels again, it was never going to happen. I felt like I was in a prison – not allowed out or on a visit home – and the weeks stretched out in front of me while I wasted my life and missed out on my kids and husband. Sometimes they felt so far away from me, and as the weeks passed, I could sense the boys were changing from boys to young men. I don't know if it was the time they were spending with Lee, or just the knowledge that I had nearly died, but it seemed as if they were growing up almost overnight and an irrational part of me felt almost put out by it. I'd always thought the family would fall apart without me, but it obviously hadn't and the reason for our separation – all this hard rehab work – was pointless, because I still looked like Mrs Overall from *Acorn Antiques*.

Even Dr Shakir still occasionally mentioned 'the hump'. Maybe he was right. Maybe creeping along with my bum out, shoulders hunched and back crooked was the best it was going to get. But no one seemed to listen – day after day the nurses and therapists arrived to encourage me, and they would shower me with congratulations during the meetings we had every two weeks about my progress. I'd reached every goal expected of me, I was a real classroom swot, but I couldn't be bothered any more, because it didn't seem to make any difference. With 4-inch roots in my highlights, no make-up on, overgrown eyebrows and leg hair, I didn't care. I'd lost interest in myself and didn't think my body deserved any tarting up.

The other feeling that filled me was anger. I'd never known anything like it. I hadn't really thought about the MSSA when I first talked to Janice, our lawyer, about it. I'd just felt sad. But now I was angry as my legal case got underway to try to establish exactly what had gone wrong. I shouldn't be like this. All the signs were there that I had an infection, so why hadn't someone acted on them? My life had changed for ever because of something as basic as keeping things clean.

Then there was all the newspaper stuff. I knew the police were still investigating the alleged assault on Debbie – they had to because of the pressure the press were applying – but I couldn't help feeling upset when they asked to see me. I found it appalling that people were causing so much pain and heartache when our defences were at an all-time low. But I'd calmed down by the time two officers arrived at the Wellington, and, in fact, they seemed more nervous than me.

'We're so sorry to intrude,' they said, walking into my room.

They were with me less than half an hour as they asked about the night of the birthday argument with Debbie and I told them what had really happened. But I wasn't so calm a couple of weeks later when Lee was arrested at seven o'clock in the morning and taken in for questioning – despite several previous offers from our lawyer for him to go in voluntarily. He was released on bail, and however much he told me it didn't worry him, I knew it would. He'd done nothing wrong and now this was hanging over him. Of course the story somehow made it into the papers.

It was probably about mid-June, a month into my stay at the Welly, when Lee and Max arrived with a picnic lunch. Well, a sandwich and bottle of water, actually, but it's the thought that counts.

'Shall we go out?' Lee said, as he bent down to kiss me.

'Where?' I asked.

'Well, I don't know. How about the park?'

'What?'

'Regent's Park. It's a lovely day and it isn't far.'

I stared out of the windows at the sunshine. The sky was blue, the park would be green, but I didn't want to go. I hadn't left my bubble for so long and this was all a bit quick. I felt safe in the protective shell of my room – I couldn't just suddenly leave; I had to think about it, prepare myself more.

'Oh, no,' I replied. 'It'll cause too much hassle. Let's not make a fuss.'

Lee looked down at me.

'Come on, Mum,' said Max. 'It'll be nice. It's boring being stuck in here all the time.'

'Yes, come on, Les. It will do you good.'

'What will?' Agnes asked, as she walked in with a smile.

'Coming out with Max and me for lunch in the park,' Lee said. 'It will be good for her, won't it, Agnes? She needs to get out a bit.'

'Of course it will,' she said to me. 'You can go. There's no problem. We can get you into the car. You'll be fine.'

'Well, OK, then,' I replied uncertainly. I knew when I was outnumbered.

The first challenge was getting into the car, so Agnes called Catherine, who came to give me an occupational therapy lesson in the car park. The passenger seat looked so high as I sat in my wheelchair. We've got a four-by-four and the seat looked like Mount Everest.

Here goes, I thought, picturing myself toppling back and falling like a beetle with my legs in the air as Lee, Max and Catherine looked on.

But it was easier than I thought. Soon I heard the thump of the boot as Max closed it after putting my chair in. He was obsessed by the bloody thing and headed straight for it during visits so that he could practise his wheelies. Beside me, Lee looked so familiar in his sunglasses and baseball cap, but it felt strange doing something so normal. Excitement bubbled up inside me as I talked to Max about school, his friends, the latest computer game he wanted. I was out and about, in the real world again.

A few minutes later we pulled up outside the entrance to the rose garden at Regent's Park and I could see children running around, people admiring the flowers, teenagers chatting as they sat on the grass – a normal day.

Panic gripped me.

'I can't get out,' I said in a rush.

Lee turned towards me.

'I'm sorry. I can't. I'm exhausted. I just can't get out. Do you mind if we sit in the car?'

'Of course we can,' Lee replied. 'But why? We can get you out, Les. You'll be fine. There won't be a problem.'

'I can't,' I pleaded. 'I just can't, OK. Don't make me.'

'Of course I won't. It's fine. But why not? Why don't you want to get out?'

I stared back at him. He looked so worried, so confused and I wanted to cry.

'Because I don't want anyone to see me like this,' I whispered.

I thought I'd come so far, but looking out of the car window, I realised that my world in hospital was a million miles from this normal one. Mine moved at 5 miles an hour, while the real world started at 100 and only got faster.

CHAPTER 16

Home Sweet Home

I believe there comes a point in anyone's recovery when you have to make a decision, and it was after the trip to Regent's Park that I made mine. I felt so down when I got back. I'd been right all along – I was never going to be part of the real world again, be back to normal. I'd got as far as I was going to get and that was it. I just wanted to lie back and give in.

But I was still in hospital, and as images of the real world on that sunny day kept replaying in my head, I slowly began to realise that I had a choice – just as I had when I'd seen the woman in the mirror at the Charing Cross. I could either give up and accept I was never going to walk or keep trying and hope that one day I would. When you've got a family, there really isn't any decision to make – you've just got to keep trying – and it was that which changed things for me.

'Think of everyone else, not just you,' a voice started whispering inside. 'You've got to get home to Lee, Max and Joe.'

It got louder every day and soon, instead of just going through the motions, I was working harder at the gym and things were starting to click. As I walked with Rachel, I began to realise that rehabilitation was just like being in rehearsals for a musical – there's a dance routine, a song, a melody and some lyrics. They are all completely disjointed at the start, but you keep practising until one day you've got the words, pitch and tempo right and you're performing, baby! I'd just been paying lip service to my recovery for a long time: swinging from 'I can't do this' to believing that – bang! – it would happen. That had to change.

For the first time I realised that I had to accept I was never going to walk like I had in my former life. I was different now – just as I was different after my marriage, the birth of my children, my mum's death, this was another life experience and I had to change with it. This wasn't about getting back to the old Leslie but becoming the new one, and I had to forget how things once were. My body was a whole new person that I had to learn how to use in a different way – not through feeling, but muscle memory, sight, placement of my legs and awareness of my core muscles.

'Your recovery is up to you,' Rachel would tell me day after day. 'You've got to realise that I can help you so far but only you can remind your body of all it once knew.'

Lying in bed moping was never going to get me better. My nerves were never suddenly going to come back to life, and I'd get nothing for nothing. I had to work to wake up my body, and to do that, I needed to get control over my feelings because all I'd done was cry since my accident. It was bloody depressing apart from anything else.

When you leave this place, you'll be at home: Agnes won't be there to be nice all the time; Rachel won't be there to make you do your exercises; Catherine won't be there to open the dishwasher door if you can't reach it, I thought as I realised how self-indulgent I'd been.

Dr Shakir hadn't been horrible to me – he'd just told me how it was. I was always going to have some sort of disability, but how much of one was down to me. I was looking down two paths: one would be travelled in a wheelchair and the other on foot. I told myself I was lucky to even have a choice – a lot of people didn't.

Just see how far you can push yourself, I said to myself. And if all else fails, you can bluff it.

I finally started working really hard when I realised my recovery was there for the taking. It wasn't enough to make do with a crappy shuffle. I started trying to refine my movement using the lessons Rachel was teaching me, the control I'd had drilled into me as a child in ballet classes and a lifetime of being able-bodied. I didn't want to shuffle along for the rest of my life and use a wheelchair when it all got too tiring. I wanted to walk tall.

Gradually my body started responding – my feet went where I wanted them to, I relied less on my arms as I walked along the bars, and my legs didn't weave around so much. I still couldn't feel anything in the places where it really mattered, like my hips, knees and ankles, but I knew when my stomach muscles were working and everything led back to that.

To keep myself going, I focused on the family holiday we had booked in Ibiza on 1 August. It was now the end of June and that bloody holiday was all I could think about.

'Do you think I'll get there?' I started asking Rachel every day.

'We'll have to see. We'll keep working hard and assess you,' she'd reply.

Just the thought of being on a plane got me out of bed in the morning – plus the fact that my insurance was going to run out at about the same time – and I also kept returning to other mental goals: walking around at the Chelsea Flower Show next year; walking on a beach; walking down the King's Road looking in the shop windows. Walking, walking, walking – it was the only thing that mattered to me.

Funnily enough, it was getting up after a fall that proved to me that all the hard work was paying off. I was standing at the window one day thinking about nothing much, looking down at Lord's Cricket Ground and up at the beautiful sunny sky, when I suddenly found myself on my arse. That happened occasionally when I stopped concentrating – I had to think about it all the time, otherwise I'd keel over. So there I was with no one around to pick me up and I had to try to get up. Rachel had shown me a technique, but I'd never used it alone until now. Fifteen minutes later I'd done it, and I felt so pleased when I told Agnes.

'Leslie, you've got to call me if you fall,' she said.

'But there's no harm,' I told her, and she smiled.

Agnes knew how much getting up meant to me – and not just physically. In fact, everyone at the Wellington was far more aware of my mental state than I ever was. For instance, around a month in I picked up a hand mirror and realised that something had to be done.

Poor Lee's got to see this, I thought, as I looked at my roots and pale skin.

I'd always taken pride in my appearance – especially my hair – and seeing myself looking so bad made me realise I had to make a bit of effort, not just for my sake, but my husband's too. I was more Marge Simpson than Jessica Simpson, and it wasn't a good look. After all, there's only so long a man can stare at hairy legs, bristling eyebrows and a surgical gown. It was time for a change, and for the first time since my accident, I felt the need to reach for my make-up bag.

I laid everything out on the table across my bed. All my old friends were there – creamy all-in-one powder foundation, rose blusher, plum lip-liner, kohl eye pencil and sugar-pink lip gloss. Picking up my hand mirror, I started work. It felt strange to watch my face transforming. At first I found it hard to apply everything properly, but then I tasted the lip gloss, smelt the powdery smell of the foundation and relaxed. It was like riding a bike – a woman doesn't forget how to make the best of her assets. Finally I brushed my eyebrows and pulled my hair back into a ponytail. I felt so feminine again. I'd been adamant about not looking after myself for so long, but it was almost as if I had a new woman pulsing through my veins.

'You look lovely,' a nurse said as she came in. She was the first of many people that day who noticed how different I looked and it proved to me that just a little effort can go a long way.

'It's an important hurdle you've crossed today, Leslie,' Dr Shakir told me when he came in for his visit. 'You might not have meant to do it, but you've naturally got over it and that's great news. It's an important psychological moment in your recovery when you're interested enough in yourself to worry about how you look.'

It was almost as if those doctors and nurses knew what was going to happen before I did at times. Spooky!

I don't know if it was my new-found positivity or just old-fashioned healing, but a couple of weeks later Dr Shakir came running into my room.

'I've just read your notes,' he said. 'What wonderful news.'

'What do you mean?' I asked.

He looked very smiley. 'Your notes from last night,' he replied.

It was still as clear as mud. The previous evening I'd been examined by his colleague and the only difference to every other night was that my toes had gone down instead of up when the doctor had run the end of his hammer along the sole of my foot.

'Your toes are flexing downwards in response to stimulus, instead of up, which means your reflexes are changing,' Dr Shakir continued. 'This is very important, Leslie – a real milestone in your recovery – because it proves to us that your nerves are regenerating and that means there is recovery in your spine.'

I stared up at him, not quite daring to hear what he was saying.

'Some of the damage is beginning to mend itself, Leslie,'

the medic said. 'It's what we've been waiting for.'

Finally, after all the work, the uncertainty and the pain, there was some good news. My feeling was returning.

I was walking forward – smooth, flowing steps, like I never thought I'd feel again. My back was straight, and for the first time in months I didn't feel like I was dragging my heavy limbs.

'This is amazing,' I said, turning to Rachel, who was stood beside me.

'I know.' She smiled back.

We were in the Welly's hydrotherapy pool and I was walking down the middle holding on to a polystyrene tube in front of me. My body felt light, my movement easy as the water closed around me. For the first time since waking up, I felt as if I could control my legs. Of course, it only lasted as long as I was in the water. Back on dry land, I weaved around like a drunken sailor again. But it felt fantastic even for that short time as the water held me and I almost believed I could feel again. Six weeks into my time at the Welly, I was moving on to the next stage of my recovery. Kind BUPA had thankfully extended the number of weeks they'd cover my bill, but everyone knew the countdown to home was looming. My insurance would only last so long, and while I might not be able to walk properly, I could now move about in a wheelchair, my muscles were stronger, and I was learning to adapt to my new body, so at some point I had to go it alone. But a question mark still hung over whether I'd have to go on to another rehab centre or would be well enough to go on holiday. Given the choice of a physio gym or lying by a pool, I knew which one I wanted and so I worked as hard as I could in hydrotherapy and to tackle new challenges like the stairs, which felt like Everest when I first tried them.

Part of me was so excited at the thought of going home. I'd be back with my family, in my own bed, eating my own food, living a normal life again. At times it was all I could think about, but I was also aware of another part of me which didn't want to leave. I felt happy and safe in hospital, and as much as I was looking forward to seeing the real world, it also terrified me: I wouldn't be able to cope; it would all be too fast; I'd fall; looking after my family again would be too much.

Don't get me wrong, I loved Lee and the boys and they loved me, but I also did a lot for them. 'Where are my trackie bottoms?', 'What's for lunch?', 'Can you give me a lift?', 'Where's that envelope I left on the kitchen counter?'

The three men in my life needed constant attention and I feared they'd make demands on me in every department – domestic, emotional, physical – as soon as I walked through the door. They'd think things were normal again – Mum's back, Leslie's home, let's carry on where we left off – and I was scared I'd disappoint them. I might have drunk a bit too much in the past, worked a bit too hard and argued a bit too loudly, but I'd always been good at domestics, like cooking, cleaning and caring. Now I was scared I wasn't up to it, and while I knew Rita would be there to help me, I was frightened of being a failure in my own home.

The other thing I began to think about as the time to leave the Welly beckoned was my relationship with Lee. Between the crisis, the hard graft and his constant support, I had almost forgotten we'd had any problems before I'd gone into hospital, and in some ways I knew we were now closer. Organised and dedicated, he hadn't fallen apart without me but had kept everything together, and without too much vodka or too many late nights, we'd been far nicer to each other than we had been in a long time. We watched TV, laughed at each other's jokes, chatted about stuff and even regularly locked the door to my room so that I could practise my pelvic tilts on him! But the most important thing he'd done was allow me to focus on my recovery without having to worry about Joe and Max. I knew Lee was there for them, and that between school and their father, my absence was hard but not too hard for them. They still seemed fine when I saw them – so fine in fact that I kept wondering when one of them might look in the least bothered! But a lot of that was down to Lee. He'd stepped in to care for them and it seemed like we'd all learned something in the process. I'd always been the one in charge domestically, but Lee had proved that parenting – practical details and all – was about two people and not just me. I'd been taken out of the equation in a way that would never have happened without my accident and Lee had almost been like a single dad. He'd risen to the occasion brilliantly, and as I prepared to leave hospital, I realised that in a way it was time for me to step back from my sons. Now they needed to be guided more by their father as they moved towards becoming adults. I'd always been a bit of a soft touch and it had done them good to have their father in charge and learn that no sometimes really does mean no.

If any more proof were needed about how committed Lee was to me, it came when he decided to sell our shares in Teatro. I'd long felt there was a third person in my marriage – although it was a club instead of a woman – but Lee had resisted giving up on his baby. He'd been thinking of selling for a while, but my accident made the decision for him. He knew how much time he was going to have to spend with me and realised he needed to find a buyer. From now on he'd concentrate personally on me and business-wise on Souk.

Despite all that, there was still a part of me that worried about going home – would the closeness we'd rediscovered fall apart again?

Team Leslie sat looking at me. It was our regular fortnightly meeting, and once again I'd been a good girl and done all they'd asked. A couple of days before, I'd even got up on crutches for the first time. Rachel was leaving for a new job and was anxious to fulfil the one promise she'd made to me – to get me upright without parallel bars, polystyrene tubes or her arms holding me. She wanted to be the one to see me on crutches for the first time.

So, a couple of sunny mornings before, I'd wheeled myself down to the gym, where she was waiting with a pair of crutches lined up. Excitement filled me. Knowing my nerves were beginning to heal gave me a real boost and I felt more confident because I could feel some kind of sensation creeping back into my body. The joints were still dead, but I could feel more of the bits in between. Now I was going on to crutches, and if I could do this, then maybe one day I wouldn't have to use a chair any more, maybe I'd go from two crutches to one and then on to a stick. That was all I wanted – to walk with a stick however stiffly. My dad's wheelchair was quite enough for one family.

I put my left crutch forward, moved my right leg and took a step.

'Relax your shoulders, Leslie,' Rachel told me. 'Remember you can't let yourself slip into bad habits now.'

I felt myself move forward – I was walking on my own for the first time. My bum might be sticking out, I might be unsteady, but I was standing up!

'You're doing it, Leslie, you're doing it,' Rachel almost cheered.

Now I looked around the room at Team Leslie as the meeting came to an end.

'Is there anything else?' Eileen, the administrator, asked everyone.

'Well, there is one thing,' Rachel said, as she looked at me. 'Leslie's done really well this week. She's got on to crutches, and her hydrotherapy is going well.'

I looked at her – please, please, please say I could go on holiday.

'And because of all that, I think she'll be ready to travel to Ibiza,' I heard her say.

I'd have jumped up and kissed her if I could. Instead, I just sat and laughed as everyone congratulated me – no more hospital food for me. I was off on holiday.

I sat on my bed holding a bag that Agnes had put together for me – tablets, make-up, all I needed for my first weekend visit home. I'd done my hydro and physio for the day and was feeling excited but apprehensive because Lee was on his way to take me home for two whole nights with my family.

I checked the bag three or four times, making sure everything I needed was there. Had Agnes forgotten my sleeping pills or my painkillers? Of course not, but still I felt anxious, scared about leaving my bubble. It was about 1 p.m. when Lee came through the door.

'Ready to go?' he asked.

I nodded and put myself into my chair.

As Agnes waved us off into the lift, I felt like a nervous teenager going on a first date, almost a bit self-conscious. I'd be sleeping with Lee in our marital bed, where my accident had happened before all this had begun and from where I'd been carried away by paramedics all those weeks before.

'The boys will be home later,' Lee said.

I thought of the flat. My nerves shifted to joy when I thought of seeing Charlie. I hadn't seen her for an eternity and I'd missed her so much. Soon I'd be able to cuddle up to her and kiss her little head, and then the boys would come home and I'd kiss their little heads too.

Soon we pulled into the underground car park and Lee got my chair out for me. Manoeuvring myself into it, I pushed myself through the door to the lift and thought of my dad. I'd done this journey with him and his chair so many times.

The lift moved slowly upwards until the doors opened and I heard Charlie snuffling under our front door a metre away.

She hurled herself into my chair as soon as it was opened – crying in excitement and wiggling her bum as I stroked her.

'Charlie,' I squeaked. She was beside herself.

Rita stood behind her – almost as pleased to see me, but not quite – and I wheeled myself into the flat. The place was spotless, just the way I liked it. The only thing not quite right was the dining table – all Lee's papers were scattered across it. I wanted to whizz around, tidy everything up, but I couldn't. Ah, well. I was home.

'Maaaaaaaaaaaaaax,' I shouted, 'have you got my chair?'

It was Sunday afternoon and I was trying to get up from the sofa. Yet again my younger son had taken my chair away to play with.

'Sorry, Mum,' he said as he appeared and bent down so that I could give him the thousandth kiss of the weekend. It was so lovely to be at home with him and Joe, comforting to finally lie down again beside Lee, settle into the crook of his arm and fall asleep.

It seemed as if I'd spent most of the previous day calling out to someone or other: 'Can you do this?', 'Can you do that?' 'Can you get me this?' 'Can you get me that?' And to my amazement they'd done it. We'd had a quiet day in the flat because I didn't want to go out in public and give the paparazzi the chance of a picture – I didn't want to send out the wrong message because that wasn't how my recovery was going. I was learning to walk on crutches and getting better all the time.

So we'd stayed in, got a takeaway in the evening, and Sunday had come too soon. Guess what? We had another takeaway for lunch and now I was on my way to see my dad before going back to the Wellington. I had to be there by 6 p.m. so I could have my final horribly painful blood-thinning injection of the day. I wasn't looking forward to going back, and needless to say I cried my eyes out when I said goodbye to the boys. They looked so sad as I left. Joe was waving Charlie's paw at me and that was the tableau as the lift doors closed.

Soon we arrived at the Pines Nursing Home. I was looking forward to seeing Dad. Debbie had been due to pick him up on his birthday a couple of weeks before and hadn't managed to show up, so I'd been worried about him. I was also anxious for him to see exactly how I was. We'd spoken on the phone a few times and he'd always done his best to cheer me up, but I wasn't sure if he realised just how much things were going to have to change.

He was sitting in his wheelchair as the door to his room opened, and just as he did every time I arrived, he turned his head to look at me. His eyes gazed upwards to find my face, until he remembered himself and dropped his gaze down to the wheelchair.

'Hello, darling,' he said with a smile that was more of a shocked grimace.

'Hi, Dad.'

'So, how are you, love?'

I started chatting about my weekend until he suddenly interrupted me.

'We can have a race now,' he said, looking at my chair.

'Well, yours might be called a Quickie, but mine will go faster – it's from a private hospital,' I joked.

We'd laughed at no end of stupid jokes when we realised his chair was called a Quickie, but it didn't seem quite so funny now we were both sitting in them.

We had a cup of tea as I showed Dad what I could do like some kind of performing seal – cracking jokes and smiling so hard my face ached – and he chatted much more than usual, almost as if he wanted to cover up a feeling of discomfort. I didn't know if it was sadness, disappointment or what.

'Have you heard from Debbie?' I asked when there was a lull in conversation.

'Nope,' he said quickly. 'So how are you coping, Leslie?'

'I'm OK. It's just day by day, really. But it's going to take a while and I won't be able to drive you for a bit.'

'Well, that's OK,' he replied. 'You just take your time and get yourself better.'

Soon it was time to go and Dad turned towards the television as I wheeled myself towards the door. It felt strange to be wheeling myself out when I'd spent so much time wheeling him in – usually at high speed because I was always late and he couldn't stand bad timekeeping. Tears tightened my throat. I couldn't believe he'd had to see me like that. Dad had always been so proud of me, but everything he'd seen me achieve – like riding a bike or balancing on ice-skates – had gone and I felt as if I'd thrown it all away.

Lee opened the door for me and I turned back to focus on Dad's face, taking a snapshot of it in my mind as always because Mum's death had taught me how easily I could lose people.

'You'll be fine, love,' Dad said, as he turned back to me. 'You're doing well, girl. Keep going.'

Why did I feel like all he really wanted to say was, 'Look at the state of you'? I started crying as we went back to the car. Tears ran down my face during the whole journey back to the Welly and didn't stop when I got there.

I worked harder than ever as the days ticked down for me to leave. I knew I had to be as good as possible at using my crutches, even though I was still using my chair quite a bit. My new physio, Suzanne, took Rachel's place in teaching me. I was leaving on Friday, 23 July and it was all I could think about.

I tried to be as positive as possible, but there were still times when it all threatened to get on top of me. For instance, there was the day when my in-laws came to visit – my sister-in-law, Denise, her partner, Tom, their twins, Scarlett and

Charles, my mother-in-law, Gill, and her partner, Bill. They came to the gym to see me walk on crutches because I wanted to show them how far I'd come. But the room seemed so quiet as I took my first steps and felt my eyes fill with tears. Who was I kidding? This was my audience now and there'd be no laughs or applause, just stunned silence, as they watched me shuffle down the room.

Then there was the day when Catherine came to see me with brochures for wheelchairs and bath aids. It made it all so real. My life was going to have to change, even my home was going to have to change because there would be a disabled person in it.

'Do you need a ramp up to the front door? Is there lift access to your flat? What happens if it breaks down?'

The depressing questions were endless, but I knew I had to answer them. It felt as if there'd never be any spontaneity in my life again – everything would have to be planned. But I forced all the anxious thoughts out of my head and concentrated on leaving. Then I was given a real boost when the lingerie company Playtex approached Michele, my agent, to ask if I would front an advertising campaign for them.

'Are they mad?' I asked when she rang me. 'I'm still in hospital.'

'No, they really want you,' she insisted. 'They want you because it's a new range for the older woman with a fuller bosom. I've told them where you are, but they know you're coming out soon and want you to be involved.'

So the deal went ahead and I was absolutely thrilled I had a job to do straight after leaving hospital – work had been on my mind a lot and I'd worried it would take a while to get back into. Now it seemed I'd been right to hope, and if that didn't give me the incentive to look and feel good, then nothing would.

Knowing we were going on holiday also forced me and Lee to think about another aspect of the real world – the newspapers. Lee had known all along that there would be no escaping the interest when I left hospital, but I'd finally realised how bad it might be when he'd taken me to see an acupuncturist in Harley Street.

'You get paparazzi here all the time,' he said worriedly, as he wheeled me along the pavement.

'Oh, don't be so paranoid,' I replied breezily.

Half an hour later I'd had the acupuncture and was feeling pretty relaxed as we left.

'Hold on,' Lee said. He wheeled me out through the front door, turned the chair round and – bang! bang! bang! – we thumped down the steps before hitting the pavement with a thud.

'For God's sake,' I said to him. 'I've got a spinal injury.'

I'd also just had countless needles stuck into me and could feel the g-force as Lee pushed me down the pavement. I'd go flying if we hit the kerb.

'Come on, come on,' he kept muttering as we sped towards the car.

Sunglasses on, hat over my eyes and travelling at the speed of light, I couldn't see a thing. He bundled me into the passenger seat. He was right, though, and sure enough pictures of me appeared in the papers. We'd had loads of requests for interviews while I was in hospital, but had always said no. Now, though, we felt that article after article had been written about our marriage and we wanted people to know we were still together, still happy, so we agreed to talk to the *Sunday Mirror* on our first day in Ibiza – an interview, some pictures and then we could concentrate on the next stages of my recovery because although I was leaving hospital, it was far from over.

From now on it would be down to Lee and me. Without my physios and the safe environment of the hospital, he would be the one getting me out of bed, up from the sofa and into the shower. Lee was literally going to have to learn to be my carer – how to support me using his weight, how to offer me an arm and not pull me, how to pick me up if I fell, how to help me across the road and up kerbs. But the most important thing he'd have to do was walk with me. I was still using two crutches, and the only way I'd learn how to go down to one – and eventually hopefully none – was with his help. First, he'd steady me and then gradually do it less and less as I got stronger, until one day I might walk unaided. It was the one goal I had to achieve after leaving the Welly, the most important one of all, and even though I'd arranged to see Rachel, my old physio, twice a week at home when I got back from Ibiza, Lee would be the main person to help me reach it.

So one day we were taken outside to an area that had everything we needed – paving stones and a kerb, plus a walking stretch of about 30 metres – and Lee was given a demonstration of how to help me. Then it was time for us to go it alone. He towered above me as I held on to my crutch for dear life and leaned on him with my other arm. I started to walk shakily forward. I looked down at my little legs and wanted to laugh because Lee's huge ones beside them were taking these slow, little steps.

'Don't go too fast,' I told him.

'I'm not going to,' he replied.

We were off – it wasn't exactly a walk into the sunset, but it was a start.

CHAPTER 17

Hello and Goodbye

I was sitting in a people carrier with Lee, Max and Neil Reading, the guy who helped us with media work. I'd left Agnes and the Welly the day before and, after getting my highlights done and having a good night's sleep, we were on our way to City Airport. We were off on holiday! Well, poor Neil wasn't – he was just coming with us to see us off because we were flying with the *Sunday Mirror* to Ibiza to do our interview on the first day of our holiday. Our friend Kevin Harper was coming over with us to meet his girlfriend, Georgia, on the sunshine island, and we'd meet up with Joe there because he was already in Spain with friends who were also coming to stay with us. Phew! Life in the real world was complicated.

The car slowed to a halt and *Sunday Mirror* journalist Maggie O'Riordan opened the door.

'I'm worried another paper will get a shot of you getting on to the plane,' she said in a rush.

I wasn't even out of the car yet.

'We're going to have to move quickly,' she continued. 'So they don't get a chance.'

'Well, that's the one thing I can't do,' I replied. 'You need to give me a lot of notice about what you want me to do because I'm pretty slow.'

'Yeah, that's fine,' she said anxiously. 'We need to get you into a chair and whizz you through to the plane. Other photographers will be around somewhere, so we can't let them get a picture.'

Of course I knew that newspapers were very protective of exclusive interviews with people, but I hadn't realised quite how bad it would be.

I started shuffling out of the car on my crutches.

'Get back, get back!' Maggie screamed. 'I can see a pap.'

I stopped moving and waited for my next instruction. Max stared at me wide-eyed from the seat behind. I was terrified I was going to fall and disgrace myself, and he was wondering what on earth his mother was up to.

Maggie got my wheelchair out of the car, then disappeared. She returned clutching about six brightly coloured umbrellas. Everyone was handed one as I got into the chair and the umbrellas were opened up to shield me. It was like the transformation scene in *Cinderella*. I didn't know whether my chair and the umbrellas were going to change into a pumpkin coach and horses at any second. It just looked ridiculous and I wasn't sure whether I should laugh or cry.

Things got a whole lot better as we boarded the private plane taking us to Ibiza. Its padded leather seats were like big armchairs and everything was so luxurious. Just as we started to relax, though, Maggie dropped the bombshell.

'There's been a slight change of plan,' she said. 'We're not going to Ibiza – we're going to Alicante instead.'

'What?' Lee replied.

'Well, we've had word that a press agency has staked out Ibiza Airport and my editor wants us to divert to a villa in the middle of nowhere so that we can do the photos in privacy. Then you can travel to Ibiza tomorrow and all this will be a distant memory as you start your holiday.'

It obviously wasn't so much a question as a command – we'd been hijacked by the *Sunday Mirror*! Then came loads of discussions between Lee and Maggie, Maggie and Neil,

Neil and Lee, and Lee and the editor until everything was sorted. I could see our friend Kevin inwardly combusting even as he smiled. He was supposed to be in Ibiza tonight, not on mainland bloody Spain. When we took off, though, everyone soon relaxed, the interview started, and the champagne flowed for them and the water for me.

We landed in Alicante at about 5 p.m. to find two people carriers waiting to take us all to the isolated villa. It turned out, though, that the secret location was in fact so secret no one could find it and the one-hour drive stretched on and on. Up until then, I'd still only sat upright for about an hour at a time so I was in agony. My back went into spasm, the journey went on and on – and on and on – and three hours later we were still going. I was in pain, Lee was panicking, and Kevin was pissed off with hearing me complain. We finally arrived in the small secret town. Home, sweet home at last. No such luck. It took another hour to find the shop where the keys to the villa were held. We then went round one roundabout approximately eight times and got stuck in a one-way system so we didn't get to the villa until about 10 p.m.

I was so pleased to be able to lie down at last, but things didn't get any better the next day when we woke up at our secret rural location to find we were smack bang in the middle of a residential estate with houses on all sides and weren't allowed to open any of the curtains in case someone snatched a picture of us.

Is this another bloody Gotcha Award? I started asking myself.

But it wasn't and soon the pictures were done, the interview was in the bag, and we were on our way to Ibiza. Hooray. A few hours later we touched down and said goodbye to Kevin – well, I think it was him, but he moved so fast he was a blur. We were on our way to the villa that was going to be our home for two weeks.

*

I sat with my legs dangling in the turquoise water. I was sitting by the side of the pool and could hear voices inside the house, where the boys were. Our villa was beautiful – in the middle of nowhere, surrounded by trees and really quiet. I loved it; in fact I loved Ibiza as much as ever. It's a chilled-out place, slow and relaxed, so it suited me brilliantly, even though Lee had enjoyed it for just a few days before getting itchy feet. Once he's got a tan, he loses interest.

He'd taken a while to relax because the trip hadn't got off to a great start when we'd seen the *Sunday Mirror* article. It all looked a bit clichéd and desperate. Ah, well, we'd agreed to do it. The final straw had come, however, when the whole thing also ended up in *Hello!*. We hadn't known a thing about it and weren't very pleased that people would think we were on some massive publicity campaign, rather than doing just one interview.

But then we'd all started to relax, and it was great being with my boys again. Lee was doing really well looking after me – lifting me in and out of the bath, helping me get down all the stairs, that kind of thing – and Joe was having a good time with the two friends he'd brought along. Max was OK, but a little upset that his mates had pulled out of coming.

'It'll be too much for you,' their mums had told me.

I couldn't help wondering if they thought it would be too risky leaving their kids with me – I could hardly look after my own children after all, let alone someone else's – but I didn't think about it too much. Max, though, was really grumpy on the nights when Lee took Joe and his friends into the main town to have a look at the nightlife and he had to stay behind with me.

'Why can't I go?' he'd moan.

'Because Joe is fifteen and you're only twelve,' I'd reply, as he huffed and puffed.

Poor Max. There was his dad and brother out having fun and he was with me – woozy from medication from about 4 p.m.

when the pain got too bad and in bed by 9 p.m. No wonder he was fed up.

I felt so far from the Welly as the days melted into one another. No more hospital food, smells or routine; instead, I got up, had breakfast by the pool and topped up my tan on a sunbed for the rest of the day – only getting off it to shuffle to the edge of the pool on my bottom. I didn't feel safe enough to go in on my own and was too unsteady on my crutches to get down the steps into the water, so Lee had to help me when I wanted to swim. But I wasn't being lazy all the time and had kept up with the exercise programme Suzanne had given me. I still got really tired and used the wheelchair a lot, but was looking forward to seeing Rachel when I got back and carrying on building up my strength.

The only hard thing was that the boys sometimes got impatient with how slow I was back in the real world.

'Come on, hurry up, Mum,' they'd say.

'Don't say that, because I can't,' I'd tell them.

They had to get used to my world just as much as I had to get used to being back in theirs again. Things had changed and it would take time.

Otherwise, I was having the most relaxing holiday I'd had since having them. Instead of jumping up to make food or clear up, I just had to lie on my sun lounger, and I quite enjoyed saying the words 'Sorry, I can't' if they asked me for something.

'Mum, where's my swimming shorts?' they'd shout.

'Don't know, can't look,' I'd shout back.

It's a thankless task being a mother and it was nice to have people running after me for a change!

I flexed my feet in the water as Lee sat down beside me.

'Will you take me for a swim?' I asked.

'In a minute,' he replied. 'I've had some news. I've just had a phone call. Teatro's been sold. It's all gone through. That's it.'

Relief washed over me. Part of me couldn't believe I'd never cross that threshold again – my last memory of it was running up the stairs in a pair of stilettos, and Teatro had been such a big part of our lives – but mostly I was glad. It was the end of all the partying, the craziness, the fighting for attention with a business.

'Are you all right?' I asked.

'Yes, fine,' Lee replied.

I knew he'd be upset about the end of Teatro, however well he hid it.

'We'll be OK,' I said, as I turned to him. 'You'll be busy. There's still Souk to run. It's good that Teatro's gone.'

'I'm fine, Les,' he replied. 'Really, I'm fine.'

'Well, that's good,' I said, and leant across to kiss him. 'Because now I've got you all to myself.'

I looked at the bed a metre away. Just a couple of steps and I'd be there. I held on to the chest of drawers behind me and glanced quickly at the bedroom door to make sure no one was around.

You can do it, I thought, as I stared at my feet.

I felt sick, nervous. I loosened my grip, raised my right leg and guided it forward, knowing my left would follow through behind. It felt strange having nothing to hold or lean on to after such a long time.

Arches up, knees straight, weight even, I told myself as I put my foot to the floor.

It was a big moment for me. Four long months after my accident, I'd started believing – instead of just hoping – that I would one day walk unaided.

I hadn't told anyone what I was about to do – particularly not Rachel, because I knew she'd tell me off. She always worried about me pushing myself too hard and hurting my ankles because you can easily go over on them when you can't feel.

But I was so impatient. I'd got much steadier on my

crutches while we were in Ibiza, and in the three weeks since getting back, I'd been almost as busy with my recovery as I had been in hospital. Rachel and I had been practising hard during our twice-weekly sessions together, and where before we'd 'danced' between the parallel bars, we now moved across the living room as I laid my arms on tops of hers to feel my way. I looked a bit like Frankenstein – stiff and jerky, my legs weaving in front of me as I walked – but at least I was giving it a go.

I was also going swimming once a week with my personal trainer, Wendy, having regular massages and acupuncture, and practising my exercises as I lay in bed, on the sofa or walked around on my crutches – flexing and pointing my feet or pulling in my stomach muscles to lift my leg and hold it out in front of me for as long as possible. I had to make sure that my feet were properly aligned, because my right one tended to turn out a lot, and that my weight was spread evenly between both.

My recovery was racing forward again. Even though the paraesthesia meant I still couldn't feel my joints, I was finally regaining partial feeling in some of my muscles and had sensation in my little and big toes, which was really significant because it gave me a much better idea of where I was placing my feet. Most importantly, I was no longer relying on feeling alone. Sight and core-muscle sensation were just as important to me now as my damaged nerves. Admittedly, I could still only do short distances on my crutches and spent most of my day lying down, but the more I used them, the better I'd get. To make sure I pushed myself, Lee and I had taken my wheelchair back to the Welly a couple of weeks before.

I was also coping far better without Team Leslie than I'd ever imagined I would. I'd been so scared about leaving them, but life was easier than I'd thought it would be. When it came to housekeeping, Rita did big domestic things, including washing, shopping and cleaning, while I helped out – very slowly – with little bits like making the bed. For everything else, Lee was by my side. If I made a cup of tea, he'd carry it for me; if I sat on the sofa watching telly, he'd work at the dining-room table so he could get me what I needed; if I went to have a shower, he'd keep an eye on me in case I fell over when I closed my eyes to wash my hair.

Even the boys were getting more used to the changes – in fact, I think they quite liked some of them. For instance, I couldn't get around the kitchen to cook, so we got takeaways or ate at restaurants far more often than ever before, which went down well. They'd also worked out that I'd never be able to surprise them again – the metallic clicking noise of my crutches could be heard way before I appeared in the bedroom doorway – so they were always nowhere to be seen when I wanted to ask them to do something.

I looked at the bed in front of me and prayed that no one would come in as I brought my leg forward. I didn't want to try walking for the first time in front of an audience. I needed to do this alone. This was something private, and if I messed it up, then no one would have to know. I wouldn't have to look at the doubt in their eyes.

My left leg swung into view just as my right foot hit the floor. I stared down as I willed it forward – just one more step. One, two, that's all that was needed to make a walk. I just had to see those steps in my mind's eye and my body would follow.

Slowly, slowly, my left foot touched down on the carpet and I fell against the bed. I'd done it! I'd taken two steps. I'd walked unaided.

I couldn't wait to return to work, get out there and let people know I was back. I'd earned my own money since I was 16 and had never really been unemployed, so I was keen to get back on the circuit again. Six weeks after leaving the Welly, I got my chance when the Playtex shoot was done. I was really looking forward to it. Life was going well and I felt ready to think about something other than my recovery.

We'd got a boost a few weeks before, when the police had finally announced that the investigation into Debbie's accusations had been dropped and no charges were being brought against Lee. Even though we'd always known it would come to nothing, it was still horrible having it hanging over our heads, and I finally felt as if we could put the whole thing behind us – the accident, the hospital, the lies. Her name was never mentioned any more in our house, and even Dad and I didn't talk about it when Rita took me to see him. We did the trip at least once a week, and he'd been really pleased to see how well I'd done when I'd first left hospital.

'Hi, Dad,' I'd said, when I walked into his room for the first time on crutches.

He'd looked downwards as he turned his head, expecting to see me in a wheelchair, but then his eyes had travelled up – in exactly the opposite direction that they had on my awful weekend visit from hospital – and I could see how pleased he was.

'Hello, love,' he said. 'Look at you. Nice to see you up and about.'

Body bent forward in a long straight line and looking like I had four legs instead of two, thanks to the crutches, I was moving at a snail's pace and looked a bit like a giraffe, but Dad was beaming as we sat and chatted. No one mentioned Debbie. Throughout the whole ordeal I'd kept thinking about what I'd do if something like that ever happened with Joe and Max and I knew I'd still love them both whatever. So I felt that Dad and I shouldn't talk about what had happened. I didn't want him to feel he had to pick a side – Debbie was his daughter. He didn't mention it, so I didn't either. I knew I would never speak to my sister again and I didn't want him to be upset. Sometimes silence really is golden.

The final piece of the moving-on jigsaw was a TV interview we'd agreed to do with Sir Trevor McDonald at the end
of September. We'd felt so disappointed with the *Sunday
Mirror* article – I thought it looked fake and was worried we'd
only made the problems worse – that we'd agreed to do an
interview with Sir Trevor. There would be no headlines or
pictures to worry about – just Lee and me setting the record
straight and then we could get on with our lives.

It finally seemed as if we were about to close that horrible
chapter and I felt ready to move on. In order to do that, the
first thing I needed was to get a few job offers and for that I
needed people to see I was available for work. And, boy, was
I going to be seen, thanks to the Playtex campaign! I'd had a
meeting with the company a few days after getting back from
Ibiza and they'd shown me the lingerie I was going to model.
There were four different designs in red, white, blue and
black and they were all lovely – but just a bit see-through.

'Is there anything you can do about that?' I enquired politely, while gesturing at my boobs.

'Oh, we airbrush the pictures,' a voice replied. 'Don't
worry.'

'But what will I do during the shoot? Surely there'll be a
photographer and his assistant there?'

'No, no, no,' a soothing voice said. 'You'll wear nipple covers under the bra and a flesh pant under the Playtex pant.'

That's what they say in lingerie language, but who calls it
'a pant'? I'd been hearing that word for years – ever since
starting modelling – and could never understand it. They're
'pantsssss' and I hadn't got to where I had in comedy by calling them 'a pant' – that would never have got the laughs we'd
got each week filming *Men Behaving Badly*, when Neil,
Martin, Caroline and I had tried to weave the word 'pants' at
least once into every episode and usually we'd managed it.

I didn't tell the Playtex ladies that, of course, and had
arrived at the photographic studio on my crutches a few

weeks later. After all that gym time and a good holiday, I was slimmer, browner and more toned than I'd been for years and felt great when my hair and make-up had been done.

We got down to work and soon the photographer had pictures of me wearing a black suit with the red lingerie peeping out, me in a cashmere cardigan with my fluffy sheepskin boots on and me standing against a wall in a white silk dressing gown revealing the white set.

'They're great,' I said, when I was shown some test shots at the end of the day.

I almost couldn't believe it was me. There I was on film looking just like my old self. Better even! The woman in the mirror at the Charing Cross popped into my head as I pushed her out again. I didn't look weak or have that ill hospital look in my eyes – the shadow of a traumatic experience lingering there. My sparkle had finally returned and now all the world would see it.

'So have there been any calls for me?' I asked Michele.

'No,' she replied. 'But I've got a few meetings coming up and I'll have a chat with people to see what's out there for you.'

'No one's been in touch about doing a one-off episode or anything? I used to be asked to do stuff like that all the time.'

'No, sorry,' Michele told me. 'I'll make some calls and come back to you.'

'OK, then. Speak soon.'

I put down the receiver and stared around the living room. The house was so quiet – the boys were at school, Rita had left for the day, and Lee was working. Everyone was busy doing something.

It was late October – weeks since I'd done the Playtex shoot – and there was still no work on the horizon. What was wrong with people? What was wrong with me? Didn't they want me any more?

Don't be stupid, I kept telling myself. They've just got to realise you're available and then you'll get something. Think of all the people you know, all the directors you've worked with over the years. They know what you're capable of, what you can do. You've come so far and they'll realise that.

But I knew other people weren't so sure.

'You shouldn't push yourself too hard, just let yourself carry on getting stronger and the work will come in time,' Lee said to me when we talked about it.

I didn't want to wait. I could play a patient lying in a hospital bed – I knew that part off by heart, after all – or a boardroom bitch sitting behind a desk, or do voiceovers. I just needed to get out there again. It annoyed me that everyone seemed to think I'd dropped off the face of the earth. I was up and about again – ready, willing and able!

I looked around for the TV remote control. Fuck. It was over on the bookshelf. I reached for my crutches, stood up and started to edge my way across the room.

'We've got a little bit of a walk to the studio,' the girl said to me.

'That's fiiiiiiiiiiiine,' I replied in a perky voice, as one word echoed in my head: 'Shiiiiiiiiiiit!'

'Well, just follow me,' she said, and showed me through a door.

I was at the BBC studios in West London to do a documentary voiceover. It was only going to take an hour or so, but at least it was a job. I'd got myself extra-specially ready for the day, and Lee had dropped me off right outside the building.

'It's not too far,' the girl said cheerily, taking me into a paved area where people were eating sandwiches and drinking coffee.

I looked down at all the bumps and lumps in the paving stones that I had to get across.

'Oh, please don't worry,' I said as the girl looked at me. 'I'm absolutely fine. I'm a bit slow, but it's really no problem. I just need to be steady and I'll get there...'

She smiled as I chatted away, hoping a stream of words would cover up the time that it was taking me to move from A to B.

'Only another minute,' I kept laughing as I edged along. 'I'll speed up. I'm so sorry. It's lovely here. I haven't seen it before like this. When was this done?'

I carried on smiling while the girl told me about the BBC's facelift. I hadn't even got across the courtyard yet, and who knew how much more there was to say about it and how far it would be to the studio?

On and on, I kept up the chat until finally running out of things to say. I needed to look at the ground more and talk less if I was going to speed up, and there was only so long the poor girl could keep up the conversation. We smiled nervously at each other as we continued our journey to the studio. I was so pleased when we eventually arrived.

'How did it go?' Lee asked when he picked me up later.

I started laughing. 'Oh, really well,' I giggled. 'I took longer getting to the studio than doing the actual voiceover. I think they loved me.'

My stomach twisted with nerves as the car drove through the studio gates. It was early morning and my breath appeared in white clouds in front of me when I got out. Everything on set was just as it always had been – chippies and electricians running around, set designers and props people putting the final touches to things and the smell of bacon sarnies in the air.

'Hi, Leslie,' Pumba, a hair stylist I'd known for years, said as I was shown into my dressing room.

'Hey, there,' I replied.

My make-up artist friend Katie came to give me a hug. 'How are you?' she asked. 'I haven't seen you since the day I came in to do your make-up when you were leaving the

Chelsea and Westminster. I couldn't believe what happened. I'm so sorry. Are you OK?'

It was the beginning of the shoot for the final ever Homebase commercial and it was good seeing familiar faces. We'd all known we were living on borrowed time for ages because *Men Behaving Badly* had been finished for almost six years, but I was really excited about doing some acting – even if I would only be on screen for 30 seconds. We were doing a Christmas commercial I'd been contracted to do before I fell ill and it would feature scenes of me helping Neil inside with bags of DIY shopping, us decorating the tree and playing charades together.

I changed into my costume and had my hair and face done. Then the call came that the director wanted to start and I set off for the studio. A massive yard lay between it and me and I knew I'd take for ever getting across.

'Why don't you stick me in there?' I asked, pointing to a shopping trolley.

'Health and safety,' came the reply.

Well, my health was pretty ropey and I wasn't exactly safe on my feet at the best of times, so stick me in the trolley! But of course they wouldn't. Everyone must have been waiting for ages by the time I reached the studio.

'All right?' Neil asked as I hobbled in, feeling conscious of holding everyone up. 'How are you? Lovely to see you. You've been through it, haven't you? So what happened, then?'

We started chatting as people bustled around us.

'OK, stand by,' the director shouted.

We took our positions by the Christmas tree.

'I'll just grab those for you,' a voice said, and my crutches were taken away.

Fear filled me as I felt myself begin to sway – I was going to fall over if I wasn't careful. Bollocks. I couldn't fall over. I just couldn't.

I grabbed on to the tree and held on for dear life. Neil

started laughing as he saw my knuckles go white and my teeth grit. I was fucking well going to stay upright.

'What are you doing?' he said, staring at me.

'Holding on,' I laughed. 'Just don't move, otherwise I'll fall over.'

'I didn't realise.'

'Don't worry. No one does.'

We carried on giggling and the director started shouting instructions.

'Can you move two inches to your left, Leslie?'

No.

'Can you step away from the Christmas tree?'

No.

'Can you hold up the gold ball in one hand?'

No.

'Er...so you have to hold on to the Christmas tree at all times?'

You've got it.

I ended up wedged between the set wall and the Christmas tree during that scene, and against a door frame for the next – all I can say is that it was a blessed relief to do the charades because I could finally sit down. I carried on laughing at myself – telling people I was fine, insisting that everything was OK – but slowly I could feel my sense of humour drying up. I couldn't carry on seeing the funny side as I stood holding on to whatever was near – a tree, a door, a chair back – while people rushed about around me.

What kind of dream had I been living in? I didn't belong to this world any more, couldn't be part of it in the state I was in. There wasn't any going back for me. I was 44, the age when most actresses' careers get more difficult, and I was disabled. Double whammy. There were younger, stronger women out there who could easily fill my shoes without all the problems I'd bring on to set. I was not going back to work for a long time, and time's just what I didn't have, because people would forget me if I waited. Memories are short in my industry.

Face it. Being on a set – the long days, the cold, the hard work, the moving around – was too much for me. How could I have been so stupid? And how could everyone have allowed me to think like that, instead of saying, 'No one can employ you. You can't walk.' I had to admit to myself what I was really like: I sat on the sofa most of the day, was spaced out by medication and asleep just as most three-year-olds were dropping off. I couldn't cook a meal, walk more than 50 metres or sit in a chair for more than two hours. I'd been making a fool of myself as I tried to arrange lunches with faces from my past. Why hadn't I realised? Why hadn't I listened to the silence which had only got louder with each day that passed? Instead, I'd just ignored it and now I was standing on a set, holding on to a Christmas tree for dear life and reassuring everyone I was fine.

I fought down tears. I felt out of control, like I was slipping away. Who was I trying to kid?

It was 2 December and I was running late to see Dad when the phone went.

'Damn,' I said as I went to grab it.

I'd arranged to see him after lunch and I knew he'd be getting wound up that I wasn't on time. It was one of those beautiful, sunny winter days and I was going to take him into the garden to have a bit of fresh air with his cigar. I had to hurry up, otherwise it would get too late and cold.

'Hello, Mrs Chapman. It's the Pines here,' a voice said.

'Hi,' I replied. 'Is Dad asking where I am? Can you tell him I'm on my way?'

'It's not that. I'm afraid your father's had a fall and we'd like you to come now if possible.'

My heart lurched as I heard panic in the woman's voice.

'Yes, of course,' I told her. 'I'll leave right now.'

I told Lee what had happened and a few minutes later we pulled into the drive of the nursing home. I could see an ambulance waiting.

I phoned back. 'Is that my father?' I asked, while someone was being loaded into the ambulance.

'Yes,' I was told. 'He's being taken to Kingston Hospital.'

'OK,' I replied.

Panic filled me and Lee started following the ambulance as it drove away.

Oh, God. Not my dad.

'What's going on?' I asked Lee. 'Why won't they tell me what's wrong with him?'

'I don't know,' he replied. 'We'll be there in a minute and we'll know everything then.'

I tried to stay calm on the way to the hospital. What had happened? Was it another stroke?

'Can I help?' a receptionist asked when we arrived at A&E.

'My wife's father has just been brought in,' Lee replied. 'His name is Moe Ash.'

'Ah, yes. Would you like to come into the family room?'

I'd prepared for this moment, of course. Dad had had so many strokes that I knew this was bad, and I sat down and waited with Lee until a nurse came in. She looked straight at me and I knew what she was going to say. Her words sounded so far away as she spoke, but I could clearly make out one word: 'died'. I couldn't believe Dad had actually gone. Lee held me until I was shown into a room to say goodbye. Dad was warm and, just like Mum, looked like he was sleeping as I bent down to kiss him. He'd had a massive stroke and there was nothing anyone could have done for him.

Later I went back to his room and saw a cigar resting on the edge of an ashtray. It had been cut ready to smoke and he must have just got up to look for a light when he collapsed. Sadness washed over me. My last link with my childhood had gone. Of course you always know your parents will die, but it still felt unreal that they'd both gone. Maybe now they were together again. I didn't know, but I hoped they were.

Knowing their luck, though, Mum would have just got chatting to Frank Sinatra or something when Dad turned up.

I stared straight ahead as the words of 'Ave Maria' filled the air. Nine days after Dad's death, we were in Putney Vale Crematorium to say goodbye to him. My fingers dug into my pocket and closed around one of his handkerchiefs.

The place was packed with family, Dad's friends from Mitcham Golf Club, and even ex-staff from Unidec had turned up. Debbie and her daughters were sitting two rows behind Lee, Joe, Max and me. I'd spoken to my sister just once, on the day of Dad's death.

'It's Leslie,' I said when she picked up the phone. 'I've got some bad news. Dad passed away today. He had a major stroke. He wouldn't have known anything about it.'

The line went quiet for a moment, and then I continued: 'I'm on my way to get the doctor's certificate and then I'll start arranging the funeral. I'll ring you back when I know what's happening.'

'Don't you want me to give you a hand?' Debbie asked.

'No,' I replied calmly. 'No, I don't. I can sort it out.'

'All right, then.'

'I'll phone you back when I know what's happening.'

'OK.'

Late in the afternoon Lee drove me to the GP's surgery to get the paperwork needed for the death certificate.

In the end I texted Debbie the details of the service. It may sound harsh, but I won't apologise. I felt her article could have destroyed my family. I was going to pull myself together, give my dad a good send-off and honour the last family tie I had.

I had felt so strong as I arranged the funeral – the certificates, the coffin, the church, the crematorium – but as I stood listening to the music play, I tried not to break down in front of everyone. The man singing on the CD was an opera singer called Tony Dali, who'd owned an Italian restaurant in Marbella that we'd gone to for years, and every time we'd eaten at his place when I was young I'd asked him to sing 'Ave Maria'. I told myself that I mustn't shed a tear as I listened to it. If I cried, then all I'd be doing was feeling sorry for myself, and Dad would have hated to see me a blubbering wreck. He'd had a good life and now it was time to say good-bye. Anyway, I knew what people were thinking as they looked at me hobble into church, and if I couldn't be strong physically, then I could be mentally. I didn't want to buckle under the strain and look weak.

After the service ended, we all went outside. I could see Debbie out of the corner of my eye as I thanked people for coming and looked at the messages on the flowers. I was glad she wasn't coming up to me because at least there wouldn't be any scenes. But suddenly I felt arms slide round me from the side and turned my head to see her clinging on to me. She didn't say anything as she looked at me with tears on her face. I froze. Looking straight ahead, I didn't move or speak. I didn't know what to do.

'All right, Mum?' Joe asked, as I carried on staring, saying nothing and just wishing she'd go.

I didn't move as Debbie finally let me go and walked away. Later my younger niece, Holly, came to say hello and I gave her a hug.

'Keep in touch, won't you?' I said. 'Let me know what's happening, how you are.'

She might only have been a teenager, but I knew she understood.

The next day pictures of my sister and me appeared in a newspaper under the headline 'Bitter Leslie Ash snubs sister at father's funeral' with quotes from a 'friend' of Debbie's. Three weeks later my sister did another interview in which she repeated her accusations against Lee. She said she wanted to give me a 'wake-up call'.

I stared at the empty chair at the table. It was Christmas Day and Lee, the boys and I were having lunch in a pub because I still wasn't up to cooking. I'd called to say we would only be four instead of five and they'd taken Dad's place setting away, but the chair was still there and I couldn't stop looking at it.

I'd tried to get into the Christmas spirit, count my blessings and all that, as Gill helped me round the shops to buy presents and I'd wrapped them before putting them under the tree. Earlier that morning Lee and I had been woken up by the boys playing Mariah Carey's 'All I Want for Christmas' at top volume and I'd felt really touched. But now I just couldn't get into the mood. It was like I was at the bottom of a pit as I stared at that chair and ate a Christmas meal that someone else had made. I was useless and Dad had given up on life when he'd realised that. I'd been the one he depended on, and when he saw that I couldn't look after him any more, he'd just let go.

I'd felt worse and worse ever since the funeral. I just wanted to get the year out of the way, forget all that had happened. But as I sat around waiting for my body to heal, I had too much time to think. Once again, it seemed like my recovery had reached its limit. There'd been no real improvement in my movement for months – I was still only taking a few steps unaided as I walked behind the back of the sofa, my fingers tracing its edge in case I fell. Nothing was happening – even my legal case against the hospital didn't seem to be moving anywhere. Reports were being done, specialists were examining me, but the whole thing was taking ages. It was simple, wasn't it? I'd caught an infection because of poor hospital hygiene and now I was disabled. I wasn't going to work again, be the woman I once was, so what was there to argue about?

I was beginning to feel as if I was never going to get rid of

my crutches. I'd tried anything and anyone that might help my recovery since leaving hospital – faith healing, osteopathy, acupuncture, different types of massage, changing my diet, vitamins. I'd even considered doing yoga in a hot room, but I couldn't balance enough to do it. Everyone seemed to have an idea about what I should try. You know how people recommend creams for cellulite or wrinkles? Well, it was the same thing as they very kindly kept giving me their ideas on how to repair the damage to my spine. I knew I was clutching at straws. My spine was permanently damaged, that was it, and however anxious I was to leave no stone unturned, I was never going to find a magic cure. I couldn't work, run my home or even concentrate on reading a book because of the medication. I just had to sit there and wait, sit out the depression, sit out the grief. At least in hospital I'd had something to aim for, something to achieve, but now life seemed like a wide open space and I was lost.

CHAPTER 18

That's All, Folks!

'Lee, have you seen my glasses?'

Pause.

'Joe, have you?'

Another pause.

'Max?'

Silence.

'Hellooooo? Is anyone there?'

'Yes, Mum. We can hear you, but we don't know.'

'Well, can someone help me, then? Can someone do something? Can someone get up off their arse?'

'All right. Calm down. So where did you last see them?'

'I don't know, otherwise I wouldn't be asking, would I? Can't you just come here and look for them? Why do I have to beg to find my glasses? Is it too much to ask that one of you helps me?'

Lee looked at me. 'You need to get a diary and write things down. That's the second acupuncture appointment you've missed. I don't mind taking you, but I don't know when you've made the appointments, so I don't know if you're missing them.'

'But it's the medication. It makes me forget things.'

'Les, I know the pills are strong, but if that's the way it is, then you've got to start writing things down.'

'Well, so what if I forget? If you knew what I'd been through, the pain, the effort it takes just to get out of sodding bed, it's no wonder things go out of my mind. It's not fair of you to shout at me.'

'I'm not shouting at you. I'm just telling you to get a diary.'

'Oh, fuck off, Mr Know-It-All.'

I hit the ground and heard the smash of crockery as the meat plate crashed down beside me.

'Mum, are you all right?'

'No.' I started sobbing.

'Don't cry. I'll help you.'

'My hip. I fell on my hip.'

'Let's get you up,' Joe said.

'I can't believe I've smashed the meat plate. My favourite meat plate.'

'It's too heavy for you. You should have asked Max or me to help you.'

'Well, I couldn't, could I? You're watching the football, and, anyway, I'm not that bloody pathetic. I can carry a dish.'

'Of course we can help you. Stop crying. Please. Let's get you off the floor. Why didn't you put your hands out to stop yourself?'

'Because I don't know when I'm going to fall, do I? One minute I'm up, the next I'm on the floor. I've had enough of this shit.'

'You'll feel better on the sofa. We can finish the lunch.'

'I'm useless. I can't even cook a roast any more.'

'Of course you can, Mum. You're just having a bad day.'

Queen Bee giving out orders, mother from hell, crazy wife – I was all those things as 2005 got underway. I snapped at everyone, shouted or cried in seconds and could hardly be bothered to get off the sofa because I only seemed to get it wrong when I did. I felt as if I'd lost every role I'd ever had – efficient wife,

well-known actress and now dutiful daughter. Sometimes I doubted whether I was even a proper mum any more. I couldn't do all the practical stuff Joe and Max needed doing when they came home at weekends; in fact, it was like they'd suddenly grown up without me noticing. Joe, who'd just turned 16, had really changed. He didn't want quite so many kisses, was a bit more distant, and I'd got really upset one day when we had an argument in the lift after I'd mentioned how big his muscles had got.

'Ooooh, look at you,' I'd said, poking his arm.

'Get off me, don't touch me,' he'd shouted. 'Mum, you can't just do that.'

I didn't see that he was just letting off steam, being a teenager, and I'd invaded his space. Instead, I was hurt that my boy had grown into a man and didn't seem to want me around any more. Even Max wasn't so much a child as a nearly teen and was far more interested in Joe and his friends than me. Jealousy filled me as I realised that they just wanted to be with Lee, talk to him about man stuff and leave me sitting on the sofa.

'Give us a cuddle,' I said to Joe one day.

'Mum, stop it,' he replied, and walked away.

I started crying. I'd lost my buddies. All I wanted was a hug.

'Just stop it,' Joe shouted. 'Don't do that. Don't try to make me feel bad.'

I couldn't see it at the time, but he was right. I was being selfish, trying to make my own son feel guilty so that he would comfort me. What a mess. All I can say in my defence is that I felt no one needed me any more now Dad had gone – in fact, it seemed at times as if my sons were getting bored with me.

'Could you get my glasses?' I'd shout to Max if I'd just sat down. It took so much effort getting back on to my feet that I hated doing it.

'No, I'm busy,' he'd shout back.

'But, Max, I'm on the sofa and I need my glasses.'

'Well, get them yourself.'

Oh, my God. The novelty really had worn off.

No wonder. From being a mum who worked and lived away during shoots, I was now at home the whole time. As Lee ran Souk and the boys went to school, all I did was walk from one seat to another. I couldn't go out unless I was taken, and when I did, I got sick of telling the same bloody story all the time.

'I cannot walk because I caught a superbug because I was in hospital because I broke my ribs.'

Not only was I moving slowly, but I had to repeat and repeat myself as well. It was so boring and I couldn't be bothered to socialise – particularly not with people who were drinking. Occasionally I went down to Souk with Lee, but I just couldn't face being in a crowded room full of people getting pissed. They were on to their second or third when all I could think about was ending my day with a sleeping pill. It had also become obvious that Teatro had been the only thing I had in common with some friends. I was no longer the fun that I had been when I was drinking. There was no more party girl, life and soul; instead I was sober, dull and slow. I knew what they were thinking: I could remember going out in the old days with people who didn't drink and wondering what on earth was the point. Now suddenly I was that person, and sure enough I didn't get another call from some people.

The most I could manage was forcing myself to go out for supper with Lee, but even then I wanted to leave as soon as the meal was over. I could still only sit up for so long, shallow-breathing because I didn't have the muscle power to inflate my lungs properly, and was still on strong medication. Poor Lee. I knew he'd signed up for in sickness as well as in health, but he was getting a whole lot more of it about 30 years earlier than he'd bargained for.

Back at home, I sat for hours staring into space or at some rubbish on TV as people passed by.

'Are you all right? Do you want a cup of tea?' they'd ask, and that would be it.

I was like some sort of maiden aunt they had to stop and say hello to before moving on again.

I was pissed off with relying on people all the time and interrupting them. I just couldn't understand why they didn't see how much help I needed. It would take me five minutes to get up and get my glasses if I left them in the bedroom, whereas it would take them seconds. Why couldn't they help me more? I did my best, after all – glasses on a chain, mobile phone on a string round my neck, pills in a bag that I hung off a crutch handle – but I couldn't do everything.

I was still seeing Rachel, of course, and going swimming, but my heart wasn't in it. I'd been so desperate to try walking unaided, but something in me had given up. I'd been pushing the barriers of my recovery ever since my accident, but there was no getting away from the fact that I was too unsteady and unbalanced to ever walk without help. Yes, I could sit up; yes, I could stand up; yes, I could use crutches. But what was the point of trying to use the stick in preparation for throwing it away when that wasn't going to happen? So instead of trying to give up the crutches, I just stayed on them – I was happy and steady. Why should I go on to something unstable like a stick when I'd never get to the end point?

I tried to be good at times; but making a meal like a simple stir-fry took me an hour instead of 20 minutes, and I was tired two aisles into shuffling round the supermarket with Rita. I felt like I should be wearing L-plates telling people to give me a wide birth as I used the trolley like a Zimmer frame, my legs jerking out stiffly and my shoulders hunched. It was Lee who was keeping everything going – getting my pills, organising doctors' appointments, driving me to the gym, watching while Wendy walked me up the stairs to the

swimming pool, picking me up and asking how my lesson had gone. I was like a child he had to take everywhere.

I couldn't be bothered any more. I'd just get back on the bed as soon as Rita had made it and watch TV. I'd still be there when Lee got home.

'Come on, Leslie. We've got to go. We're late.'

'I'm not coming.'

'Why?'

'I'm just not. I'm too tired.'

'What do you mean?'

'What do you think I mean? I can't be bothered, OK?'

I was lying in bed as Lee got ready to go to the gym. I'd been horizontal for about four days – not really getting up properly, not bothering to exercise and feeling sorry for myself.

'It's up to you,' Lee said. 'But remember that you're going to lose muscle tone and you'll only have to build it up again.'

I lay there silently.

'You've got to keep working, Les. The more exercise you do, the better your endurance will be. You can't just give up. I know you're tired, but you've got to keep going. You'll get there.'

'Oh, just leave me alone,' I exploded. 'What do you know about it, anyway? I won't get there. I've been like this for ages. This is it, Lee – just accept it.'

'But you've been moping around for weeks. You've got to sort yourself out and get out of that bed. Enough is enough.'

'Go away,' I screamed. 'I'm sick of you telling me what to do. I don't think you realise how much pain I'm in. You think I'm better now I'm out of hospital, but I'm not. Every step I take still hurts, the nerve pain is as much agony as it was the day I woke up, if not more because I'm not so numb any more.

'I can't just take a paracetamol and it's all fine, Lee. Why do you think I'm taking all this medication?'

'I know you're in pain, Les, but lying there won't help.'

I turned away from him. I couldn't even bloody well storm out of the room any more.

'All right, then. Stay there,' Lee said as he walked towards the door. 'But remember it's up to you. For every day you lie in bed, it will take three to get back to where you were.'

He left the room and soon I heard the front door slam. I lay staring up out of the window. I knew he was right of course. I didn't have any more excuses. I was just feeling sorry for myself and everyone had had enough of it.

'Where are my crutches?' I shouted, as I went to get up off the sofa.

Lee walked into the living room, pulling on his jacket.

'Why don't you try using your stick tonight?' he asked.

We were going out for dinner to one of our favourite Italian restaurants, called Aglio e Olio on the Fulham Road. Lee had been going on about my stick for weeks now, saying I was too dependent on the crutches and needed to break the habit.

'You're just scared of not having them,' he'd say to me. 'There's no reason why you can't go on to the stick. You're in a comfort zone and you've got to challenge yourself, Leslie, because otherwise you'll never get any better. I'll help you.'

Hmm. Lee, like lots of men, meant what he said now, but I knew he might well end up four steps ahead of me while I weaved about the pavement with only a piece of wood to hold me up. Rachel was a great believer in better to be safe than sorry and was worried I could do some damage if I went on to a stick when I wasn't ready. I agreed, but Lee was determined to get me using it.

'You look so much better on the stick,' he'd tell me. 'So much stronger, more upright, you've got to get there. You've got to break the habit, test your body, trust your body.'

He walked out of the room to go and get the car keys, and I stared at my crutches. I knew he was right. It was another

of those times in my recovery when I just had to take a deep breath and do something I was scared of. I was glad Lee was pushing me. It was as if he couldn't accept that I wasn't going to get well and refused to believe it would be for ever.

'You're not disabled – you're in recovery,' he'd say.

It might sound corny, but his belief kept pushing me on when I'd all but lost my own.

I looked up at him when he walked back into the living room.

'All right, then,' I said. 'I'll try it. But you've got to make sure I'm safe. I've never gone that far on a stick or outside with it.'

'Of course,' he replied. 'I'll just phone Adriano and ask him to meet us outside the restaurant so he can walk you in while I park the car.'

As we drew up outside the restaurant, I began to feel really nervous. I'd be on my own. Would I fall and make a prat of myself? I opened the door and edged off the seat as Adriano walked up to meet me. Staring down at my feet, I knew I was far slower at walking like this than I was on crutches because I had to concentrate so much more on placing my feet. I didn't have the same support without the crutches. It was just me and a crappy old stick holding me up.

Adriano walked patiently beside me as I neared the restaurant door, holding the stick in my right hand because my left leg was the stronger and needed less support. I was scared, though, because my weaker right leg kicked out behind me. Would it knock my stick and I'd fall?

The restaurant was packed as we walked in. It's a real traditional mad Italian with tables everywhere and people chatting and laughing as they eat big bowls of pasta. The noise hit me. I wasn't use to life being so loud.

'You're just over there,' Adriano gestured.

I felt like a drunken old man as I weaved around. There seemed to be people everywhere, and a lot of them stared

when my stick got stuck on a woman's chair leg.

'Sorry,' I smiled, as I tried to wrench it back into position.

Why the hell had I listened to Lee? It would have been so much easier to do this using my crutches. What was the big deal about a stick, anyway?

You won't look like a sick person any more, Leslie, I told myself. That's why you've got to do this – and maybe after the stick comes walking unaided. Just one more stage until you're back to normal. Remember that.

At last I reached the table and I breathed a sigh of relief as I sat down.

'OK?' Lee asked, sitting down and picking up the menu.

'Fine,' I replied.

He was playing it very cool. If I didn't know better, I'd have thought he'd chosen that restaurant deliberately – knowing he couldn't park outside and I'd have to walk in alone.

After that night, I kept on using the stick and within weeks the crutches had gone. It made an immediate difference to life – I was quicker getting down stairs and moving around in general, could feel my right leg strengthening as it was forced to work harder and was holding myself more upright now that I didn't bend forward on the crutches. But even though I'd like to say it was a huge, happy moment, getting on to the stick wasn't like I'd hoped it would be. In hospital, I'd thought it would be the answer to everything. If the doctors were telling me I might not walk again, then getting on to a stick was my dream. But life never really measures up to the fantasy, does it? Every time you reach a goal, you look past it to the next one, and now all I wanted was to regain enough feeling to walk unaided or put normal shoes back on. My feet still couldn't grip slip-ons and I was way too unsteady for high heels, so I wore trainers all the time with either a track-suit or jeans. It really depressed me. I wanted to have a reason to dress up again. Sometimes I'd get all my shoes out of the wardrobe and line them up in the bedroom. One day I

decided to put on my pink Jean-Paul Gaultier cowboy boots. Leaning heavily on the stick, I took about two steps before my arches caved in and I fell over. I didn't try again.

All in all, moving on to the stick felt like just another stage in my recovery. I still had spinal damage, couldn't go out alone and had to have someone with me to make sure I didn't fall. So, yes, I made the effort – got out of bed, got on to the stick and tried to get a grip – but I was sick of the whole thing. Whatever I did would never make everything all right.

'I don't know whether you'll be interested in this or not, but I've just been contacted by an organisation called the Patients Association,' Michele said on the phone one day. 'They want to know if you'd be interested in launching their campaign for cleaner hospitals.'

'What is it?' I asked.

'It's a charity that works on behalf of patients and they're holding a conference in April to highlight the issue of hospital-acquired infections like MRSA and MSSA. They want you to be involved because you're a high-profile sufferer.'

'Well, I'm not sure how much help I can be,' I said. 'But could you ask them to send me some more information?'

Let's just get one thing straight. For almost a year after my accident, I thought that I'd just been very, very unlucky. I hardly knew a thing about superbugs and thought an infection like mine was something rare – only affecting vulnerable people like the old, babies and the odd person like me. Then I was contacted by the Patients Association and realised how wrong I'd been.

They sent me an information pack and I couldn't believe what I read. At least 5,000 people a year were being killed by these infections – the equivalent of a 747 plane crashing every month. A dozen air crashes a year and no one was really talking about it. The problem wasn't going away either. Like a lot of people, I'd trusted the system and assumed that

medical staff washed their hands properly, equipment was sterilised, and wards were thoroughly cleaned – that everything possible was being done to solve the problem. But it wasn't. Underfunding, cuts, lack of training and resources and, in some cases, plain old bad practice meant these bugs were spiralling out of control and doctors were running out of antibiotics to stop them.

At first I felt sick when I realised how bad the problem was, and then I felt angry. I mean, really angry – the kind of twisting-in-your-gut rage you get maybe once every few years – and it was like having a rocket put up my arse. I'd known I was angry about something for a long time, but I'd pushed it down, allowed it to eat me up, because I didn't know what I was angry about. Now I did. After all those days, weeks and months of asking what had happened to me, I finally understood. I wasn't alone. It felt as if there'd been a big cover-up and I was angry at how stupid the people in charge must think we all were. Didn't they know that we'd realise what was happening? That underfunding, wage cuts, trying to get cleaning done on the cheap and getting rid of matrons meant people were dying because standards had slipped.

How could our hospitals be in such a sorry state? Other countries had tackled the problem, so why hadn't we? How could this be happening in this day and age? Why was no one jumping up and down and screaming about it? It wasn't right that people's loved ones weren't being protected and were dying just because hospitals weren't properly clean. People were going in with something minor and possibly not coming out. It was a disgrace. And how many more people like me were out there – patients who hadn't ended up as part of the official death statistics but whose lives had been ruined? I was lucky – I could have my say because newspapers were interested in me, but a lot of other people couldn't, and the more I read, the more I felt like I had to stand up for them. It was as if I'd finally been given a soapbox

to stand on to shout about this scandal, and I was bloody well going to do it. Sod sitting around feeling sorry for myself: I had to do something.

I picked up the phone to Michele.

'I'll do whatever they need,' I said to her.

I looked down at the seat beside me, where my new walking stick lay. If I couldn't wear good shoes, then at least I could have a good walking stick. I'd found the perfect one in a famous shop called Smith & Sons on the corner of New Oxford Street. It was the shop that had apparently provided John Steed's famous brolly for *The Avengers* and Sherlock Holmes's walking stick. Mine was mahogany with a silver handle and had cost me about £400. Bloody expensive, but I was so pleased when I'd bought it. I was never going back to crutches and all I could think was thank goodness that metallic clicking would never echo around the house any more. Even today, if I hear that sound, it can still take me back to that horrible time and send a shiver down my spine.

All I could feel were nerves and excitement as I sat in the car on that April day in 2005. I was on my way to the Patients Association's Clean Hospital Summit at a London hotel and I'd been on the go since 6 a.m. doing interviews – I'd done *GMTV*, ITN and even the bloody *Today* programme! It's usually wall-to-wall politicians, but there was me having a chat on Radio 4.

I didn't feel tired or in too much pain after it all. I felt like some kind of missionary – preaching to the unconverted, trying to convince them of how important the problem was. A few weeks before, I'd had lunch with agony aunt Claire Rayner, president of the Patients Association and herself an MRSA sufferer, and become more and more excited about the whole idea of helping them out. They'd told me I could help because my case was high profile, would attract a lot of media

interest and that in turn would bring attention to the whole issue.

Now, though, I felt like a rabbit trapped in headlights as I got out of the car with Michele. I was on my way to do a question and answer with journalists. I kept reminding myself these were people who wrote about real news facts – not showbiz fantasy – as I walked into a room to see them sitting on chairs, notebooks in hand and tape recorders at the ready.

'So, how are you getting on, Leslie?' someone asked.

'Can you tell us your story?' another voice said.

'How do you feel now? What are you doing here today? How did you get involved? What are your thoughts about the issue?'

My mind went blank as questions were fired at me. What on earth was I doing here? I was Leslie Ash, the girl-next-door, the comedy blonde, the dizzy bird – not a health campaigner.

Get a grip, I told myself as I stared at the faces.

Here goes...

'We should all be in fear,' I said, as the reporters looked down and started scribbling. 'This problem is getting out of hand.

'I don't think there is a lot of pride in the cleaning of hospitals, and there should be.

'It is a good idea to bring Matron back, but the cleaners underneath her need to be properly trained and proper disinfectant cleaning fluids need to be used, not just cheap spray polish.

'I count myself pretty lucky because my infection could be treated with antibiotics. If you are diagnosed with MRSA, then you face a pretty bleak future.'

I must have done something right because they all seemed to be listening, and when the conference was finished, I went outside to do TV and radio interviews and have pictures

taken before doing another question and answer with health professionals.

'I'd like to say that I am proud of the hospital I work in,' one nurse told me. 'We have a very good record of cleanliness and work hard to maintain it.'

'I'm not doubting that you have,' I replied. 'I'm not saying that every hospital has poor hygiene, but there are those that do and I know from personal experience the terrible consequences it can have. We need more hospitals like yours – good, clean hospitals that take this issue seriously – and more checks on those that don't.

'The only way this situation will change is by getting someone to answer for it, get back to basics, bring back Matron.'

Finally the day finished and my work was done. I felt elated. I'd helped highlight an important issue and spoken up for all those people out there who'd been affected but had never spoken out or been able to speak out. I just hoped that someone, somewhere, would listen to all the voices.

'You did brilliantly,' Michele told me, as we got into the car at the end of the day.

I hoped I had, and I didn't feel exhausted and weak either. I felt energised, happy and useful. I hadn't had that feeling for so long and it felt great. Even if it was for just one day, people needed me to help and I had done. I also hoped that the press coverage the next day would reflect that. This wasn't about accidents, arguments, cosmetic surgery or illness – this was a serious subject that I had something to say about, and I just hoped to be in the papers for a more positive reason.

I sat back in my seat as London slipped by the windows. I'd been on the go for more than ten hours, and testing my body had told me something I'd never have known if I'd carried on sitting at home. I was getting stronger, my endurance was getting better – my recovery might not be as quick and noticeable as during those first few months in hospital, but

things were slowly changing and today had proved it.

I was wiped out after it, of course, and had to rest a lot, but whatever I did for other people on that day, it brought me far more in return. Finally I realised I had to keep trying, carry on pushing myself and working at my recovery. Finding a channel for my anger, doing something useful and speaking out all helped, but what really spurred me on were the letters I got in the weeks after from members of the public telling me about their experiences of spinal injuries and MRSA. Some I will never forget – like the husband whose wife had gone in for a routine operation and died. She'd left two daughters behind. Or the man who went in with a minor leg injury and ended up having an amputation. These were the people whose voices deserved to be heard. MRSA wasn't just some vague issue that we had to accept and shrug off: it wrecked lives and left families devastated, and it could all be avoided.

Enough of my moping around – I was one of the lucky ones. I was alive and able to walk and there were many people in my position who would never be able to. Either spinal injury or hospital-acquired infection would have been too much for their bodies, and I realised that my selfish self-pity had to stop.

It might not have been a *Secret Garden* moment, but soon I started working harder at the gym and generally putting a lot more effort in. The results might have been small, but they meant a lot. I kept moving until I really had to sit down, instead of lying down after exercising; I started cooking much more and got into a routine of going supermarket-shopping with Rita every Friday; and I also concentrated on keeping as straight and tall as possible when I walked with my stick. Believe me, it's scary to stand in a straight line when you have nerve damage, because you feel as if you'll fall, but I forced myself to trust my body – and my new sense of judgement – more and more. Sometimes I'd even lift up my stick for a few seconds to walk unaided – it might only be a few

steps at a time, but each week I could do a couple more, and who knew where I might end up? Acorns really do make oaks, and I had to carry on believing that in time my steps might eventually become a walk.

I knew things were getting back to normal with Lee when he shouted back at me during an argument. Just as we had done for years, we'd started rowing in the car when I tried to navigate.

'Turn left here,' I said suddenly, as we drove through town. 'You'll avoid all the traffic that way.'

Lee swung the car into a side road, only to find it completely blocked.

'Shit!' he exploded. 'I knew I shouldn't have listened to you.'

'I was only trying to help,' I shouted back. 'And how was I to know there'd be all this traffic here as well? I'm not a bloody psychic.'

'Well, we all know that now. But that's the point, isn't it?' he moaned. 'I should have known better than to listen to your traffic advice.'

Blimey. Mr Angry from Chelsea was back in town – complaining about the roads and me as well.

Later that day I smiled to myself when I realised what had happened. Lee and I had argued just like we always had done. Eureka! He wasn't treating me with kid gloves any more – I was finally strong enough for him to shout at. For months after coming out of hospital, I'd burst into tears if he'd so much as raised his voice a notch and so he'd always shut up. But now it was time for things to really start getting back to normal.

In some ways, though, they never would, and I mean that in the nicest possible way. As summer 2005 approached and I rediscovered the power of being positive, I began to realise just how much both Lee and I had gained from the terrible

previous year. Instead of always seeing the downsides of my accident and recovery, I'd started noticing the good – and my relationship with my husband was among them.

Just as we had done all those years before up North, Lee and I were living in each other's pockets again and it did us good. If I wanted to cook a meal, then he'd pass me things out of the cupboards and chat to me; if I wanted to go shopping, he'd drive me really slowly down the King's Road so I could look in the shop windows before he took me back to the place where I'd spotted something; and if he wanted to go and see some weird, arty, subtitled French film that I'd never have watched in a million years before, then I'd go with him.

Children, work, drink, partying, money and moods had got in the way for such a long time before the accident – you name it we'd argued about it. But now we had time together and didn't go head to head like we used to. I could no longer storm out of rooms when the going got tough: instead of flouncing off, I had to sit and talk. I also had to listen and gradually I realised that the things that had annoyed me about Lee – like the fact that he always answers the phone in a restaurant in the middle of dinner or chats when you're trying to watch *Deal or No Deal* – really didn't matter so much. I'd mellowed, grown up and I understood for the first time that not every battle needs to be won, and I think he did too.

Our relationship was like it had been all those years ago and I felt so much closer to Lee. It was as if I finally remembered what I liked about him – he's a funny, shy and kind man who I fitted with really well – and I think he also found a new respect for me.

'I'm so proud of what you've done,' he told me one day. 'You've come so far. Not many people could have done it, and you've achieved so much more than anyone ever thought. You've kept at it, never given in. You've done so well.'

All the worries I'd had before my accident didn't exist any more. I'd been insecure, anxious, tired and work-focused.

Now I knew that we would be together for ever and all the insecurities had disappeared. In the end, I think it came down to one lesson that we'd both learned: life is fragile, precious and short. You should treasure it.

'Are you ready to go?' Lee asked, as he sat across the table from me.

We'd been out for dinner and had just finished our food. It was 9 p.m. – time for bed. I might have made some progress, but I was still knackered by early evening, longing for my sleeping pill and liable to get grumpy if anyone crossed me.

'I'm just going to go to the loo,' I said.

'What?' he said. 'But it's downstairs. Wait a minute and you can go at home. The stairs are too narrow for you.'

'I know, but I'll be fine,' I reassured him. 'I'll get down OK.'

'Well, I'll come with you.'

'No. Really, I'm fine. I can do it myself.'

He didn't look convinced as I got up from the table and leaned on my stick. After all those months of looking after me, Lee was finding it difficult to let go sometimes, but I was sure I could get down the stairs all right.

I edged down step by step, foot by foot, as I clung on to the stick in one hand and the banister in another, and thought of the day so many months before when Rachel had stood with me at the top of the Welly staircase. I'd thought I would never learn how to get down, but, just like so many other things, I had in the end.

On the way back up from the loo, though, I began to think that maybe Lee was right and that I had set myself too hard a task. My legs felt heavy, it was difficult moving them, and each step took for ever as I lifted up my feet inch by inch. It was as if they didn't want to move any more, and I couldn't understand why going down – the hardest bit – had seemed so much easier.

'All ready,' I said to Lee, when I finally got to the table.

'OK, then,' he said, and stood up to walk out with me.

'I must be really tired or something,' I said, looking down at myself. I was wearing a long, black wraparound skirt with sheepskin boots – hardly restricting – and couldn't understand why my legs felt so heavy.

'Well, you did a lot at the gym today,' Lee replied, as we walked to the car.

'Yes. Maybe it's that. I just need some sleep.'

I opened the passenger door when I heard the click of the locks. Lee climbed into the driver's seat. As I lifted my leg to get into the world's highest-off-the-ground car, however, I found I couldn't move my legs properly again.

'I can't get my leg up on to the step,' I exploded. 'This is ridiculous. My leg is so heavy, and I can't believe we have a car that I can't even get into.'

I tugged at my leg, but it just wouldn't get on to the step, no matter how hard I pulled it.

'I've had enough of this!' I shouted. 'This is stupid. We've got to get another car.'

In the end, Lee had enough of my moans and got out to help me. As he stood beside me, I tried to lift up my leg yet again and my skirt fell slightly open at the knee.

'Leslie,' he said quietly.

'What?' I snapped.

'You've got your pants round your ankles, you silly cow.'

I stared down and there they were. My smalls were snagged round the top of my boots. I had left them there after going to the loo and hadn't been able to feel them round my numb legs. I'd just walked through an entire restaurant with my pants down!

'Oh, shit,' I laughed.

I didn't care if it was a chilly May day. I was bloody excited. Lee and I were at the entrance to the Chelsea Flower Show

and I couldn't wait to get inside. It was an important day for me – a year ago I had been lying in a hospital bed fearing I might never walk again and the TV coverage of Chelsea had kept me going. My mum, my childhood, another beautiful world full of sunshine and colour, and the memories of my trips with Lee had all combined to make the flower show the one bright spot in the darkness. I'd never have believed back then that I'd be here again.

'Can you see her?' I asked Lee, as I looked for Rachel in the faces milling around.

I'd invited her along to say thank you because I'd never forgotten how much she and I had talked about the show during my first days in the gym.

Suddenly she appeared out of the crowd.

'Hi, Leslie,' she said, as she went to give me a hug.

'Hello,' I replied. 'You look lovely. How are you?'

'Fine.' She smiled. 'You're looking well too.'

My stick tapped in front of me as we walked through the entrance and down to the long road that wound round the perimeter of the show gardens.

'So, how have you been getting on?' Rachel asked, as we looked around, our eyes stopping every so often to gaze at something that really stood out.

'I'm good,' I replied. 'Very good, in fact. I'm here with you and Lee, I'm on my stick, and I haven't got that bloody hump that Dr Shakir kept going on about.'

Rachel laughed.

Everything was so lovely: people had put an incredible amount of work into their gardens, and there was colour everywhere – pinks, oranges, creams, greens, reds and yellows all lit up briefly whenever the sun came out from behind the clouds. Last year my life had been about hospitals, white walls and pain – now it was a slower one in which I could literally stop and smell the roses again, concentrate on the good things and forget the bad.

A couple of weeks before, I'd been for another MRI scan and Dr Shakir had shown me a picture of an upside-down question mark on my spinal column – it was permanent scarring. Of course, deep down, I'd always hoped that my nerves and spine would suddenly and miraculously heal completely, but in that moment I had finally known it would never happen and had felt sad but calm as I looked at the scan. I would always have problems with my proprioception, but I had a choice whether to fight against my body or work with it. Slowly, slowly, my nerves were regrowing, and I knew how much more secure I now felt on my feet. If I'd come so far in just a year, then who knows what I would be like in another? I'd just carry on as I was, keep on trying and maybe one day I'd finally walk unaided.

I took a deep breath as we stopped in front of a really striking display. Flowers in bursts of vibrant colour covered the beds, the grass was so green it almost shone, and I could hear water moving somewhere close by. It was perfect.

'Shall we go on?' I heard Lee ask. As always, he was standing close to me – he might have learned to let me do my own thing, but he was still always nearby.

'No,' I replied.

There was no need to rush on to the next moment, when we could savour this one. We had all the time in the world. My mind flashed back once more to that thin, sad, sick woman lying in bed last year. I couldn't recognise her any more. She had gone for ever.

'Let's just stay here another minute,' I continued. 'It's so beautiful. I want to remember it.'

I breathed in a lungful of fresh, clean air as the sun moved out from behind a cloud and warmed my face. I couldn't believe I was actually here. I'd done it, got through and was alive to see this beautiful day.

'Shall we go?' I said, turning to smile at Rachel and Lee, and the three of us started walking on to the next garden.

AFTERWORD

Being disabled has shown me a whole new side to life. Of course, I knew it existed before my accident, but it wasn't my problem. Then it happened to me and I felt almost invisible when I was in a wheelchair. It seemed to bring out both the best and the worst in people – some were so kind and I've been overwhelmed by how much support I've got from strangers, while others could hardly be bothered to move out of the way as I tried to negotiate every bump, kerb and crack in the pavement. You just want to be given the chance to move properly in an able-bodied world and it's amazing how stupid people can be, like the well-known TV soap actress who once said cheerily to me, 'Well, you can't really tell when you're sitting down, can you?' But at least I was lucky enough to have a chance to leave the wheelchair behind.

Just one thing stands out as I look back on the past three years and that is how well Lee has cared for me throughout it all. From the first moment I woke up after my operation, he has been positive, quietly confident and encouraged me to accept the challenge of my recovery. I can still remember the look on his face in the moments before I was put under for the operation to save my life and it said so much. It might sound strange, but it was the same look he'd given me when I walked in with Dad to the registry office in Jersey to marry him. It was pride, belief, but most of all love, and it made my heart jump on my wedding day because it told me Lee was with me for the run, the whole trip. That's what his look said again as he gazed down at me moments before I went into surgery.

He's protected me from the press and outside world, visited me three times a day while I was in hospital and always been there to speak to the doctors and specialists, get all the information and translate it back to me. He's also dried the tears, made me laugh and held me close when I was scared. After everything that has been said about him, he still holds his head up high. Everyone has had their say, but they've all got it so wrong. If only they knew what a truly loving man he is. All I know is that I couldn't have wanted for a better person to be with through this traumatic time and I'm looking forward to our future together.

I continue to campaign for cleaner hospitals by talking to the media about the problem and doing other bits of work as and when I'm asked. One highlight was delivering a speech at the House of Lords in January 2006 to a meeting of NHS Trust representatives, and I've also become a businesswoman by helping develop a range of antibacterial products, like a hand wash and hand gel, called Matron, which I hope will do their bit to stem the spread of infections. Even so, it can feel like a lonely fight at times – especially when I think about the fact that hospital-acquired infections are only getting worse. The number of deaths linked to MRSA rose by 39 per cent in 2005, and deaths linked to a second superbug called clostridium difficile went up by 69 per cent.

I believe the only way we'll overcome these problems is to go back in time to the days when there was a matron to answer to, who had a standard of cleanliness that has somehow got lost. It's all put down to money, of course, it always is, and while I think that is true in a lot of ways, I also believe the excuse is being overused. It is scandalous that so many lives are being affected by hospital-acquired infections and the people at the top should be taking it far more seriously – there is no excuse for a dirty hospital. It's also an issue that everyone can do something about and we just have to be cleaner to stop the spread of infection. It's that simple. I think

there should be protocols about how to enter hospitals on visits, hand-washing rules and information about basic hygiene. We've all got to work together to fight the problem.

I contracted an infection that responded to antibiotics, but there are many that don't and we've got to find new ways of fighting them. The Centre for Healthcare-Associated Infections at Nottingham University is one of the places working to do that and I was proud to become a patron of it in early 2007. Scientists there are working towards new ways of fighting these microbes by disarming them, but the centre needs funding because it can cost millions of pounds just to get a new antibiotic on to the market. Again it all comes down to money, but can you really put a price on health and life?

I still haven't returned to work, but, however sad I feel about it, my illness and recovery have also allowed me to look at the acting business from another angle. I realise now that what I thought was my entire life and soul isn't. There's so much spin and PR involved in being an actor and a celebrity about how great your life is, and it's just not like that. You have to live up to this image all the time and it's hard. It's a strange world, because you're pretending to be so many people that you forget who you are, and I was guilty of that. I wasn't sure if I was a mother, a famous person or what and I ended up not really liking myself.

Alcohol is the other thing that affected my life and it's the little details that remind me of how much it cost me – like the fact that so many of the photos of Joe and Max growing up were taken by my mum and mother-in-law. I was just too busy working or having fun to stop long enough to get a camera out. My sons are always reassuring me that I was around, I was a fantastic mum, but I think mothers often feel they could have done better and I'm the same. I don't think you're ever prepared for the moment when they start to move away from you into their own adult lives and that's what my sons

are doing at the moment, so it makes me think back. But I also remind myself that I wasn't away all the time and didn't have a glass of wine permanently stuck in my hand. I took them to school, wiped their grazed knees and cheered them on at football, so even if I made some mistakes, I also did the important stuff with them. Recently they've had to learn the painful but valuable lesson that people are fallible, their mother included, and we've been drawn closer together because of it.

I enjoy my life so much more now that I'm not drinking. I feel I'm giving myself a chance of seeing things as they really are. I don't need to drink any more, and the longer I don't do it, the more I realise how strange it is to numb your feelings with alcohol. It also affects your proprioception, and why would I want to make mine any worse than it is? Most importantly, I don't need to drink any more, because I want to remember absolutely everything. I don't want to forget another day. It's scary sometimes, of course, not having that fallback and the thought of getting old like this frightens me. But then I'll just have to ask for help, won't I?

Perhaps that's the biggest thing all this has taught me. I was always so independent before my accident – working, keeping a home and family together – that I didn't really let people into my life. My dad always taught me to have your cab fare home and house keys in your pocket when you went out because then you only had to rely on yourself – and I carried that lesson into life in general. I looked after myself almost too well. After my accident, I could no longer do that and it taught me something very precious – it's OK to ask for help, and even if people don't do things exactly the way you would, then just shut up and appreciate that they're doing them.

You see, my life has changed for the better since the accident – as well as the worse – because I can't run away from things or think about them tomorrow: I have to deal with

problems straight away. My world isn't crammed with stuff as I try to ignore what I don't want to see, and today I feel like a nicer person – more thoughtful and honest – because my life is more intense and compact. I concentrate on what's important and live each day as it comes.

My legal action is still ongoing, and I look forward to spending time with Lee and the boys and continuing to rebuild my new life. Yes, I have regrets, but life's too short to spend too much time on them – I've learned the hard way that we never know what is round the corner. All I can do is trust that I've hit the lowest point and that now the only way is up. Hopefully there'll be a lot more good times, only a few bad ones and, of course, just enough behaving badly to keep things interesting.

INDEX